*The Mexican American:*
A Critical Guide to Research Aids

**FOUNDATIONS IN LIBRARY AND
INFORMATION SCIENCE, VOLUME 1**

*Editor:* Robert D. Stueart, Dean, *School of Library Science, Simmons College*

# FOUNDATIONS IN LIBRARY AND INFORMATION SCIENCE

### A Series of Monographs, Texts and Treatises

*Series Editor:*  Robert D. Stueart, *Dean, School of Library Science, Simmons College, Boston*

## Publisher's Acknowledgment

*The publishers wish to acknowledge the valuable assistance in the development of this Work to Hans Weber, formerly affiliated with the University of California Library at Riverside, and the late Warren Boes, Director of Libraries at Michigan Technological University.*

# The Mexican American:

## A Critical Guide to Research Aids

*by* BARBARA J. ROBINSON
*Bibliographer for Latin American
and Mexican American Studies
University of California Library,
Riverside*

J. CORDELL ROBINSON
*Department of History
California State College,
San Bernardino*

*Foreword by* CARLOS E. CORTES
*University of California,
Riverside*

 JAI PRESS INC.
*Greenwich, Connecticut*

**Library of Congress Cataloging in Publication Data**

Robinson, Barbara J
   The Mexican American.

   (Foundations in library and information science; v. 1)
   Includes indexes.
   1.  Mexican Americans—Bibliography.
2.  Bibliography—Bibliography—Mexican Americans.
I.  Robinson, Joy Cordell, 1940-     joint
author.  II.  Title.  III.  Series.
Z1361.M4R63    [E184.M6]    016.973′046872
ISBN 0-89232-006-0    76-5643

*Copyright © 1980 JAI PRESS INC.*
*165 West Putnam Avenue*
*Greenwich, Connecticut 06830*

*ISBN NUMBER: 0-89232-006-0*
*Library of Congress Catalog Card Number: 76-5643*
*Manufactured in the United States of America*

# CONTENTS

# Foreword

When the Chicano Movement exploded onto the American scene in the 1960's, it issued myriad challenges to U.S. society. One of these challenges occurred in the area of scholarship. Chicanos wanted their story told, their problems examined, and their issues addressed by persons equipped with the tools and skills of scholarly research.

Not that scholars had totally ignored Chicanos prior to the Movement. For decades, relatively small numbers of scholars had devoted sporadic attention to Chicano culture, experience, and problems. Yet, for the most part, Mexican Americans had not yet become academically "legitimate" as a research topic nor had Chicanos gained entry into mainstream textbooks, whether at the elementary, secondary, or collegiate levels. And even where inclusion had occurred or research had been conducted, the results often reflected insensitivity, stereotyping, distortion, and mainstream ethnocentric misinterpretation.

The long overdue demands for inclusion, accuracy, balanced presentation, and new perspectives on Mexican Americans generated the Chicano scholarly movement. However, researchers soon found that they were limited by available sources. Chicanos had suffered not only by research neglect and textbook omission, but also by inconsistent and often incorrect inclusion in society's official documents themselves. Even when materials did exist, scholars confronted the massive task of identifying, locating, and collecting them.

As a result, during the first stages of the Chicano scholarly movement, a major emphasis was placed on the development of research guides, such as bibliographies, directories, dictionaries, and other basic tools of investigation. For a time, in fact, it seemed as if bibliographies on Chicanos might ultimately outnumber books on Chicanos. These guides came in many forms, with differing emphases, and of varying quality. Soon even the knowledgeable scholar had trouble separating the bibliographical wheat and chaff.

Then along came Barbara and J. Cordell Robinson. Undertaking a task of massive proportions, the Robinsons identified, collected, examined, analyzed, categorized, and annotated the diverse sources and guides available for Chicano-oriented research. The result—*The Mexican American: A Critical Guide to Research Aids*—marks a major breakthrough for Chicano scholarship.

As a basic scholarly reference, this book is invaluable. The mere listing of these many bibliographies, guides, directories, dictionaries, and other sources would in itself have been a major accomplishment and contribution to Chicano research. But the Robinsons have gone far beyond the gathering and listing of references. They have also provided logical categorizations and insightful annotations, which should enable researchers to determine more quickly the most useful sources for their particular projects and interests.

Moreover, their chapter introductions are themselves contributions of note. In some cases they comprise "state-of-the-art" surveys of sources, and they often contain intriguing research suggestions which should prove useful to veteran and novice scholars alike. Even those who have spent years in Chicano-related research can benefit from their discussions of sources, library holdings, and the current status of materials. Some provide insights into the very development of scholarship about the Mexican American people. Introductions to the chapters on education, history, folklore, labor, linguistics, literature, and women shed light on the historical evolution—including successes and failures—of research on these topics. Moreover, at times their discussions become mini-social histories of scholars' attitudes toward Mexican Americans as reflected in research paradigms, interpretive assumptions, and available materials.

The Robinsons are to be commended for their honesty and forthrightness. They have lauded when they felt it was deserving, yet have not hesitated to criticize what they consider to be poorly conceived, inaccurate materials or to warn researchers about weaknesses in the various sources. While I might not agree with all of their interpretations and conclusions, I found their analyses, whether in chapter introductions or in annotations, to be consistently clear, considered, useful, and at times provocative.

Overall, *The Mexican American: A Critical Guide to Research Aids* is a fine piece of research, analysis, and conceptualization. With the publication of this book, Chicano scholarship has taken a giant step forward. For future researchers interested in any aspect of Chicano experience, culture, or societal problems, this work should be the natural starting point.

Carlos E. Cortés
Professor of History
Chair, Chicano Studies
University of California, Riverside

# Acknowledgments

We express our deepest gratitude to the many individuals who so generously provided assistance and encouragement during the work on this bibliography. In particular, we would like to thank the following: Hazel Schupbach and Deborah Lipton (Inter-Library Loan office, University of California, Riverside); and Lyn Young (Inter-Library Loan office, California State College, San Bernardino), who assisted in locating many sources and in unraveling bibliographical snarls; Penny Jones and Gail Carbis, who typed seemingly endless drafts and chapters of our manuscript; Francisco García-Ayvens (formerly Head of the Chicano Studies Library, University of California, Los Angeles and now at Berkeley) and the staff at the Chicano Studies Library at the University of California, Berkeley, who made available the resources of their fine collections; colleagues in the Library at the University of California, Riverside, especially Judith A. Ganson (Acting Head of Technical Processing Department) for sharing her bibliographic expertise, reading the final draft of the manuscript, and offering helpful suggestions in general; and Ruth Halman (Head of Reference Services, General Library) for her professional advice on the subject index.

We also thank Hans Weber, editor, and Herb Johnson, publisher, for their professional assistance, patience, and faith over the years. And finally, we would be remiss if we did not mention our children, Lisa and Hilton Robinson and their grandparents, Beryl and Beulah Potter for enduring with us the process of writing and for giving so much of their time. Their unfailing cooperation and assistance facilitated the completion of our work. This book is for them.

Barbara J. Robinson
J. Cordell Robinson

# Introduction

In the early 1960's, when interest in the Mexican American began to develop at all levels of society, there were only a few recognized reference works which provided access to sources on this ethnic group. The situation soon changed in the latter part of the decade and throughout the 1970's as the demand for information on Mexican Americans grew. This demand was initially felt in colleges and universities as a result of Chicano Studies courses and programs, but later spread rapidly to public libraries, school districts, governmental agencies and ultimately to business and other professional groups.

In recent years numerous bibliographies and other reference tools have been published to satisfy some informational needs and to facilitate research on Americans of Mexican heritage. Although specialized bibliographies, dictionaries, and archival sources existed prior to 1960, their proliferation since then clearly reflects the impact of the Chicano Movement on scholarly and bibliographic efforts.

Among the sources now available are general and special subject bibliographies; guides to library and archival collections; genealogical, biographical, and statistical sources; directories of organizations; dictionaries and vocabularies; newspaper and periodical listings and indexes; and guides to films, tapes, sound recordings, and other audiovisual materials. Because a good many of these are unknown or unfamiliar to all but the most diligent and expert researchers, we have attempted to bring together in an organized, analytical fashion, the pertinent bibliographies and research aids which related to the study of the Mexican American.

In the course of four years of investigation, from 1974 to 1978, we collected and evaluated nearly 2,000 works of varying quality, scope and accessibility. From this vast array of sources, 668 items were chosen for inclusion. Selection was based on the relevancy of the content of each work to the Mexican American experience. Thus we cited all titles which deal exclusively with Mexican Americans or Chicanos, as well as those with a cross-cultural or multi-ethnic perspective. Additionally, a number of sources with a thematic emphasis were included to complete the bibliographic picture, e.g. those integrally related to the socioeconomic, political, and historical milieu of Mexican Americans—agricultural and migrant labor, the historical and cultural background of the Spanish and Mexican periods, and bilingual-bicultural education, to mention just a few.

The selections consist of published and unpublished works: books, chapters in books, government publications, periodical articles, pamphlets, bibliographies appended to other works, theses and dissertations, and mimeographed manuscripts. Limiting the scope to only separately published works would have neglected numerous fine contributions and ignored the fact that in certain fields, such as history and literature, many of the landmark works have been published in periodicals and anthologies. All the items cited in this bibliography are available in major research libraries and archival repositories in the West and Southwest.

Progress on this work was occasionally incumbered by difficulties with terminology, periodization, geographical limitations, and incomplete and inaccurate bibliographic reporting in other sources.

Although the terms "Mexican American" and "Chicano" are used more frequently and often interchangeably throughout the bibliography, many other labels referring to this ethnic group are utilized in the sources cited. Titles relating to Mexicans in the United States, Hispanos, Spanish Americans, Spanish-Speaking, Latin Americans, and *La Raza,* contain valuable references to Mexican Americans. Preference is given to "Mexican Americans" in the title over other terms since it connotes, in our opinion, a broader spectrum of resources.

Periodization posed problems in selection because authors and compilers perceive differing chronological parameters in their works. Some limit their coverage to the twentieth century, others refer back to pre-Columbian times or the conquest and colonization of the Southwest, while others choose 1848 as their point of departure. In our selections we concentrate on the nineteenth and twentieth centuries, but include a few historical and genealogical works on earlier periods.

Geographical focus is limited to the United States, except in certain fields such as history, folklore and linguistics. These are closely intertwined with Mexican influences and cannot be easily restricted to artificial national boundaries. Only the most relevant and essential titles relating to Mexico are included since Mexico's bibliography is extremely extensive and adequately covered in other specialized works.

A final concern is the perpetuation of errors in bibliographic references. By examining each of the sources first-hand, we endeavoured to provide the user with the most complete and accurate bibliographic citations possible. It is unfortunate that some of the compilers of recent works cited herein have not shared this same concern. The lack of other desirable features in a reference source, i.e. annotations, selection guidelines, indexes, etc., creates certain problems for the user, but the bibliographic errors are the most disconcerting.

The selected works are organized in seventeen chapters in two major sections: general works and subject bibliographies. Some of the sources defy precise categorization but this arrangement offers advantages to the researcher not provided by strictly ennumerative bibliographies. These include ease in identifying types of reference sources available and in analyzing the state of the literature in particular fields.

Each chapter is introduced by an essay which discusses the sources and places them within the context of research on the Mexican American. Following the essays the works are cited in alphabetical order. All entries are critically evaluated according to arrangement, scope, content, coverage, and usage. ED numbers are provided, when known, signifying that the work has been acquired and distributed by the Educational Resources Information Center (ERIC).

We offer this bibliography as testimony to the diligence of the many scholars and bibliographers who have undertaken the task of documenting the Mexican American experience and as a response to those who have unjustly claimed that there is no body of literature on this ethnic group. The resources and tools actually emcompass a period of more than a century, the earliest dating back to 1857. A majority were produced during the past twenty years; and one-third between 1974 and 1978. However, Mexican American bibliography, when compared to that of the Afro-American, is still in its infancy.

In 1974 what appeared to be a possible task, now seems unending. New works, revised editions of earlier works, and reprints continue to appear, and though welcomed, frustrate the bibliographer's attempts at comprehensiveness. We hope that this work provides new insights into research on the Mexican American and serves as a useful guide to scholars, librarians, teachers, and laymen.

Barbara J. Robinson                         J. Cordell Robinson
Associate Librarian                     Associate Professor
University of California,               California State College,
Riverside                                   San Bernardino

# Part 1

# GENERAL WORKS

# Chapter 1

# *General Bibliographies*

General bibliographies, covering various aspects of the Mexican American experience, the history, politics, culture, folklore, religion, education, and literature were among the first types of reference works produced on this ethnic group. Although most of these bibliographies focus on the Mexican American, occasionally other minority or Spanish-speaking groups are represented. Some of these bibliographies are separately published works, others appear as periodical articles, as chapters in books, or as supplements to monographic studies or anthologies. The works listed in this chapter were published between 1929 and 1979; however, the peak period of bibliographic production was from 1970 to 1975, during which time an average of six or more were issued per year. Many of these were completely new works and others were reprints or revised editions of earlier works. The proliferation of this type of bibliography was indicative of the growing interest in the Mexican American in many sectors of society and of the growth and diversity of scholarship in the field.

Motives for the preparation of these compilations are as numerous as the works themselves, but a common thread unites them all. During the 50-year period in which these bibliographies were produced, many of the compilers stressed the importance of increasing the understanding of Mexican Americans and their culture through the literature. The earliest bibliographies were prepared by Anglo-American scholars concerned with the problems and adjustments of the Mexican immigrants in the United States. Prior to the 1950s Lyle Saunders, Emory Bogardus, and Robert Jones were among those who attempted to stimulate readers to inquire more openly and to explore more fully the role of the Mexican in the United States. By recording and preserving the sources on their cultural heritage, these scholars hoped to stimulate future research and studies.

From 1944 to 1960 there was a hiatus in which no identifiable bibliographies of this general type were published. In 1960, Charles Cumberland's excellent guide to scholarly literature on the borderlands presaged the bibliographic activity that was to come. By the latter part of the decade a significant number of works had appeared and the bibliographic activity began to gain momentum. Guides were prepared for the purpose of promoting intercultural understanding, strengthening pride in the cultural identity of Mexican Americans, and bolstering the claims of the Chicano movement. During the 1970s nearly half of the compilers were of Mexican or Hispanic origin and their works singled out the overlooked contributions of Mexican American scholars and writers.

3

The materials cited in the general bibliographies cover not only a wide range of subjects, disciplines, and types of resources, but also a broad time span—from the earliest Indian civilizations in Mexico and the Southwest to the present. At least half of these bibliographies were prepared by academic institutions. Various of these focus on a particular type of material (e.g., government publications, theses and dissertations, or specialized bibliographies) in an attempt to accumulate as many relevant sources as possible for the study of the Mexican American. The majority of sources cited in these works are scholarly in nature and, as such, provide tools for the serious researcher. A few of the general bibliographies were issued by state and federal agencies or trade publishers and were aimed at the general public or the informed laymen. Other bibliographies were compiled to assist librarians and teachers in selecting materials. Certain works, such as that by REFORMA, the National Organization of Spanish-Speaking Librarians, offer core collections in the humanities and social sciences. And school districts with bilingual-bicultural programs prepared several resource lists of current books, periodicals, children's literature, and audiovisual media for use by teachers in the primary and secondary grades.

Many of the general bibliographies, particularly those published since 1960, were hastily and somewhat carelessly produced and, thus, present problems for the user. Hensley C. Woodbridge has aptly pointed to a number of these in his critique of various Chicano bibliographies.[1] Commonly found problems include the lack of a stated purpose or clearly defined scope. Frequently, no criteria are given for the selection of items listed and some of the titles seem marginal or irrelevant. Particularly obvious to those familiar with Latin American literature are the large number of citations to works from Mexico, Chile, Argentina, Colombia and other countries which have very little significance, or none at all, to the study of the Mexican American. A few of the entries are for works that were never published and some citations perpetuate errors found in other bibliographies. Inaccuracies, misspelled words, lack of accents, and improper editing plague most of these bibliographies on the Mexican American. Finally, annotations and indexes, although highly desirable and helpful to researchers, are often not found in many of these general compilations.

In spite of these shortcomings, a number of very fine basic bibliographies have been prepared. Keeping in mind the problems and limitations, readers can use the following guides to gain an overview of the literature on the Mexican American.

1. Hensley C. Woodbridge, "Fourteen Chicano Bibliographies, 1971–1975," *Modern Language Journal,* 61 (January–February, 1977):20–25.

1. Barrios, Ernest. *Bibliografía de Aztlán: An Annotated Chicano Bibliography*. San Diego, CA: Centro de Estudios Chicanos Publications, San Diego State College, 1971. 157 p. Annotated. Indexes.
Barrios attempts to remove "stereotyped views" of Chicanos in this bibliography. A cross section of materials on the Mexican American, including books, articles, journals, and newspapers, is arranged in 15 somewhat disorganized and overlapping subject divisions. The coverage is general and a number of the entries are on Mexican history, philosophy and literature. The lengthy annotations are the most notable feature of this work. They provide articulate evaluation and criticism, often lacking in similar general bibliographies.

There is a long introduction which seeks to define the terms Chicano and *La Raza,* and a list of members of the Chicano Press Association, with addresses. Author and title indexes are appended.

2. Bogardus, Emory S. "Literature and Research." In *The Mexican in the United States,* pp. 99–123. New York: Arno Press, 1970. (Reprint of 1934 ed., Los Angeles: University of Southern California Press.) 126 p. Annotated.

This bibliography is one of the most important selections of books, reports, and articles on or about the Mexican Americans published prior to 1934. The selections, ranging from scholarly studies to popular interpretations, include the best works available on the cultural background of the Mexican immigrant, local studies of particular Mexican communities in the United States, and the integration of Mexican immigrants into American society. Many of the items are sociological and anthropological. Short descriptive annotations are provided.

This bibliography, part of a classic work on the Mexican American, was prepared by a noted American sociologist.

3. _____. "The Mexican Immigrant: An Annotated Bibliography." In *Mexican American Bibliographies*, edited by Carlos E. Cortés. New York: Arno Press, 1974. (Reprint of 1929 ed., Los Angeles: Council on International Relations. 21 p.) Annotated.

This is the earliest identifiable general bibliography compiled on the Mexican American. As a classic, it is useful for its perspective and historical approach to the literature in the field. The titles listed indicate the scope and interest that was placed on the social adjustment of the Mexican immigrant during the early part of the twentieth century.

The coverage includes approximately 200 books, articles, and chapters from books arranged in three sections: Cultural backgrounds, Studies in the United States, and Interracial adjustments. Bogardus indicated, in 1929, that there was a need for Americans to have a more thorough understanding of Mexicans. The bibliography, prepared with this idea in mind, cites only titles in English.

4. Cabrera, Ysidro Arturo. "General Bibliography" and "Doctoral Dissertations." In *Emerging Faces: The Mexican Americans,* pp. 85–95. San Jose, CA: W. C. Brown, 1971. 99 p.

Two separate bibliographies which supplement the text are contained in this work. The first is a listing of 90 books, chapters from books and reports, and the second is a list of 96 doctoral dissertations relating to the history and culture of Mexican Americans. The selections in the general bibliography date from Justin H. Smith's *The War with Mexico,* 1919, to Ernesto Galarza's *Spiders in the House and Workers in the Field,* 1970. History, social science, folklore and literature are selectively represented. Some items are only about Mexico.

The dissertations were identified principally in *Dissertation Abstracts* and only those completed after 1960 are listed. The order numbers for the dissertations were included when available. The author's hope is that the text and the bibliographies will stimulate readers' interest in Mexican Americans.

5. _____. *Mexican-American/Chicano Doctoral Studies Abstracts: A Comprehensive Guide to 1976*. Ann Arbor, MI: Xerox University Microfilms, 1976. 124 p. Indexes.

This is a general bibliography of 584 doctoral dissertations which have some bearing on the contemporary concerns of Mexican Americans. The compiler made selections based on the abstract content in *Dissertation Abstracts International*. The titles are arranged in broad subject categories used in *DAI:* Education; History; Language, Literature, Linguistics; Miscellaneous; Political Science; and Sociology. Dissertations on Education comprise the majority of the entries and are subarranged by Administration, Curriculum General, Guidance and Counseling, Higher, Psychology, Special, Teacher Training, Theory and Practice.

Many of the studies listed are directly related to the Mexican American but others only serve as background material. The Miscellaneous section contains studies primarily in other areas of the social sciences such as labor, economic conditions, health, psychological and sociological problems, and women. The section devoted to political topics is short but valuable since no separate bibliography exists to date on this area of Mexican American studies.

Cabrera's introduction includes a subjective discussion of education and the Mexican American along with conclusions based on the dissertations in the bibliography. This work, in conjunction with other listings of dissertations on the Mexican American, provides access to many unpublished scholarly resources. Annotations and a subject index would certainly enhance the usefulness of this bibliography.

6. Cárdenas, Gilbert. *Selected Bibliography Pertaining to La Raza in the Midwest and Great Lake States, 1924–1973*. Rev. ed. South Bend, IN: Notre Dame University, 1973. 23 p. ED 091 141.

Mexican Americans in the Midwestern states are the focus of this rather unique bibliography. It is arranged in one alphabetical listing and includes dissertations, theses, periodical articles, state publications, transcripts of hearings, and federal reports published between 1924 and 1973. The works cited are primarily on labor trends in migrant farm areas, but a sampling of items on religion, culture, language, health, education, population, and general living conditions of Spanish-speaking people of the area are also included. In all, there are 184 citations, the vast majority of which are relevant to the study of Mexican Americans. Thirteen Spanish newspapers, magazines, and periodicals published in the Midwest are also mentioned. An earlier and less extensive eight-page edition of this bibliography was compiled by Gilbert Cárdenas and Ricardo Parra in January, 1973.

7. Caselli, Ron. *The Minority Experience: A Basic Bibliography of American Ethnic Studies*. Santa Rosa, CA: Sonoma County Schools, 1970. 61 p. ED 038 221.

This general bibliography was prepared for teachers and students of ethnic studies by the author and members of the Sonoma County Ethnic Studies Curriculum Committee. Listed are approximately 950 books and periodical articles published between 1940 and 1969 on the three major ethnic groups in the United States: Afro-Americans, Mexican Americans and Native Americans. The section on the Mexican American contains 190 entries mainly in the areas of sociology, economics, and psychology. Following the section for each ethnic group is a list of relevant periodicals. Most works provide a historical approach to current problems. There are no annotations nor indexes.

8. Chicano Coordinating Council on Higher Education. "Select Bibliography." In *The Plan de Santa Barbara: A Chicano Plan for Higher Education*, pp. 73–81. Santa Barbara, CA: La Causa Publications, 1970. 154 p.

The primary purpose of this work is to strengthen pride in the cultural identity of Chicanos. The "Select Bibliography," which supplements the text, supports this with a basic but critical selection of sources. The bibliography is subdivided into 14 subject areas. It includes the cultural and historical material usually present in other general lists as well as items in the areas of literature, law, justice, psychology, public health, and statistical sources. This is a good basic list but it is by no means complete. Only three journal titles are cited and very few works in Spanish. There are no annotations and no indexes.

9. Clark y Moreno, Joseph A. "Bibliography of Bibliographies Relating to Mexican American Studies." *El Grito,* 3 (Summer, 1970): 25–31.

10. _____. "A Bibliography of Bibliographies Relating to Studies of Mexican Americans." *El Grito,* 5 (Winter, 1971–72): 47–79.

Together these two bibliographies of bibliographies include 546 items relating to the various aspects of Mexican American life (history, education, politics, sociology, economics, etc.). The selections were published between 1928 and 1970. Each bibliography is arranged alphabetically by author. After examining all of the titles cited, some items seem to be of marginal relevance or none at all to Mexican American studies. All of the pertinent items in Clark y Moreno's lists have been incorporated into this reference work. Those titles which were rejected generally related to Blacks or other minorities.

The attempt to identify sources for the study of the Mexican American is praiseworthy but annotations would have made the selections more useful to students and scholars. No indexes are included.

11. Cumberland, Charles Curtis. "The United States–Mexican Border: A Selective Guide to the Literature of the Region." In *Mexican American Bibliographies*, edited by Carlos E. Cortés. New York: Arno Press, 1974. Originally issued as supplement to *Rural Sociology*, 25 (June, 1960): 1–236. Annotated. Index.

This superb scholarly bibliography should serve as a model for bibliographers who are preparing guides to the literature in the field of Mexican American studies. The primary purpose of this work was to assist researchers by indicating the state of the scholarly literature on the Mexican borderlands from the Mexican Independence period up to 1958. Excluded are materials on the discovery and conquest, the Mission period, and colonial Texas and New Mexico.

The arrangement is by topic and each section is subdivided by books and monographs, theses and unpublished material, and journal articles. The following topics are covered: Bibliographies and guides; Diplomatic relations; Description, travel and geography; Spanish-speaking population of the United States; Immigration to the United States from Mexico; History; Education; Land use; Economic activity; Aspects of culture: general values; Religion; Folklore; Health; Government and politics; and Indians of the border area. The bibliography concludes with a list of 115 journals cited in the bibliography.

12. Flores Durán, Daniel. *Latino Materials: A Multimedia Guide for Children and Young Adults.* Santa Barbara, CA: ABC-Clio in association with Neal-Schuman Publishers, 1979. 249 p. Annotated. Indexes.

Current materials particularly suitable for Mexican American and Puerto Rican children from elementary level through the twelfth grade are covered in this general bibliography. Many of the titles in the secondary school section are also appropriate for college level although this is not indicated. The 473 items reviewed include books, films, and journals. These are arranged in four parts: Essays, General resources, Mexican American resources, and Puerto Rican resources.

For the convenience of the user, the materials are subarranged by elementary, secondary or professional materials and then by format. For each bibliographic entry the price and grade levels are also indicated. The selection of fiction and nonfiction is well balanced and demonstrates attention to literary quality, accuracy, and cultural relevance.

13. Ford, Mack E. *Americans of Mexican Descent: A Selected Bibliography of Materials on Mexicans and Mexican-Americans in the U.S.A.* San Francisco: California State College, 1969. 31 p. Annotated.

Compiled for a history course, this bibliography contains material on the Mexican Americans in the Southwest. The titles were selected from the holdings of the libraries of the city of San Francisco, the University of California, Berkeley, and San Francisco State College. It is arranged in three sections and includes a list of bibliographies; books and articles on the Mexicans and Mexican Americans in the United States; and books and articles on Mexican American education in the Southwest. The list is mimeographed and was prepared for limited use only. Location symbols for each entry are provided. The list is only partially annotated and the annotations consist of one-line descriptions of content.

14. Gómez-Quiñones, Juan, and Alberto Camarillo. *Selected Bibliography for Chicano Studies.* 3rd ed. Los Angeles: Aztlán Publications, 1975. (Bibliographic and Reference Series) 52 p.

15 _____, and Alberto Camarillo. *Selected Bibliography for Chicano Studies.* Los Angeles: Aztlán Publications, 1974. 38 p.

16 _____. *Selected Materials on the Chicano.* Los Angeles: Mexican American Cultural Center, University of California, 1970. 14 p.

In an effort to emphasize current writings in the field of Chicano studies, these bibliographies were produced. The third edition is an expanded version of the 1970 and 1974 editions. It lists approximately 900 titles of recent books and articles. The selected items are listed under 25 sections that are thematic or disciplinary. These include bibliographies, reference works, statistical materials, journals and magazines, and general interest works (anthologies, surveys, biographies, and autobiographies). There are sections on the Mexican background, U.S. influence, Economics/labor, Education/schooling, Fine arts, Folklore, History, Law and justice, Library science, Linguistics and language, Literature, Media and communications, Migration, Philosophy and social critique, Politics, Psychology, Public health, Society, Social structure and change, Women, and Mexican writings. This bibliography appears to be well selected and the various sections cover nearly every major aspect of Mexican American life. Furthermore, it indicates the growth and diversity of scholarship on the Chicano since 1970, particularly in areas such as creative writing, history, and political science. Annotations and indexes are lacking.

17. Grebler, Leo, Joan W. Moore, and Ralph Guzmán. "Bibliography." In *The Mexican-American People, the Nation's Second Largest Minority,* pp. 677–742. New York: The Free Press, 1970. 777 p.

This bibliography is most useful for study of the contemporary period of Mexican American history. It contains a general interdisciplinary selection of materials that supplement the text. Included are books, pamphlets, government publications, periodical articles, dissertations, other unpublished materials, and bibliographies. Arranged in five sections, it offers good coverage in the areas of economics, education, politics and religion of the Mexican American community. There is no introduction, no stated criteria, no annotations, and no index. Nevertheless, it is a good basic selection of resources for students.

18. Hyland, Anne. *A Mexican American Bibliography: A Collection of Print and Non-Print Materials.* Toledo, OH: Public Schools Curriculum Office, 1974. 90 p. Annotated. Indexes. ED 103 331

Resources on the Mexican American available in the curriculum office of the Toledo, Ohio, Public School System are listed in this bibliography. The materials were gathered between 1971 and 1974 for teachers and students. The titles are arranged in one alphabetical list. The collection includes books, records, filmstrips, tapes, 16 mm films, and periodicals which focus on the social sciences. The final pages of this bibliography include a list of addresses of publishers, producers, and distributors of the materials cited. Author-title and subject indexes assist the user in locating the materials desired. The annotations provided for some items are short content descriptions.

19. Jones, Robert C. "Mexicans in the United States: A Bibliography." In *Mexican American Bibliographies,* edited by Carlos E. Cortés. New York: Arno Press, 1974. (Reprint of 1942 ed., Washington, DC: Pan American Union. 14 p.)

The purpose of this bibliography is to supplement the work produced by Emory S. Bogardus, *The Mexican Immigrant: An Annotated Bibliography,* 1929. It lists over 200 books, periodical articles, government publications, and reports concerning urban settlements and industrial labor, agricultural labor, and the social problems of Mexicans in the United States. This is one of five bibliographies, reprinted in 1974 by Arno Press and included in *Mexican American Bibliographies,* edited by Carlos E. Cortés.

Jones's work is historically significant in that it demonstrates the state of the art of Mexican American bibliography up to 1942. There are no annotations and no indexes.

20. Jordan, Lois B. *Mexican Americans: Resources to Build Cultural Understanding.* Littleton, CO: Libraries Unlimited, 1973. 265 p. Annotated. Indexes.

Geared principally for young adults, this highly useful reference work is arranged in three parts. Part one covers printed materials, primarily books, which deal with the background history of Mexican Americans, their life in the United States, their art and literature. The majority of the sources cited in this first section are concerned with Mexico and its cultural influences rather than with the Mexican Americans themselves. Part two provides a list of

16 mm and 8 mm films; 35 mm filmstrips; recordings (tapes and discs); maps, transparencies and other audiovisual tools. The content of these materials, directly relevant to Mexican American studies, focuses on cultural heritage and contemporary social, economic, and political problems.

The unique part of this volume, however, is the final section which consists of four appendixes. Appendix *A* provides brief biographical sketches of distinguished Mexican American personalities in government, business, education, social movements and also those of artists, writers, sports figures, and entertainers. Appendix *B* is a directory of Mexican American organizations with addresses and brief descriptions of membership, scope, and purpose. Appendix *C* lists the membership of the Chicano Press Association and periodicals and newspapers of interest to Mexican Americans. Each entry includes the address, price, language, frequency, original date of publication and a brief description of the type of publication. Appendix *D* is a selected list of reference works including bibliographies, directories, guides, and handbooks, along with a few general works about the Mexican American.

The titles are well annotated and author, title, and subject indexes are provided.

21. Kratzert, Mona Y., and Evelyn K. Thornberry. *An Alphabetical Listing by Author of Periodical Articles Pertaining to the Chicano.* Fullerton: Library, California State University, 1973. 57 p.

This is an alphabetical listing of articles by or about Mexican Americans dating from the early 1930s to the early 1970s. All subjects are represented. In perusing the bibliography, we note that the articles were obtained from periodicals, both scholarly and popular, and from a few newspapers as well. Since no introduction is provided it is not possible to ascertain the criteria used in the selection. It is assumed, however, that this is a selection from the Fullerton collection for use by library patrons. Although the work demonstrates extensive effort on the part of the compilers, the absence of a subject arrangement or a subject index lessens the usefulness of this specialized list.

22. Lamb, Ruth S. "Bibliography." In *Mexican Americans: Sons of the Southwest,* pp. 149–196. Claremont, CA: Ocelot Press, 1970. 198 p.

This general bibliography cites a selection of books and articles arranged by such subjects as civil rights, political activities, education, folklore, the arts, history, labor, sociology and children's literature. The section on history is by far the most extensive. Other items, such as magazines and newspapers which are of interest to Mexican Americans, are also mentioned. Although part of a greater work, this list of materials is useful as an independent source for beginning research on certain subjects relating to the Mexican American and Southwest history.

23. Maciel, David R. *Mexico: A Selected Bibliography of Sources for Chicano Studies.* Los Angeles: Aztlán Publications, 1975. (Bibliographic and Reference Series) 38 p.

Prepared for use in Chicano Studies courses, this compilation contains background materials on Mexican Americans. The sources selected include books, articles, and a few dissertations, published both in Mexico and the United States. Works from the 1960s are predominant. The materials cover the historical period from pre-Columbian times to the twentieth century. They are divided into the following general categories: Reference works, Bibliographies, General works on Mexico, History, Politics, Economic aspects, Women, Social conditions, National characteristics, Cultural aspects, Schooling, Arts, Literature, and Philosophy. The bibliography is a basic guide to the secondary sources on Mexico which may serve as a point of departure for students involved in independent research on the Mexican American.

24. Martínez, Gilbert T. *Bibliography on Mexican-Americans.* Sacramento, CA: Sacramento City United School District, 1968. 45 p.

This is an example of an early general bibliography of some of the most basic and notable works on the Mexican Americans. It contains a few materials on every major subject area with an emphasis on the social sciences and education. Included are approximately 600 books, bulletins, and pamphlets arranged in one alphabetical list. However, no annotations and no indexes are provided. Presumably it was compiled for use in the school district at the secondary level, but an introduction is lacking.

25. Martínez, Julio A. *Selective Bibliography of Chicano Bibliographies.* San Diego, CA: Department of Reference and Institutional Services, Malcolm A. Love Library, San Diego State University, 1974. 16 p.

Bibliographies relevant to Chicano Studies are enumerated in this work. Included are 151 unannotated entries for works published between 1959 and 1974. Arrangement is alphabetical by main entry. Coverage is mainly in history and the social sciences, i.e., cultural identity, political awareness, socioeconomic conditions, psychology, and history of Chicanos. Reference is made to the bibliographies of Clark y Moreno and Talbot and Cruz for sources on art, literature, and education, etc., and Ray Padilla's bibliography for retrospective materials.

Call numbers and location symbols are provided for the items in the Malcolm A. Love Library. A revised and expanded edition of this work is in progress.

26. Mickey, Barbara H. *A Bibliography of Studies Concerning the Spanish-Speaking Population of the American Southwest.* Greeley: Library, Colorado State College, 1969. (Museum of Anthropology Miscellaneous Series, no. 4) 42 p. ED 042 548.

The purpose of this bibliography was to gather references useful to an anthropological study of the Spanish-speaking population of the American Southwest. Arranged in alphabetical order by author is an array of materials dealing with the social problems, language, employment, immigration and migration, sociology, and education of the Mexican American. There are 544 entries focusing mainly on the post-1930 period to the mid-1960s. Books, articles, travel accounts, theses, and dissertations are included in this listing. The selections generally relate to the Mexican American. There are no annotations and no indexes.

27. Miller, Wayne Charles. "Mexican Americans: A Guide to the Mexican-American Experience." In *A Comprehensive Bibliography for the Study of American Minorities,* pp. 911–953. New York: New York University Press, 1976. 2 vols. Annotated. Indexes.

This immense bibliographical effort provides a general comparative approach to the study of minorities. Twenty-nine thousand three hundred titles have been collected on all major minority groups in America. The work is divided into sections by the various ethnic and minority groups. Each section is preceded by a historical-bibliographical essay presenting an overview of the most useful studies on the particular group. The section on Mexican Americans lists approximately 600 titles arranged in the following categories: Bibliographies, Periodicals, History, Sociology, Immigration and labor, Education and language, Psychology and medicine, Politics and social issues, Religion, Literary criticism, Biography and autobiography, Painting, Sculpture and architecture, Anthologies, Drama, Novels and short stories, Poetry, Folklore, and Music. In keeping with the overall approach, there is a concluding section in volume two on Multi-group studies which also contains material relevant to the Mexican Americans.

This is one of the better general bibliographies for the study of the Mexican Americans. Annotations, subject arrangement, and indexes enhance the usefulness of the work.

28. Nichols, Margaret S., and Margaret N. O'Neill. *Multicultural Materials; A Selective Bibliography of Adult Materials Concerning Human Relations and the History, Culture and Current Social Issues of Black, Chicano, Asian American and Native American Peoples.* Stanford, CA: Multicultural Resources, 1974. 49 p.

Four ethnic groups are covered by this general bibliography in the areas of history and current social issues; biography; fiction, poetry, drama, legends, collections; art and music; and periodicals. The selected items are arranged by ethnic group, subdivided by topic, and listed in alphabetical order. There is a special section of approximately 110 items on the Chicano. This is a revised edition of the *Bibliography of Multicultural Materials* (California State Department of Education, Bureau of Intergroup Relations, 1973). A helpful directory of publishers and their addresses is included. No annotations and no indexes are provided, but the topical arrangement facilitates access to the materials cited.

29. Nogales, Luís G. *The Mexican American: A Selected and Annotated Bibliography.* Stanford, CA: Stanford University, 1971. 162 p. Annotated. Index.

This bibliography is a revised and enlarged edition of *The Mexican American; A Selected and Annotated Bibliography* (Center for Latin American Studies, Stanford University, 1969). The new edition covers a selection of over 400 of the most significant works on Mexican Americans with emphasis on scholarly publications. The selected works are in the areas of anthropology, economics, education, history, linguistics, literature, philosophy, political science, psychology, public health, and sociology.

Included are books, periodical articles, and dissertations which focus principally on contemporary concerns of the Mexican American community. The long, descriptive, and critical annotations aid the researcher in selecting the appropriate source. A special feature of this bibliography is a listing of Chicano periodicals by state. An adequate field index with cross references is also provided. This is a very useful and well-balanced general bibliography on the Mexican Americans for the specialist and the informed layman.

30. Oaks, Priscilla. *Minority Studies: A Selective Annotated Bibliography.* Boston: G. K. Hall, 1975. 303 p. Annotated. Index.

Sources on Mexican Americans, Asian Americans, Native Americans, and Afro-Americans are covered in this bibliography. In total, there are 287 entries. They include the usual and familiar bibliographies, periodical articles, and books on the various minority groups. The subjects covered by the items on the Mexican Americans are also commonly found in other bibliographies: history, geography, politics, economics, agricultural labor, education, bicultural programs, general culture, and literature. Annotations are provided but are poorly written. The index covers authors and titles.

31. Ortego, Philip D. *Selective Mexican American Bibliography.* El Paso, TX: Border Regional Library Association and Chicano Research Institute, 1972. 121 p.

The purpose of this bibliography is to show the extent of the Mexican American literary tradition by bringing together books, articles, and government publications authored exclusively by Mexican Americans and Mexicans. The citations are arranged alphabetically in 15 subject categories covering nearly every aspect of Mexican American life, i.e., history, politics, civil rights, literature and folklore, economics, public health, sociology, labor, and agriculture. Of particular value is the lengthy section on literature and folklore. Supplementing the main work is a list of reference sources including bibliographies, directories, guides, documents, and special collections. The bibliographical entries are in abbreviated form and no annotations are provided.

32. Ortíz, Ana María. *Bibliography on Hispano American History and Culture.* Springfield: Education Services Department, Illinois State Commission on Human Relations, 1972. 35 p. Annotated. ED 080 270.

This work includes 145 books written between 1945 and 1969 on the Hispano Americans. Approximately 21 of the selections are directly relevant to the Mexican American experience while the rest concern the history and culture of Mexico, the Puerto Ricans, and other Hispanic groups. Perhaps the most unusual feature of this bibliography is a list of 23 resource and story books for children, most of which are in Spanish. No guidelines for selection of the material are given. The work is only partially annotated and no indexes are provided.

The bibliography was designed for students, teachers, parents, and librarians with an interest in Spanish-speaking people. The section on children's literature would be useful for bilingual-bicultural programs.

33. Padilla, Ray. "Apuntes para la documentación de la cultura chicana." *El Grito,* 5 (Winter, 1971–72): 3-46.

This issue of *El Grito* is devoted almost entirely to Chicano bibliography. The major part consists of Padilla's bibliographical essay covering 1846 to 1972. It is arranged in three historical periods and discusses approximately 125 titles. Following the essay is a short bibliography of 56 bibliographies related to Chicano studies. It supplements Joseph A. Clark y Moreno's *A Bibliography of Bibliographies Relating to Studies of Mexican Americans,* published in this same issue. Most of the works are relevant to Latin American history, the history and culture of the Southwest, as well as to the study of the Mexican American experience. This essay is a good analysis of the state of Mexican American bibliography up to 1971.

34. Pino, Frank. *Mexican Americans: A Research Bibliography*. East Lansing: Michigan State University, 1974. 2 vols. Index.

A vast amount of research material on the Mexican American is covered in this comprehensive computer-produced bibliography. The two volumes contain approximately 8,692 entries arranged in 35 different areas and provide an interdisciplinary selection for the serious researcher. In spite of its coverage, this bibliography must be used with caution because of the numerous deficiencies, inaccuracies, duplications, and the inclusion of unnecessary and non-existent titles. As a truly valuable reference work, it is something of a failure; with corrections and proper editing it might have been published in one volume. Using the coded cross-reference scheme is cumbersome and time-consuming.

In spite of the shortcomings there is a wealth of resources including theses, dissertations, articles, special studies, and government publications. Of particular interest is the unique section on "Images" which lists sources that relate to the vision of the Mexican American as conceived by himself and others.

35. Quezada, María. *Chicano Resource Materials*. Washington, DC: Montal Systems Inc., 1970. 90 p.

This is a compilation of materials gathered from educational laboratories, libraries, distribution centers, and Chicano studies programs for the benefit of participants in Chicano studies institutes. It includes a list of bibliographies, periodical articles, and books. The books are classified under ten headings: Economics and labor, Education, Art, History, Literature, Philosophy, Psychology, Political science, Public health, and Sociology. Also included is a list of audiovisual aids (films and slides), a list of Mexican American newspapers and magazines, and two separate lists of educational materials relevant to the Mexican Americans, although a number of items pertain to Mexico. There are no annotations and no indexes.

36. Quintana, Helena. *A Current Bibliography on Chicanos, 1960-1973; Selected and Annotated*. 2nd ed. Albuquerque: University of New Mexico, 1974. 47 p. Annotated. Index.

The purpose of this bibliography is to provide teachers with a list of supplementary materials on the Chicano for use in the classroom. Included are 246 books and monographs published since 1960, with a few exceptions. There are quite a number of literary entries but most items are on general culture and history. Each citation indicates the recommended educational level: elementary, junior high, high school, junior college, or college. The bibliography also contains a list of Chicano periodicals, names of publishers, addresses, and acquisitions information.

This edition adds new titles and publisher information not in the first edition, prepared in 1973.

37. REFORMA. Arizona Chapter. *A Core Collection of Print Material for Libraries Serving the Spanish-Speaking of the Southwest*. Tucson: University of Arizona Libraries, 1978. 83 p. Annotated.

Designed as a guide to the development of a core collection for public libraries serving the Spanish-speaking in the Southwest, this general bibliography was produced by a chapter of REFORMA, the National Association of Spanish-Speaking Librarians. Although the list is not research oriented, many of the titles are essential to a basic research collection on the Mexican American. The 550 books and periodicals are arranged in four parts: General reference, Subject areas, Juvenile literature, and Periodicals. A list of publishers and distributors of the material cited in the bibliography appears at the end of the work. It includes addresses and evaluative comments on the services provided. The subject categories in section II cover applied sciences, the arts, astrology and the occult, biography, education, folklore and customs, health and medicine, history, language, literature, Spanish language fiction, mathematics and science, philosophy and religion. Audiovisual materials are excluded. It is evident that the titles have been selected with care and attention to quality. Most of the titles are current and readily available. Prices are indicated for many of the items.

This list is particularly useful for both information on Mexican background and contemporary Chicano culture. Supplements are to be published in the occasional newsletter of the Arizona Chapter of REFORMA.

38. Revelle, Keith. *Chicano: A Selected Bibliography of Materials by and about Mexico and Mexican Americans.* Oakland, CA: Latin American Library, Oakland Public Library, 1969. 21 p. Annotated.
This work was designed for use by the general public interested in Mexican Americans or for librarians wishing to establish core Mexican American collections. It covers basic works—books, newspapers, periodicals, articles, reports, and speeches—which any library should have if interested in Mexican American culture and problems. The citations are abridged and the annotations are generally descriptive of the content of each work.

39. ———. "A Collection for La Raza." *Library Journal,* 96 (1971): 3719–3726. Annotated.
A working aid for the public librarian, this bibliography is divided into four general sections. The first is an alphabetical list of books containing fictional materials in Spanish and English; "how to" and "self-realization" materials in Spanish; historical works; biographies of military and political figures; and materials in English on the Mexican Americans. The second section provides a list of Spanish language magazines and newspapers. The third lists the Chicano Press publications and the last section is an annotated list of audiovisual materials.

This highly selective listing was designed to make Chicano materials more accessible and to offer a variety of resources which have proven successful with Mexican American patrons. The annotations are brief content descriptions; a few give the English translations for titles in Spanish.

40. Saldaña, Nancy. *Mexican-Americans in the Midwest: An Annotated Bibliography.* East Lansing: Rural Manpower Center, Michigan State University, 1969. (Special paper, No. 10) 60 p. Annotated.
The focus of this work is on Mexican Americans in the Midwest. The materials are listed under 13 topical headings which include Acculturation and assimilation; Attitudes and world view; Demographic analysis; Distinctive cultural components; Education; Employment and income; Marriage and family, General discussion; Housing; Migration and

immigration; Language; Political behavior; and Social status. It is not an extensive bibliography, but the 125 items are well selected and analyzed.

There is a good introduction analyzing the state of Mexican American bibliography in the United States, organized by historical periods. Critical annotations are in essay form. Although this is one of the best bibliographies on the Mexican American in the Midwest, the emphasis is on the social sciences. Literary works are not included.

41. Saunders, Lyle. *A Guide to Materials Bearing on Cultural Relations in New Mexico*. Albuquerque: University of New Mexico Press, 1944. 528 p. Annotated. Indexes.

This impressive bibliographical effort by the School of Inter-American Affairs, University of New Mexico, although somewhat dated now, is one of the few works of this extent and kind. It was motivated by the desire to provide scholars with a useful guide to materials on New Mexico, to preserve the bibliographical heritage of the state and to stimulate future studies and compilations of this type.

The guide is arranged in three basic sections followed by an addenda and the author and subject indexes. The approximately 5,000 selections include books, articles, and unpublished manuscripts. The opening section, the Dictionary-Guide, consists of 263 titles that are the most relevant to the study of cultural relations in New Mexico. The content of each work is summarized. Following the Dictionary-Guide is the list of Selected Titles included in the Dictionary-Guide. The third and longest section is the Supplementary Bibliographies, which includes bibliographies and indexes, fiction and drama, general works, and material on the Apaches, Navajos, Pueblos, Spanish Americans and Mexicans.

Of particular relevance to the study of the Mexican American are those sources on cultural and historical background, immigration, labor, customs and beliefs, tales, dance, music, literature and language, education and social conditions. These are listed in the 32 pages in the supplementary bibliography entitled Spanish Americans and Mexicans.

42. _____. "Spanish-Speaking Americans and Mexican-Americans in the United States: A Selected Bibliography." In *Mexican-American Bibliographies*, edited by Carlos E. Cortés. New York: Arno Press, 1974. (Reprint of 1944 ed., New York: Bureau for Inter-Cultural Education. 6 p.)

One of the earliest general guides, compiled by a skilled scholar and bibliographer, it covers historical, social and economic conditions; migrants and migratory workers; education; health and nutrition; architecture, arts and crafts; folklore; music; dances; folk plays; and fiction. In addition, among the 352 unannotated items are a number of unpublished studies, periodicals, and names of organizations of interest to the Spanish-speaking community. The selection is directed toward teachers and prospective teachers. A coding system indicates which sources are suitable for use in the elementary school and which are for the high school level.

This is one of five bibliographies, reprinted by Arno Press, in *Mexican American Bibliographies*.

43. Scott, Frank, Carlos Aceves, and César Caballero. *M. A. Theses on the Mexican American in the University Archives of the University of Texas at El Paso Library*. El Paso: University of Texas, 1975. 21 p. Index.

This bibliography provides access to selected theses in a variety of subjects relevant to the study of the Mexican American. All of the theses, written between 1942 and 1974, are by graduate students at the University of Texas at El Paso. They are in the fields of education, history, literature, political science, religion, and sociology and are arranged by these fields in the bibliography. The works cited, although not of mature scholarship, cover topics and areas often ignored by larger, more professional studies. The theses are available in the El Paso Library on microform or hardcopy. Call numbers are provided in this guide for both forms. This general bibliography is indicative of the research trends and interest in Mexican American studies over three decades at the university.

44. Smith, Jesse Carney. "The Literature and Culture of Chicanos." In *Minorities in the United States: Guide to Resources*, pp. 90–112. Nashville, TN: Peabody Library School, George Peabody College for Teachers, 1973. 133 p. ED 030 133.

Intended as a guide for librarians, educators, library school students and others, this bibliography contains sources for the study of Native Americans, Black Americans, Japanese and Chinese Americans, Chicanos and Puerto Ricans. Chapter Five presents information and material on Chicanos. The introductory essay discusses the history and culture; the representative library collections in the United States with substantial Mexican or Chicano holdings; and a subject approach to the Chicano materials. The bibliography following the essay contains over 200 titles arranged under various subject headings: Library service to the Chicano, Research collections, Bibliographies and references, the Humanities, the Social sciences, and Periodicals. There are no annotations.

45. Stanford University. Center for Latin American Studies. *The Mexican American: A Selected and Annotated Bibliography*. Stanford, CA: Stanford University, 1969. 139 p. Annotated. Index.

Designed for the specialist and the informed layman, the focus of this general bibliography is on contemporary concerns of the Mexican American community. Most of the 274 books and articles listed are scholarly works in the social sciences. The entries are arranged in one alphabetical list with a subject index. The annotations, which are actually critical signed reviews, are the most notable feature of this bibliography. A revised edition of this bibliography by the same title was prepared by Luís G. Nogales in 1971.

46. Talbot, Jane Mitchell, and Gilbert R. Cruz. *A Comprehensive Chicano Bibliography, 1960–1972*. Austin, TX: Jenkins, 1973. 375 p. Indexes.

This extensive and well-researched bibliography lists books, government publications, articles, audiovisual materials, and journals dealing with such areas of Mexican American studies as history, politics, statistics, education, health, role of the Catholic Church, literature and criticism, children's literature, folklore and folk practices, music and fine arts. Of the areas mentioned, education and literature contain the largest number of entries. Prepared for the benefit of serious researchers, this tool incorporates publications both by and about the Chicano. The selection concentrates on the important works written since 1960.

This is an enlarged edition of their work, *A General Bibliography for Research in Mexican American Studies: The Decade of the Sixties to the Present*, published in 1972.

47. Tatum, Charles M. *A Selected and Annotated Bibliography of Chicano Studies*. Manhattan: Society of Spanish and Spanish-American Studies, Department of Modern Languages, Kansas State University, 1976. (SSSAS: Bibliographies, no. 101) 107 p. Annotated. Index.

This bibliography was designed for secondary school teachers and college professors who wish to establish or expand courses on the Mexican Americans. In the appendix there are brief outlines of four model courses recommended by the author and a list of publishers' addresses. Most of the 307 books, articles, audiovisuals, journals, and newspapers are current, readily available, and primarily cultural in nature. The entries are arranged by subject. Of particular strength are the sections on literature, art, music, dance, and folklore. There is also a separate section on the Chicana. Other important features are the annotations, cross references, and the author index.

The second edition of this work is forthcoming in 1979.

48. Teschner, Richard V. *Spanish-Surnamed Populations of the United States; A Catalog of Dissertations*. Ann Arbor, MI: Xerox University Microfilms, 1974. 43 p. Index.

49. ———. *Supplement No. 1 to Spanish-Surnamed Populations of the United States; A Catalog of Dissertations*. Ann Arbor, MI: University of Microfilms International, 1977.

Doctoral dissertations (1861-1974) pertaining to the several Hispanic or Spanish-surnamed populations of the United States, particularly Chicanos, Puerto Ricans and Cubans are listed in this enumerative bibliography. Some items relate to the Spanish-surnamed of Louisiana, the Sephardic Jewish groups, the New York City Galicians, etc. Cited are 1,197 items in the fields of anthropology, business and economics, geography, history, library science, political science, social work, folklore, language and linguistics, literature, mass communications, music and fine arts, religion and theology, health sciences, home economics, psychology and public health, and education. These items were gathered from volumes 17 through 32 of the *Comprehensive Dissertation Index 1861-1972* and from *Dissertation Abstracts International*, vols. 33/07-34/12 (Jan. 1973-Jan. 1974).

The supplement lists 388 titles of dissertations collected over two years and indicates the "range and depth of interest" now being shown by American universities in Hispanic topics. Covered in this supplement are volumes 35/01 (A & B) through 36/12 (A & B) of *Dissertation Abstracts International*. The same format has been used in the supplement as in the 1974 *Catalog*.

50. Trejo, Arnulfo D. *Bibliografía Chicana: A Guide to Information Sources*. Detroit: Gale Research, 1976. (Ethnic Studies: An Information Guide, vol. 1) 193 p. Annotated. Index.

Monographs on general subjects pertaining to the Mexican Americans since 1848 are found in this bibliography. Some preference is given to contemporary sources by Mexican American writers. The 349 works are arranged in five broad sections and include reference works such as guides, indexes, bibliographies, directories, dictionaries, and materials in the areas of philosophy, religion, language, literature, fine arts, education, sociology, anthropology, folklore, statistics, economics, labor, political science, psychology, public health, and history. Also provided are a directory of current periodicals and newspapers relevant to the Chicano experience; a directory of publishers of Chicano materials; and a glossary of Chicano Spanish words.

The selections have all been examined by the compiler and constitute a core collection on the Chicano.

51. Trejo, Francisco. *Chicano Bibliography*. Minneapolis, MN: Task Force on Ethnic Studies, Minneapolis Public Schools, 1972. 13 p. ED 076 475.

This bibliography was probably prepared for use by the Minneapolis Public Schools, although its purpose is not stated. The work includes 150 entries of mainly social science materials—books, journal articles, and a few dissertations from the 1960s. The selections deal with Mexicans Americans and their social, economic, political, and educational problems. Also included in this bibliography is a list of Chicano journals, newspapers, and reference materials. The items are not annotated and no indexes are provided.

52. Trueba, Henry T. *Mexican-American Bibliography: Bilingual Bicultural Education*. Urbana: University of Illinois, 1973. 26 p. ED 085 120.

General in nature, this work covers materials published between 1919 and 1973 on history, sociology, anthropology, economics, linguistics, political science, law, mental health, educational psychology, methodology, teaching English as a second language, and modern language teaching. The 306 books and periodical articles are all directly relevant to the study of the Mexican American, with only a few items on Mexico. It is arranged in three sections: Social Sciences, Education, and Bibliographies. It lacks indexes and annotations that would make it more useful, particularly to teachers in bilingual-bicultural education.

53. U.S. Bureau of Naval Personnel. Library Services Branch. *Indian and Mexican-Americans: A Selective, Annotated Bibliography*. Washington, DC: Government Printing Office, 1972. 42 p. Annotated. Index.

This work was designed to assist Navy library personnel in developing collections that would be responsive to both minority and majority groups in the society. Although the emphasis is on the Native Americans, the Mexican American portion (pp. 28–35) covers books under such subjects as history, labor, immigration, sociology, collections, youth, land grants, César Chávez, and Brown Power. The selections are familiar basic works.

54. U.S. Cabinet Committee on Opportunities for the Spanish Speaking. *The Spanish Speaking in the United States: A Guide to Materials*. Washington, DC: Government Printing Office. 1971. 175 p. Annotated. Index.

Although the majority of the materials in this guide focuses on Mexican Americans, the Spanish-speaking in this context refers to Mexican Americans, Puerto Ricans, and Cubans. The resources listed emphasize the social, political, economic, and educational role of these groups in the development of the United States. The selections are arranged alphabetically under the following categories: Books and monographs; Reports, speeches, articles; Theses and dissertations; Government publications (state and federal); Audiovisual materials. Appendixes include a list of U.S. producers or distributors of Spanish language audiovisual materials; a list of currently published serials (by state); and a list of Spanish language radio and television stations and their programs (by state).

This bibliography is a revised and expanded edition of *The Mexican American, A New Focus on Opportunity: A Guide to Materials Relating to Persons of Mexican Heritage in the United States,* published in 1969 by the U.S. Inter-Agency Committee on Mexican American Affairs and included in the chapter on Social and Behavioral Sciences.

55. U.S. Department of Housing and Urban Development. Library. *Hispanic Americans in the United States: A Selective Bibliography, 1963–1974.* Washington, DC: The Department, 1974. 31 p. Index. ED 096 089.

This bibliography was published in response to the awareness of the contributions and special problems of Americans of Hispanic ancestry. Cited are 328 books, reports, periodical articles, and bibliographies published in English between 1963 and 1974 pertaining to Hispanic Americans in the United States. The items concern their historical background and their educational, economic, and social adjustments. A good selection of socioeconomic sources are presented as well as historical and cultural materials. A special section of 211 entries pertains to the Mexican Americans. An author index is at the end of the work. No annotations are provided.

56. University of California, Los Angeles. Mexican American Study Project. *Revised Bibliography,* by Gerald Rosen, with a bibliographical essay by Ralph Guzmán. Los Angeles: Division of Research, Graduate School of Business Administration, University of California, 1967. (Advance Report, no. 3) 99 p.

One of the first comprehensive and scholarly bibliographies produced in the 1960s; it is devoted exclusively to the Mexican Americans. This is a revised edition of an earlier work published in 1966 at the University of California, Los Angeles. The newer edition, with more than 1,000 items, is arranged in five categories: Books, Journal articles, Unpublished theses and dissertations, Other unpublished materials, and Bibliographies. The coverage includes all aspects of Mexican American life in areas such as economics, sociology, politics, religion, etc. The post-1940 period is best represented in this work. This is an excellent bibliography, but annotations and indexes would have made it a more useful tool. The first edition was partially annotated.

57. Woods, Richard D. *Reference Materials on Mexican-Americans: An Annotated Bibliography.* Metuchen, NJ: Scarecrow Press, 1976. 190 p. Annotated. Indexes.

This is one of the first published bibliographies devoted to reference works on Mexican Americans. The purpose is to indicate to researchers and laymen the tools which are currently available and to point out gaps to which scholarly efforts might be directed. A total of 387 selected reference works are included which were published either in the United States or in Mexico. They cover a wide range of subjects that pertain exclusively to Mexican Americans. Worthy of special mention are those types of works not usually found in many of the other general bibliographies: e.g., cookbooks, genealogical sources, land grant sources, and church directories. The overall criteria and selection are excellent, although an arrangement other than an alphabetical listing would have enhanced the usefulness as a reference tool.

The citations, content analysis, and lengthy descriptions are accurate, for the most part, but some of the entries contain errors and misinformation. The basic orientation is toward the scholar and the academic library. There is a slight emphasis on materials from Texas.

# Chapter 2

# *Library Guides*

The Chicano Movement has had a definite impact on libraries and their collection policies. During the early 1960s college and university libraries throughout the United States, but particularly in the West and the Southwest, began to acquire research and reference materials in support of Mexican American Studies programs. Many institutions organized special Mexican American collections, such as the Colección Tloque Nahauque in the library at the University of California, Santa Barbara, or they established separate Chicano libraries, such as the Chicano Research Center Library at the University of California, Los Angeles. Portions of book budgets were designated for Mexican American resources, and subject/language specialists were assigned to develop the collections. Most libraries began to acquire types of materials that previously had been overlooked or ignored. Simultaneously, public and state libraries began to actively identify and collect materials in recognition of the informational needs of Mexican American patrons and communities.

In tandem with the collection building efforts were the attempts to identify and document what was already in the collections in order to provide better access to the materials. The librarians were often assisted in their efforts by faculty from Chicano Studies programs or by student groups such as MECHA, Movimiento Estudiantil Chicano de Aztlán. One outcome of the spirited activity in collecting and identifying Mexican American resources was the library guides or bibliographies that are cited in this chapter.

The quality and length of these guides vary considerably but they share many similarities. To avoid redundancy in the annotations, only substantial guides representing larger collections, or those containing special or unique features, have been annotated. These are identified as the Major Library Guides. The others are listed, without annotations, in the subsection entitled Minor Library Guides.

The major guides are all more than 50 pages in length and show the development of a number of significant Mexican American collections. Continued growth of these collections is indicated by the quarterly or biennial lists, the supplements, and the revised editions that have been produced since the first bibliographies were issued. Some of the library guides, although only printed or mimeographed for local use, have received wider distribution through Educational Resources Information Center (ERIC).

On the whole, the compilers of both the major and minor bibliographies prepared them with a sense of urgency or haste, often neglecting to state guidelines or criteria for the selections cited. In these works, the titles or the tables of contents must suffice as the only indications of the type of sources and subjects covered. The reader will note that these guides present a variety of approaches and solutions to the problem of identification and access to Mexican American materials. The most common approach has been the general bibliography covering numerous subjects and topics, predominately in the fields of history, social sciences, education and culture. A few of the guides have been limited to one type of material such as bibliographies or reference tools, others contain only books or articles, and still others have attempted to include all types of print and nonprint resources, both published and unpublished. Some libraries chose to produce lists which combine sources on several ethnic or minority groups. A few of the libraries have compiled guides which focus, or claim to focus, solely on the Chicano, while others have sought broader coverage by including materials on Mexico and the Southwest. However, none of the compilers claim that their guide is comprehensive, and overall the titles of the bibliographies imply selectivity. Several of the better institutional bibliographies, such as the one by Phyllis Bischoff (University of California, Berkeley) offer instruction on the use of the card catalog and other general reference tools. This enables the researcher to move independently beyond the specialized bibliography and to take advantage of other resources and services offered by the library.

The minor library guides are, with a few exceptions, ephemeral enumerative bibliographies, representing less significant collections on the Mexican American. Most lack annotations and indexes, and contain a greater number of marginally relevant materials on Mexico, on Latin America in general, and on other Spanish-speaking groups and Blacks, rather than sources exclusively on the Mexican American. Yet, many claim to be Chicano or Mexican American bibliographies. As a rule the minor bibliographies are dated and do not represent the current state of the collections. They are, nevertheless, included here in order to exemplify the recent and widespread attention that was given by libraries to Mexican American materials.

All of these guides were produced to meet the exigencies of the times. Many are inadequate for in-depth research and demonstrate the confusion that existed, even within the academic community, regarding the definition and scope of the literature on the Mexican American. Nonetheless, they indicate a willingness by many libraries to respond quickly to the new challenges and to participate in the effort to define the dimensions of the literature. These guides have served to point out lacunae in certain areas of research. The compilers, in noting these gaps, justifiably or not, filled them with marginally relevant sources, or background materials from Spain, Mexico, and other Latin American countries. This was particularly true in the areas of literature and history.

In recent years the production of the general library bibliography has diminished. The current trend is toward specialized or subject-oriented guides, highlighting such topics as health, Chicano literature, or migrant labor. Many examples of these other works can be found in the appropriate chapters relating to subject bibliographies.

## MAJOR LIBRARY GUIDES

58. Birdwell, Gladys Bryant. *Chicanos: A Selected Bibliography.* Houston, TX: Libraries, University of Houston, 1971. 60 p.
More than 30 monographs, journal articles, and government publications concerning Mexican Americans are arranged in one alphabetical listing. It appears that the selected references are of those located within the confines of the University of Houston libraries

but no stated guidelines or purpose is given. Some items in the monograph section are peripheral to the Mexican American but the articles and government publications are on the whole directly related. This general selection has been superseded by the 1974 work prepared by the office of the Assistant Director for Development of Collections, at the University of Houston, entitled *Mexican-Americans: A Selected Bibliography.*

59. Bischof, Phyllis. *Ethnic Studies: A Selective Guide to Reference Materials at Berkeley.* Berkeley: General Library, University of California, 1974. (Occasional Publications, no. 1) 52 p. Annotated. Index.
This is a selective guide to bibliographies, abstracts, indexes, and other reference works that are highly useful in ethnic studies research. All selections are held by the libraries at the University of California, Berkeley. The guide covers Mexican Americans as well as other ethnic groups. The sections listing guides to periodical literature and abstracts, general bibliographies, and Chicano bibliographies are most relevant to those interested in the Mexican American. Also helpful are the instructions on the use of the card catalogs and a general description of the library units housing ethnic studies materials. This is an exceptionally well-prepared guide with thorough and accurate annotations. An author-title index is appended.

60. California State College, San Jose. Library. *Minorities in America: A List of Books on Blacks and Mexican Americans in the San Jose State College Library. San Jose: The Library, 1969. 151 p. Index.*

This is a guide to the special holdings of the library related to the study of Blacks and Mexican Americans. The arrangement for the section on the Mexican American is by broad subject categories including History; Religion; Sociology; Psychology; Labor and employment; Health; Education; Art and literature; Mexican American youth; Mexican Americans in the Southwest, East, and West. Most of the items are those generally found in core collections. Call numbers and an author index are provided for the user.

61. California State Library. *A Quarterly Bibliography on Cultural Differences.* Sacramento: The Library, 1965+. Annotated.
A current list of materials on minority groups acquired by the California State Library are listed in this quarterly publication. The materials include monographs, articles, U.S. and California government documents, and bibliographies. Items on the Mexican American are usually found under such headings as Bibliographies, Employment, Labor relations, Education, and History. Recent issues are subdivided according to ethnic group. Entries are complete, accurate, and annotations are usually in the form of a quotation or a summary of the content.

62. California State University, Fullerton. Library. *Mexico and the Southwest Collection.* Fullerton: The Library, 1977. 316 p.
This is a revised and enlarged edition of the 1974 bibliography by the same title. It includes materials located in the California State University, Fullerton library. The headings under which the sources are listed indicate extensive coverage. There are items under General reference works, Humanities, Social sciences, History, Applied sciences, and Arts. Certain topics such as *La Chicana* and *Machismo*, the *Pachuco*, the Zoot-Suit Riots,

the Treaty of Guadalupe Hidalgo, *La Raza Unida* Party, Immigration, and the United Farm Workers Union are given in-depth coverage. Also forming part of this work is a directory of currently published Chicano newspapers and periodicals arranged by state, and a directory of Chicano publishers and media distributors. Appended is a list of audio and video taped interviews and speeches of emminent Chicanos such as César Chávez, Reíes López Tijerina, Bert Corona, and Corky Gonzáles.

This bibliography is well selected and highly useful for research on the Mexican American. Earlier works by the staff at the Fullerton contained more emphasis on Mexico. Indexes are lacking.

63. Fisher, Edith Maureen. *Focusing on Mexican/Chicano American Research; A Guide and Annotated Bibliography to Selected Resources in the University of California, San Diego Libraries.* San Diego: Instructional Services Department, University Library, University of California, 1976. 70 p. Annotated. Index.

A very basic and elementary research guide to sources of materials about Mexican Americans; it includes catalogs, subject bibliographies, biographies, dictionaries, indexes, and statistical resources located in the libraries of the University of California, San Diego. Forty-three items seem to be of direct relevance to the Mexican Americans. This work was devised as a teaching aid for students seeking resources on Mexican Americans. It is not a bibliography of the collection in the University of California, San Diego libraries.

The arrangement of this guide may be confusing to students, and the annotations are too lengthy, consisting mainly of quotations from those titles examined. The selection of subject bibliographies is too sparce, only one is provided in most instances, and some of the items included were not examined by the compiler.

In spite of the impressive title, this reference tool is a disappointment. It falls short of its twofold purpose in guiding patrons in the use of the library and in providing an annotated bibliography of selected resources.

64. García-Ayvens, Francisco, Darien Fisher, and Hilda Villarreal. *¿Quién sabe?: A Preliminary List of Chicano Reference Materials.* Los Angeles: Chicano Studies Center, University of California, 1979. (Bibliography and Reference Series, no. 11) 86 p. Annotated. Indexes.

Reference tools located in the Chicano Research Library at the University of California, Los Angeles, are listed in this special bibliography. The 86 works cited are all essential to research on the Mexican American and are important for most core collections. The library's call numbers are provided for each item. Included are bibliographies, directories, dictionaries, encyclopedias, biographical sources, and other traditional types of reference materials with particular relevance to Chicano studies. Among the nontraditional types of reference sources listed are the pictorial works, relating to the history of Mexico, the Mexican Americans, and the farmworkers.

The lengthy annotations accurately summarize the contents of each work and evaluate their usefulness as reference sources. There is an emphasis on current materials related to California. This work exemplifies the recent trend toward the production of specialized library bibliographies rather than the general type.

65. González, Héctor Aurelio, Susie García, and Andrew Villalobos. *Bibliography: A Guide to Materials in the Chicano Reference Library.* 2nd rev. ed. Palo Alto, CA: Chicano Reference Library, Stanford University, 1978. 83 p.

This work supersedes the previous bibliographies and supplement issued in 1972, 1974, and 1976 by the Chicano Reference Library at Stanford. The new edition covers over 1,900 volumes on the history, language, culture, and literature of the Mexican American. It is similar in scope and arrangement to the other bibliographies, with an emphasis on current imprints. The materials are arranged in five categories: Books, ERIC files, Princeton files, Periodicals, and Audiovisual materials. Call numbers are provided for all the books listed. The vertical file materials, the student papers collection, and the media collection are particularly noteworthy and unique. The vertical or Princeton file collection contains useful periodicals, pamphlets, government publications, and ephemera on Chicanos, but it is difficult to access. The section listing audiovisual materials is arranged by type of media. It contains 382 slides, 22 cassettes, 4 filmstrips, 3 film records, 5 films, and 17 reel-to-reel tapes. Many of the recordings were produced at Stanford. Annotations and indexes are lacking and would enhance the usefulness of this guide.

The new edition and the three earlier works (listed in the section on Minor Library Guides) are part of a series of bibliographies by the staff at the Chicano Reference Library, Stanford University. The works demonstrate the development of a fine selection of materials and a major depository in support of research on the Mexican American.

66. Indiana University, Bloomington. Libraries. *A guide to Publications on Latinos at Indiana University: The Chicanos.* Bloomington: Office of Latino Affairs, Indiana University, 1974. (Pueblo Latino, vol. 1) 108 p.

This is a well-prepared guide to the resources in the Indiana University Library on the social, cultural, and historical aspects of the Mexican American. It is the first in a series dedicated to various Hispanic nationalities. Other numbers cover Cubans and Puerto Ricans. The materials are arranged in broad disciplinary categories: Bibliographies and other resources, Chicano education, Chicano history, Humanities and publications of general interest, and Social sciences. Books, articles, theses and dissertations, and government publications are included. Call numbers are provided for most of the entries but there are no author or subject indexes. A special section devoted to periodicals is a useful feature.

Although this work is now dated it is indicative of the growing interest in the Chicano at a major Midwestern institution. The collection on the Chicano at Indiana is supplemented by an equally excellent collection on Mexico and other Latin American countries.

67. Kratzert, Mona Y., and Evelyn K. Thornberry. *A Bibliography of California State and U.S. Federal Government Documents Pertaining to the Chicano.* Fullerton: Library, California State University, 1972. 56 p.

Official documents and ERIC materials relating to the Mexican American are listed in this bibliography. Although no purpose is stated, it was presumably prepared to aid students and researchers in their quest for Mexican American source materials at California State University, Fullerton. The work is arranged in three parts: the first consists of documents published by the State of California, the second covers U.S. government documents, and the third and major portion of the bibliography includes titles from ERIC *Research in*

*Education.* Titles in the first two sections are arranged by issuing department, and in the third by author. Local call numbers and ED numbers are provided for many entries but some of the state and federal publications are not held by the library at Fullerton.

The approximately 800 entries are particularly relevant to research in the social sciences and education. Annotations and indexes, which would have enhanced the usefulness of this bibliography, have not been provided.

68. _____, and Evelyn Thornberry. *Chicano Bibliography: A Bibliography of Materials Relating to the Chicano in the California State College, Fullerton, Library.* Fullerton: Library, California State College, 1972. 112 p.
Mexican American and Mexican materials located in the California State College, Fullerton library are cited in this guide. It was produced as a result of inquiries from "concerned Chicano students." Actually more items are listed on Mexico and the cultural background of the Mexican Americans than on contemporary aspects of their life and experiences. Omitted are pamphlets, articles, documents, microfilm and uncataloged materials in Special Collections. The items are arranged by subject headings based on those of the Library of Congress: Arts; Bibliography and reference; California—history; Curriculum and texts; Early North and South American history; Education; Elements in the U.S. population of minority groups; Race and racial problems; Explorations; Conquest and colonization; Juvenile; Literature and language; Mexico—Foreign relations—U.S.; Mexico—history; Missions; New Mexico and Arizona history; The New Southwest; Social life and social problems; Spanish literature; Texas—history; United States history; War with Mexico.

This work falls somewhat short of the goal to provide adequate access to materials relevant to Chicano Studies. More recent bibliographies by the staff at Fullerton contain a wider selection of resources on the Mexican Americans. The library's call numbers are provided but annotations and indexes are lacking.

69. Márquez, Benjamín. *Chicano Studies Bibliography: A Guide to the Resources of the Library at the University of Texas at El Paso.* 4th. ed. El Paso: University of Texas, 1975. 138 p. Annotated. Indexes. ED 119 923.
Research in the field of Chicano Studies is facilitated by this updated guide to the library's holdings. More than 668 books and periodical articles, published between 1925 and 1975, are listed. These are arranged in one alphabetical listing. Call numbers are provided. There are separate sections for Chicano periodicals and newspapers, audiovisual materials, bibliographies, research aids and services. The most notable feature of this collection is the list of 56 tape recordings of speeches, interviews, meetings, and proceedings on topics relevant to Mexican American affairs.

The first two editions of this guide, entitled *Mexican American Bibliography,* were prepared by Ken Hedman in 1970 and 1971. The third edition with the same title as this work was compiled by Cesar Caballero and Ken Hedman in 1973. A supplement was later prepared in 1975 by Benjamín Márquez, entitled *Chicano Studies Bibliography; Supplement, 1974-1975.* The fourth edition supersedes all earlier works and is one of the better library bibliographies.

70. Mundo Lo, Sara de. *Spanish Speaking Minorities in the U.S.: A Select Listing of Titles in the Library, University of Illinois at Urbana-Champaign.* Urbana: Library, University of Illinois, 1974. 79 p. Index.

Prepared for an exhibit in the library on Spanish-speaking minorities in the United States, this excellent guide contains a selection of titles from the collection at the University of Illinois. Major representative works including books, masters' theses, dissertations, pamphlets, and government documents are cited. Call numbers are provided for all but the most recent additions to the collection. The appendix contains 34 relevant Chicano and ethnic serial publications that are also available in the library. Although there are 455 entries, titles are frequently cited more than once as required by the subjects.

The arrangement is alphabetical by subject, following the entries in their card catalog. With the exception of a few materials on Cubans and Puerto Ricans, the majority of the items are on the Mexican American. Topics covered include agricultural labor, bibliography, biography, education, employment, history, politics, psychology, health, hygiene, and general works with a geographical orientation. Emphasis throughout the guide is on the social sciences. Of particular interest are the various books, government publications and serials relating to Mexican Americans in the Midwestern states which are not frequently found in the library guides of the Western and Southwestern collections.

71. Nájera, Carlos. *Chicanos: A Selective Guide to Materials in the UCSB Library.* Santa Barbara: University of California, 1972. 78 p. Indexes.

This is a bibliography of 772 books, curriculum guides, and government publications on the Chicanos located in the library of the University of California, Santa Barbara, as of the fall of 1971. It consists of works covering the entire gamut of subject materials on the Chicanos. History and Mexican background are the areas with the most extensive listings.

This bibliography is a revision of the first edition, published in 1969, entitled *Mexican Americans: A Selective Guide to Materials.* It is updated periodically by the current reports entitled *Chicanos: A Checklist of Current Materials.* These issues list new acquisitions by the library and include books, periodicals, theses and dissertations on all subject areas of interest to the Mexican American. Although no periodical articles are included in this 1972 expanded edition, the earlier compilation, published in 1969, does contain articles.

72. Schramko, Linda Fowler. *Chicano Bibliography: Selected Materials on Americans of Mexican Descent.* Sacramento, CA: Library, Sacramento State College, 1970. 124 p. Index.

This revised edition of the 1969 guide to the collection at Sacramento State College contains 1,000 items. The materials are arranged by the following subject areas: Health, Psychology, Historical background, Literature, Fine arts, and Social problems, with a primary emphasis on education. Included are books, periodical articles, theses and dissertations, nonbook materials, and a listing of Chicano periodicals. A detailed subject index is appended.

A useful guide at the end of the bibliography suggests other subject headings and general periodical indexes that can provide information on Mexican Americans.

73. Tash, Steven, and Karen Nupoll. *La Raza: A Selective Bibliography of Library Resources*. Northridge; Library, California State University, 1973. [300] p. Index.

This is an extensive unpaged listing of the holdings of the California State University Library at Northridge that relate to the Mexican and Mexican American. It covers all areas of interest to students of Chicano Studies. The entries are arranged under the following headings: Reference materials, Agricultural labor, Art forms, Biography and autobiography, Chicano life style, Civil rights, Economic conditions, Education, Folklore, Geography, Health, Historical emergence of the Chicano, Housing, Immigration, Language study and bilingualism, Law enforcement, Literature, Music, Multimedia materials, Newspapers and journals, Political rights, Religion, and Theater arts. Call numbers and location symbols are provided. A personal name index and a few scattered annotations are useful features.

In preparing this guide it was the desire of the university library to better serve the Chicano Studies department and general campus community and to facilitate the use of the obviously excellent collection of Mexican American resources.

74. University of Arizona. Library. Committee on Spanish Language and Chicano Resources. *Guide to the Chicano Resources in the University of Arizona Library*, by Iliana Sonntag, *et al.* Tucson, AZ: The Library, University of Arizona, 1976. 110 p. Annotated. Indexes. ED 153 663.

Access to the resources at the University of Arizona on Mexican American history, culture, and socioeconomic development is provided by this bibliography. The emphasis is on current materials and the items are arranged under 15 subject headings: General works, Art, Economics, Education, Folklore, Health, History, Labor and laboring classes, Language, Literature, Politics and government, Psychology, Religion, Sociology and Sports. In addition to the monographs and articles, there are bibliographies, encyclopedias, dictionaries, indexes, abstracts, directories, journals, and theses. Call numbers and instructions on the use of the guide are provided.

This is one of the most important collections available on the Mexican American.

75. University of California, Santa Barbara. Library. *Chicanos: A Checklist of Current Materials*. Santa Barbara: The Library, 1972–76. (bimonthly); 1977+ (biennial). Annotated.

This current list of acquisitions is produced to reflect the expanding collection at the University of California, Santa Barbara, and updates previously published bibliographies. The lists include books, periodicals, theses and dissertations on all subject areas related to Mexico and the Mexican Americans.

Some of the issues are devoted to special topics, e.g., poetry and folklore; government publications; dissertations and theses; bibliographies, etc. Many issues contain a general section of new monographs entitled "Otros libros nuevos." Although this is primarily a selective acquisitions list rather than a bibliography it serves to familiarize students, scholars, and librarians with new publications in the field of Chicano Studies. Call numbers and location symbols are provided. This is a fine public service tool for patrons of the library. A periodic index to authors, titles, and subjects would be desirable.

76. University of Houston. Libraries. Office of the Assistant Director for Development of Collections. *Mexican-Americans: A Selected Bibliography.* Rev. ed. Houston, TX: The Libraries, 1974. 151 p. Index.

An excellent guide to the library's holdings of Mexican American materials; included are most major works on Chicano life as well as certain difficult-to-locate articles and audiovisual materials. The material is arranged under the headings of History, Sociology, Labor, Politics, Education, Literature, Fine arts, and Biography. Government documents are not included, but there is a strong section on literature and a very good section on biography and personal profiles, not usually included in other lists of this type. This guide also suggests subject headings in the library's catalog for additional materials on Mexican Americans. It is a revised and enlarged edition of a bibliography prepared in 1972.

77. University of Utah. Marriott Library. *Chicano Bibliography.* Salt Lake City: The Library, 1973. (Bibliographic Series, vol. 1) 297 p.

This guide to the Marriott Library at the University of Utah covers an extensive selection of materials concerning all aspects of Chicano life. It was produced to enable students, faculty, researchers and other users to have ready access to the Mexican American materials in the library. It contains books, government publications, and an impressive section of items from the curriculum and ERIC collections. A separate list of well-selected periodical articles, Mexican American journals, and films is also included. Although no criteria are mentioned for the selection of titles relative to the Chicano, except for the date of 1846, the items are very pertinent to the study of the Mexican American without including a great deal of Spanish and Mexican background material.

This is a revised and enlarged edition of a previous work entitled *A Selective Chicano Bibliography of Materials at the University of Utah,* 1971.

## MINOR LIBRARY GUIDES

The following bibliographies have all been examined prior to listing below. They are helpful as guides to particular library collections but not as surveys of the literature on the Mexican American. Most have fewer than 50 pages. The more lengthy works generally include a significant volume of materials on Mexico or other minorities and ethnic groups, although some items on Mexican Americans are included. Several of the works listed below have been superseded by later editions. As such they are less significant for research on the Mexican American than the Major Library Guides which are listed in the first part of the chapter. For these reasons annotations were not considered necessary.

78. Butterfield, Mary. *A Bibliography and Guide to Chicano Materials in the Eastern Michigan University Library.* Ypsilanti: Library, Eastern Michigan University, 1972, 19 p.

79. Caballero, César, and Ken Hedman. *Chicano Studies Bibliography: A Guide to the Resources of the Library at the University of Texas at El Paso.* El Paso: University of Texas, 1973. 59 p. Annotated. Indexes. ED 081 524.

80. California State College, Dominguez Hills. Library. *Chicano Bibliography.* Dominguez Hills: The Library and the Centro de Estudios Chicanos, 1973. 80 p.

81. California State College, Fresno. Library. *Afro and Mexican-Americans; Books and Other Materials in the Library of Fresno State College Relating to the History, Culture, and Problems of Afro-Americans and Mexican-Americans.* Fresno: The Library, 1969. 109 p.

82. _____. *Mexican-American Resource Guide.* Fresno: The Library, 1971, 16 p.

83. California State College, Hayward. Library. *Chicano Bibliography.* Hayward: The Library, 1970. 70 p. Annotated. Index.

84. California State College, Long Beach. Library. *Chicano Bibliography: A Selected List of Books on the Culture, History, and Socio-Economic Conditions of the Mexican-Americans.* Long Beach: The Library, 1970. 45 p.

85. California State College, Los Angeles. Library. *A Library Guide to Mexican-American Studies.* Los Angeles: John F. Kennedy Memorial Library, 1969. 14 p. Annotated.

86. California State College, San Bernardino. Library. *Black and Brown Bibliography: Literature, Art, Music and Theatre.* San Bernardino: The Library. 1970. 16 p.

87. _____. *Black and Brown Bibliography: A Selected List of Books Relating to the Culture of Afro-Americans and Mexican-Americans.* San Bernardino: The Library, 1970. 39 p.

88. _____. *Black and Brown Bibliography: A Selected List of Books Relating to the History of Afro-Americans and Mexican-Americans.* San Bernardino: The Library, 1970. 39 p.

89. California State College, San Jose. Library. *Bibliografía de Materiales, tocante el Chicano: A Bibliography of Materials Relating to the Chicano in the San Jose State College Library.* San Jose: The Library, 1971. 181 p. Index.

90. California State University, Fullerton. Library. *Mexico and the Southwest Collection.* Fullerton: The Library, 1974. 192 p.

91. *Chicano: A Selected Bibliography,* by Barbara Flynn, *et al.* Riverside, CA: Riverside Public Library, 1971. 93 p. Annotated.

92. De Anza College. Library. *Chicanos—Relevance Now: Mexican American Bibliography.* Cupertino, CA: The Library, 1970. 6 p.

93. _____. *Chicanos; A Selective Guide to Materials in the Learning Center.* Cupertino, CA: The Library, 1975. 6 p.

94. Denver Public Library. *Hispanic Heritage: A Selected Book List for All Ages.* Denver, CO: The Library, 1969. 36 p. Annotated.

95. _____. *Mexican Heritage: A Selected Book List for All Ages.* Denver, CO: The Library, 1971. 34 p. Annotated.

96. Eastern New Mexico University. Library. *A Selected List of Materials Relating to Mexican Americans.* Portales: The Library, 1970. 16 p.

97. Franco, Cristina, and Liz Bueno. *Bibliography Part II: A Guide to Materials in the Chicano Reference Library.* Palo Alto, CA: Chicano Reference Library, Stanford University, 1976. [26] p.

98. Garza, Ben. *Chicano Bibliography.* Davis: Library, University of California, 1969. 51 p.

99. Hester, Goldia. *A Select Bibliography on Mexican Americans.* Austin: Hispanic-American Institute, University of Texas, 1970. 8 p.

100. Indiana University, Bloomington. Libraries. *Mexican Americans.* Bloomington: The Libraries, 1972. 25 p.

101. _____. *Mexican Americans.* Bloomington: The Libraries, 1973.

102. Jorgensen, Venita, and Gail Neddermeyer. *Guide to Materials on Mexican-Americans in the UCR Library.* Riverside: General Library, University of California, 1970. 18 p.

103. Los Angeles Public Library. *De Aztlán a Hoy.* Los Angeles: The Library, 1970. [12] p.

104. Marin, Christine N. *Books Located in the Chicano Studies Collection at Arizona State University Library, Tempe, Arizona.* Tempe: Library, Arizona State University, 1971. 32 p.

105. Márquez, Benjamín. *Chicano Studies Bibliography: Supplement, 1974–1975.* El Paso: University of Texas, 1975. 28 p. Annotated. Index.

106. Mendoza, Edward, and Yolanda Torres. *Bibliography: A Guide to Materials in the Chicano Library.* Palo Alto, CA: Chicano Studies Reference Library, Stanford University, 1972. 16 p.

107. Michigan State University. Libraries. *Finding Chicano Materials in the Michigan State University Libraries.* East Lansing: The Libraries, 1973. (How to Find Series, no. 1). 16 p.

108. Moyer, June, Lydia Chávez, and Anthony Trujillo. *Chicano Bibliography: A Selected Bibliography of Bi-Cultural Material in the SCSC Library.* Pueblo: Southern Colorado State College Library, 1972. 19 p.

109. Salazár, José-Ramiro, and Fernando O. Córdova. *Bibliography: A Guide to Materials in the Chicano Reference Library.* Palo Alto, CA: Chicano Reference Library, Stanford University, 1974. 50 p.

110. San Diego Public Library. *Chicano: A Selected List.* San Diego, CA: The Library, 1970. 21 p. Annotated.

111. Scott, William H. O. *Spanish-Speaking Americans: A Bibliography of Government Documents.* Bellingham, WA: Wilson Library, Western State College, 1972. 7 p.

112. Seattle Public Library. *Chicano Bibliography.* Seattle, WA: The Library, 1973. 7 p.

113. Sifuentes, Octavio. *A Library Guide to Chicano Studies.* Ventura, CA: D. R. Henry Library, Ventura College, 1976. 47 p. ED 153 778.

114. Southern Colorado State College. Library. *Chicano, Hispano, Mexican-American, Spanish-American: A Selected Bibliography of Bi-Cultural Material Available in the SCSC Library.* Pueblo: The Library, 1971. 9 p.

115. Trejo, Arnulfo D. "Algunos Libros by and about Mexican-Americans." University of Arizona, Library. *Bibliographic Bulletin*, 2 (January, 1971): 1–23. Annotated.

116. University of California, Davis. Library. *Chicano Bibliography,* by the Davis Chapter of Movimiento Estudiantil Chicano de Aztlán. Davis: The Library, 1965. 51 p.

117. University of California, Santa Barbara. Library. *Mexican Americans: A Selective Guide to Materials in the UCSB Library.* Santa Barbara: The Library, 1969. 46 p. Index.

118. University of Redlands. Armacost Library. *Mexican-American Bibliography.* Redlands, CA: The Library, 1970. 14 p. Annotated.

119. University of Southern California. Library. *An Introduction to Materials for Ethnic Studies in the University of Southern California Library.* Los Angeles: University of Southern California, 1970. 198 p. Index.

120. University of Utah. Marriott Library. *A Selective Chicano Bibliography of Materials at the University of Utah.* Salt Lake City: Libraries, University of Utah, 1971. 93 p. Annotated.

121. University of Washington. Library. *Chicano Related Materials in the University of Washington Library: A Selected Bibliography.* Seattle: Library School Association and Chicano Studies Committee, University of Washington, 1970. 74 p.

122. Washington State Library. *Selected Bibliography for Spanish-Speaking Americans: Books and Periodicals in the Library.* Olympia: The Library, 1971. 18 p.

# Chapter 3

# *Biographical Sources*

In the years following World War II, a significant number of citizens of Mexican descent rose to prominence and notoriety. This was achieved through opportunities in education and the active concern for the rights of Mexican Americans. Most of these notable Mexican Americans were not known nor their heritage recognized outside a narrow circle of friends and associates. Often the Anglo-American society at large failed to acknowledge the Mexican heritage of those who managed to reach positions of influence, finding it more convenient to view them as Americans with a bit of exotic "Spanish" background. Many successful Mexican Americans contributed to this perception by retaining very little of their culture while attempting to assimilate, which was one popular goal for ambitious Mexican Americans outside the main ranks of society. This resulted in their leaving behind customs and traditions that set them apart from other Americans. For those who assimilated there were the prospects of rich materials rewards and a measure of social acceptance.

Developments in the 1960s caused the assimilationist concept to be challenged. Groups within the Mexican American community came to view it as unacceptable. They adopted instead the concept of cultural pluralism for the purpose of preserving the major features of their heritage. The notion of cultural pluralism inspired many Mexican Americans to renew their identification with their roots and to publicly acknowledge their Mexican heritage. Some felt uncomfortable with the term "Chicano," the latest designation for those of Mexican background, but most accepted it in the spirit of cultural unity.

The collections of biographical sketches listed in this chapter are the result of recent social and political activism and heightened cultural awareness among Mexican Americans. Few publications of this type existed prior to 1970. The earliest example found is *Colorado Latin American Personalities,* by Lino M. López, published in 1959. These works highlight the lives and activities of outstanding Mexican Americans in a wide range of fields including education, politics, entertainment, sports, the arts, medicine, and journalism, to mention only a few. Some are national in scope but others limit their coverage to a particular state.

The individuals listed in these works were chosen from among the most well-known and prominent contemporary Mexican Americans. In only a few cases are historical figures or lesser-known individuals included. Some of the biographical works are effective as reference tools. Others are more useful in classroom instruction or in counseling where they serve to promote cultural pride and to present role models for young Mexican Americans.

Certainly many other Americans of Mexican descent remain unrecognized although they have been successful in their respective fields and have made significant contributions to society in general. For additional information on distinguished Mexican Americans the standard biographical sources, located in many libraries, should be consulted. Some of the most popular examples are *Who's Who in America; Who's Who in the South and Southwest: Who's Who in American Politics; Directory of American Scholars;* and *American Men and Women of Science.*

Specialized sources in the chapter on Directories provide names and addresses of notable Mexican Americans in politics and various professional fields. Full-length biographies and autobiographies of famous Americans of Hispanic or Mexican origin can be identified by consulting the various general and institutional bibliographies on the Mexican American.

123. Alford, Harold J. "Biographies of Some of the Outstanding Spanish-Speaking People in the United States." In *The Proud People; The Heritage and Culture of Spanish-Speaking Peoples in the United States,* pp. 237–316. New York: David McKay Co., 1972. 325 p.

This is a collection of 60 personal vignettes arranged in alphabetical order by surname within a chapter of this volume. The individuals selected represent various Spanish-speaking groups in the United States from the time of the Spanish explorations to the present. Although a few individuals of Cuban and Puerto Rican descent are mentioned, the overwhelming majority are of Mexican origin. Most notable about these biographies is that they include many not so well-publicized individuals who have quietly succeeded in the arts, academia, business, and other professions.

124. Axford, Roger W. *Spanish-Speaking Heroes.* Midland, MI: Pendell, 1973. 85 p.

The positive contributions made by the Spanish-speaking in the United States are presented in this small selective directory. It is a collection of biographical sketches of 23 Spanish-speaking men and women. The selections cover a wide range of professions such as labor leader, entertainer, educator, politician, and athlete. Since the scope of this directory is the Spanish-speaking, only some of those included are of Mexican descent. Photographs of each individual are provided as well as bibliographical citations from which some of the data were derived. Personal interviews provided the basis for some of the information.

The directory has limited reference use but might be more appropriate for teachers and students in middle and secondary schools and for vocational counseling.

125. Institute of Texan Cultures. *Los Mexicanos Texanos.* San Antonio, University of Texas, 1971. 32 p.

Presented in this work are 48 chronologically arranged biographical sketches of Mexicans in Texas, beginning with Fray Isidro Felix de Espinoza of the eighteenth century and concluding with notable Mexican Americans of the 1970s. Photographs and illustrations of individuals and historical landmarks enhance this work which is perhaps most useful at the secondary school level. This edition is in Spanish. It is part of a series designated to point out the contributions of the various ethnic groups to the history and culture of Texas. An English edition entitled *The Mexican Texans,* 1971, is also available.

126. Larralde, Carlos. *Mexican American Movements and Leaders.* Los Alamitos, CA: Hwong Publishing Co., 1976. 229 p.

The purpose of this work is to demonstrate that the Chicano/Raza Movement has had roots in the activity and initiative of men and women of Mexican heritage for over a century. Identified are four different movements and 21 leaders among the Mexican Americans, from 1846 to the present. Lengthy biographical sketches with photographs are arranged in chronological order under each movement. Extensive footnotes indicate the use of primary and secondary sources, as well as family archives and oral histories which together introduce previously undiscovered data. The selected leaders are Juan Corina, Carlos Espárza, Santos Benavides, José Villarreal, Santa Teresa Urréa, Catarino Gárza, José Mosqueda, Nicanor Rodríguez, Luisa Garfias, Ricardo and Enrique Magón, Ancieto Pizana, Venustiano Carranza, Octaviano Larrazolo, Carmelo Franchese, Emma Terrayuca, Bert Corona, Josefina Fierro, Francisca Espárza, Corky Gonzáles, and César Chávez.

127. Levelier, Benjamin, Jr. *A Portfolio of Outstanding Americans of Mexican Descent.* Menlo Park, CA: Educational Consulting Associates, 1970. 38 p.

Presented in this portfolio are the portraits of outstanding contemporary Americans of Mexican descent. Each of the 37 figures is accompanied by a biographical sketch in English and Spanish. Among the individuals chosen for inclusion in this work were the most notable politicians, scholars, labor leaders and sports figures from the 1960s, e.g., César Chávez, Joseph Montoya, Julian Nava, George I. Sánchez, Lee Trevino, and Armando M. Rodríguez. The biographical sketches are useful for middle and secondary school level education and for reference collections in school, public, and academic libraries. This is the first work of its kind which has a national perspective. It was continued by *Chicanos y Chicanas Prominentes,* by Theodore E. B. Wood, in 1974.

128. López, Lino M. *Colorado Latin American Personalities.* Denver, CO: A. M. Printing Co., 1959. 76 p. Index.

This work contains biographical sketches of 76 contemporary Mexican American personalities and leaders from the State of Colorado. They are arranged in alphabetical order. The individuals chosen demonstrated a high degree of success or achievement in their respective fields in spite of many adversities. A significant number of the examples are women. Photographs of each person accompany the text.

129. Martínez, Al. *Rising Voices; Profiles of Hispano American Lives.* New York: New American Library, 1974. 210 p.

In an attempt to fill the void in the biographical literature of recognized Spanish-speaking heroes, the author has produced 52 biographical sketches of leading Mexican Americans, Cubans, Puerto Ricans, and Spaniards who have succeeded in sports, government, the arts, and social services as well as in other areas. More than half of those included are of Mexican descent. There is no indication of the methodology and criteria employed in the selection. The profiles are arranged alphabetically by surname and are primarily directed at young adult readers.

130. Palácios, Arturo. *The Mexican-American Directory*. Washington, DC: Executive Systems Corp., 1970. 210 p.

This is a biographical directory listing the names of Mexican Americans who are prominent or distinguished at the local, state, and national levels. The entries indicate the field of work, date of birth, education, jobs, awards, military service and address of those who are listed. The primary purpose of this directory is to provide public and private agencies or organizations with the names of Mexican Americans who have concern for and involvement with Mexican Americans. A few non-Mexican Americans are included who have made worthy contributions to their Mexican American communities. It is probably not complete, and a revised and updated edition would be useful.

131. Pinál, Mauricio del. *Who's Who in the Latin World*. Los Angeles, CA: Tribal Publications, 1975. 112 p. Index.

A guide to 204 men and women who have made notable contributions to the "Latin World" in Los Angeles is provided in this work. Many of the individuals are Mexican or Mexican American, but some are from other Latin American countries and a few are Anglo-American. They are making contributions as journalists, attorneys, actors, businessmen, doctors, politicians, teachers, librarians, and civic leaders. A short romanticized biographical sketch and photograph are included for each person listed. The information provided varies but in general the birth place, education, occupations, memberships, and names of spouse and children are mentioned.

132. Quirarte, Jacinto. *Mexican American Artists*. Austin: University of Texas Press, 1973. (John Fielding and Lois Lasater Maher Series, no. 2) 149 p. Index.

This work, although not a typical reference tool, is the only separately published source available on Mexican American artists. The author, an art historian, analyzes the work of 27 Chicano artists from 1901 to the present and places their work in the context of Spanish-Mexican antecedents. The artists, mostly all from the West and the Southwest, are arranged by periods in five sections. Some of the individuals included are Antonio García and Chelo González Amézcua, from the first decade; Edward Chávez and Michael Ponce de León, from the second decade; Peter Rodríguez and Eugenio Quezada, from the third decade; Eduardo Carrillo, Ray Chávez, Amado Peña and Glynn Gómez, from the fourth decade.

The work is heavily illustrated, includes biographical and critical comments, and a bibliography relating to Mexico, the Spanish Southwest, and Mexican American art.

The reader is also advised to consult Raymond Barrio's *Mexico's Art and Chicano Artists* (Sunnyvale, CA: Ventura Press, 1975) which contains three short chapters on Chicano artists and brief biographical sketches, although the work emphasizes Mexican art.

133. Rivera, Feliciano. "Outstanding Americans of Mexican Descent." In *A Mexican American Source Book*, pp. 117–148. Menlo Park, CA: Educational Consulting Associates, 1970. 196 p.

A selection of 32 notable Americans of Mexican background is found in this source. Each biographical sketch is presented in English and Spanish. Date of birth, education and career highlights are included. The chosen individuals represent civic leaders, politicians, educators, government officials, and other professionals. Illustrations by David L. Rodríguez accompany the biographical descriptions. No basis for the selection is stated.

134. Trejo, Arnulfo D., and Kathleen L. Lodwick. *Quién es Quien: A Who's Who of Spanish-Heritage Librarians in the United States*. Tucson: Bureau of School Services, College of Education, University of Arizona, 1976. (Graduate Library School Monograph, no. 5) 29 p.
This reference tool differs from other previous directories of librarians in that it identifies only those individuals of "Indo-Afro-Ibero-American extraction," or Hispanic heritage, who have completed degrees in library science. Of 245 librarians listed, 26 identify themselves as Chicano, 14 as Mexican, 38 as Mexican American, and 4 as Spanish American. The others are from various Latin American countries and Spain. The entries give basic data for each individual: education, birthdate, where library degree was obtained, fluency in Spanish, specialization, work experience, professional memberships, biographical directories where included, publications, honors, home address, present position and place of employment.
    The work was designed to assist in strengthening professional ties among individuals listed and to provide employers with information on professionals of Spanish heritage in the field. The introduction provides a detailed description of purpose, methodology used in collecting the information, and statistical tables on ethnic group, geographical distribution, and ratio of Spanish-speaking librarians to total population of Spanish-speaking people in the United States.

135. Tucson Public Schools. Intermediate Grades History and Human Relations Committee. *The Mexican American; A Resource Unit. Part II: Biographical Sketches*. Tucson, AZ: Tucson Public Schools, 1971. 46 p.
This is the second of a two-part unit on the Mexican American that was prepared for students in the intermediate grades. It focuses on local history and the lives of notable Mexican American citizens of Tucson, Arizona. Eight biographical sketches of individuals, from the nineteenth and twentieth centuries, relate experiences and achievements which serve as educational and inspirational models. Each profile is accompanied by a photograph of the individual, a list of vocabulary words from the sketch, and sample sentences to be illustrated by the students. Suggestions for classroom adaptation are offered in the introduction. This tool is a valuable example for teachers in other school districts. It is useful as a reference work for school and public libraries since most of these Tucsonans of Mexican heritage do not appear in other major biographical guides and directories.

136. Wood, Theodore, E. B. *Chicanos y Chicanas Prominentes*. Menlo Park, CA: Educational Consulting Associates, 1974. 24 p.
Portraits and biographical sketches, in English and Spanish, of 24 notable Mexican Americans are contained in this work. Included are both men and women who have become familiar figures in various sectors of public life. Among the prominent Chicanas included are Romana A. Banuelos, Vikki Carr, Nancy López, Irene Továr. Some of the famous men included are Frank Angel, Jr., Edward L. Barrera, José Andrés Chacón, Roberto A. Mondragón, Luís Nogales, Philip D. Ortego, James Plunkett, Ruben Salazár, and Reíes López Tijerina. This work is supplementary to *A Portfolio of Outstanding Americans of Mexican Descent,* by Benjamin Levelier, Jr., published in 1970.

# Chapter 4

# *Genealogical Sources*

The recent awakening of interest in genealogical research has prompted the inclusion of this chapter. Americans of all races, ethnic backgrounds, and social levels are now searching public archives and genealogical resources in libraries for clues to their ancestry. This is a painstaking and frustrating activity even when aided by guides to the documents and by works on the methodology of such research.

For Americans of Mexican descent the search is even more difficult. There are no collections of genealogical sources on Mexican Americans, no bibliographies, and no works on methods.[1] The existing guides and methodological works are only useful to individuals of European descent or to those whose ancestors entered the United States through eastern ports. Furthermore, Mexican Americans must follow genealogical trails leading through the records of two, and possibly three, countries—the United States, Mexico, and Spain. This may well require traveling to the location of the records since many of the sources from Mexico and Spain are unavailable in this country.[2]

The genealogical sources collected in this chapter are more relevant to those Mexican Americans who can trace their heritage to the period before 1848. In that year the territories of the Southwest, along with approximately 80,000 Indo-Hispanic inhabitants, were transferred from Mexico to the United States, following ratification of the Treaty of Guadalupe-Hidalgo. The province of New Mexico, with 65,000 people, was the most populous of the areas ceded; followed, in order of population size, by California (7,500), Texas (5,000), and Arizona (1,000). Indo-Hispanic settlers arrived in northern Mexico (today's United States Southwest) as early as the late sixteenth century. Many more came in the seventeenth and eighteenth centuries and reinforced the Spanish presence in the northern provinces of Mexico, particularly in New Mexico, Texas, and California. These settlers represented a variety of occupations and racial mixtures. They were soldiers, ranchers, priests, government officials, and laborers. Except for those who claimed to be of ''pure'' Spanish blood, they were mostly products of widespread miscegenation between whites, Blacks, and Indians.

The sources in this chapter include lists of Spanish-Mexican names, family genealogies, an early census report, and a list of Spanish immigrants to the Western Hemisphere. With the exception of the Arizona census report, the other works were produced by private researchers. A few of the authors, such as Fray Angélico Chávez and

**43**

James Padgett, are closely related to old Spanish-Mexican families of the Southwest, and it was this connection that led them to collect the information for their works.

In addition to the materials mentioned above, there are other sources, too broad for inclusion in this chapter, but which should be consulted for genealogical data. Among these are the archives of the Catholic Church and the missions of the Southwest, and the records of the civil and military governments prior to 1848. Access to these is facilitated by several of the guides and indexes found in the chapter on History.

Once the Southwestern sources about Mexican Americans are traced, it is then necessary to continue the search in the files and records of Mexico. These have been preserved and housed in archives located in Mexico City and the provincial capitals. Lyman De Platt's *Una guía genealógico-histórica de latinoamérica*[3] serves as a guide to the location of specific archives in Mexico containing genealogical information.

Mexican Americans whose ancestors immigrated to the United States after 1848 can also use Platt's guide to trace their Mexican roots as far back as the colonial days. Their family's presence in the United States can be documented by the use of conventional genealogical sources: census, immigration and naturalization files, birth records, tax rolls, etc.

Tracing family origins, particularly in the case of the Mexican Americans, where reference tools are limited, requires imagination and historical knowledge. These qualities will enable researchers to locate alternative sources where clues may be found regarding the relationships and accomplishments of previous generations.

1. Robert D. Reed, *How and Where to Research Your Ethnic-American Cultural Heritage: Mexican Americans* (Saratoga, CA: The Author, 1978), 28 p. This recently announced publication, claiming to provide complete information on all major resources for genealogical research on Mexican Americans, should be consulted although it falls somewhat short of its purpose. Designed primarily for laymen, this pamphlet presents only a small selection of the very basic sources of information.

2. Susan M. Cottler, Roger M. Haigh, and Shirley A. Weathers, *Preliminary Survey of the Mexican Collection,* Genealogical Society of Utah, Finding Aids to the Microfilmed Manuscript Collection, no. 1 (Salt Lake City: University of Utah Press, 1979), 216 p. Precise information on parish and civil records and other related holdings in the Mexican collection of the library of the Genealogical Society of Utah are contained in this recent work.

3. Lyman De Platt, *Una guía genealógico-histórica de latinoamérica* (Ramona, CA: Acoma Press, 1978), 297 p.

137. Boyd-Bowman, Peter. *Indice geobiográfico de cuarenta mil pobladores españoles de América en el siglo XVI. vol. I, 1493–1519.* Bogotá, Colombia: Instituto Caro y Cuervo, 1964. 275 p. Index.

138. _____. *Indice geobiogáfico de cuarenta mil pobladores españoles de America en el siglo XVI. vol. II, 1520–1539.* México, D.F.: Editorial Jus, 1968. 611 p. Index.

These volumes are compilations of the names of Spaniards who immigrated to the New World between 1493 and 1539. The names are alphabetically arranged under regions of origin in Spain. Each entry provides family and given names, parents' name, occupation, social status, titles of honors, date of immigration, and place of origin. There are separate indexes for surnames, occupation and status, destination, places in America, and expeditions. Many of the immigrants settled in New Spain or the region which is now the Southwestern United States. This work is useful for historical and genealogical research.

139. *California Pioneer Register and Index, 1542–1848. Including Inhabitants of California, 1796–1800 and List of Pioneers. Extracted from the History of California by Hubert Howe Bancroft.* Baltimore, MD: Regional Publishing Co., 1964. 392 p.

Three separate sections are included in this volume. The first is a list of 1,700 male inhabitants of California from 1769 to 1800. A second section is a list of pioneers entering the state up to 1848. The third and most extensive section is an index of names mentioned in the first five volumes of Bancroft's *History of California* as well as other names of individuals who played some role in California from 1542 to 1848. Entries for the index indicate the nationality, occupation, achievements, death, family connections, manner of coming to California, and the public function of each of the subjects. Information for the entries was obtained from public, private, and missionary archives, personal reminiscences, and biographical works. The *Index* was published separately in 1964 by Dawson's Book Shop in Los Angeles.

140. Chabot, Frederick C. *With the Makers of San Antonio; Genealogies of the early Latin, Anglo-American, and German Families with occasional Biographies, each Group being Prefaced with a Brief Historical Sketch and Illustration.* San Antonio, TX: Artes Gráficas, 1937. 412 p.

This is an invaluable collection of genealogies and biographies of families and persons that were closely connected with early Texas history. The work consists of three parts, one for the Spanish-Mexicans, one for the French and Anglo-Americans, and one for the Germans. Each part is introduced by a preface which describes the migration of the particular nationality into the San Antonio area. The Spanish-Mexican portion is the most extensive, comprising 254 pages and covering 99 families. In most cases their earliest connections with San Antonio are described along with their role or function in Texas history. Many of the first Spanish-Mexicans to settle in or around San Antonio were part of the Domingo Ramón expedition to the missions of the Interior Presidios in 1776. Names of spouses and children are listed and some family names are traced back to their origins in Spain. The genealogies and biographies are based on extensive research by the author in archives of Texas, Mexico, and Spain.

141. Chávez, Fray Angélico. *Origins of New Mexico Families in the Spanish Colonial Period.* Santa Fe: The Historical Society of New Mexico, 1954. 339 p.

Some of the original Spanish-Mexican families living in New Mexico from 1598 to 1821 are covered in this genealogical work. It is divided into two parts: seventeenth-century names (1598–1693) and eighteenth-century names (1693–1821). The family names are listed in alphabetical order. Under each entry are the names of prominent family members who have been selected for individual description on the basis of their position or function, dates, marriages, and relationship to others in the same family. Added to this work is a bibliography of manuscripts, books, monographs, and periodicals used in collecting the family names. A useful tool for researchers interested in the first two centuries of New Mexico's history. Reprinted in 1975 by William Gannon, Publisher.

142. _____. "Addenda to New Mexico Families." *El Palacio,* 62 (November, 1955): 324–339; 63 (May–June, 1956): 166–174; 63 (July–August, 1956): 236–248; 63 (September–October, 1956): 317–319; 63 (November–December, 1956): 367–376; 64 (March–April, 1957): 123–126; 64 (May–June, 1957): 178–190; 64 (July–August, 1957): 246–248.

Found in several volumes of *El Palacio,* this list of New Mexico family names supplements the information provided in *Origins of New Mexico Families in the Spanish Colonial Period.* After the publication of that work in 1954, Chávez located additional items and names while cataloging the Archives of the Archdiocese of Santa Fe, New Mexico. The entries include names of individuals, marriages, baptisms, spouses, children, and occasionally the occupations. This work augments the resources available to students of genealogy and history of the Southwest.

143. _____. "New Names in New Mexico, 1820–1850." *El Palacio,* 64 (September–October, 1957): 291–318; 64 (November–December, 1957): 367–380.

This is a listing of 351 new family names appearing in the pre-1850 mission registers and papers in the archdiocesan archives of Santa Fe. Each family name includes baptismal and marriage data for the period 1820–1850. Many of these surnames are of Spanish or Mexican origin. They represent a wave of new immigrants to Taos and Santa Fe during the period prior to the Mexican-American War. The source of each surname is indicated in abbreviated notes following the data. This work and the other publications by Chávez are invaluable to historians and genealogists.

144. Historical Records Survey. Arizona. *The 1864 Census of the Territory of Arizona.* Phoenix: The Survey, 1938. 210 p.

This publication includes the first census of the inhabitants of the territory of Arizona, compiled for the purpose of organizing a government. The following data were requested: name, age, sex, marital status, birthplace, length of residency in Arizona, citizenship status, family residence, occupation, and value of real estate and personal estate. Many of the 4,573 names are of Spanish-Mexicans who were living in Arizona at the time the territory became part of the United States following the Treaty of Guadalupe Hidalgo in 1848. The information in this work is useful for genealogical and historical research.

145. Maduell, Charles R., Jr. *The Romance of Spanish Surnames.* New Orleans, LA: The Author, 1967. 221 p.

Approximately 1,500 of the most prominent Spanish surnames and variations in spelling from all 50 of Spain's provinces are included in this work. They were selected from the *Guía de la Iglesia en España* which lists over 36,000 surnames of persons connected with the Catholic Church in Spain. For each name listed the entry includes a code indicating frequency of occurence, the existence of a family crest, the geographical origin, and etymology, if available. The introductory chapters review the history of Spain and the origins and characteristics of Spanish surnames. The appendixes include a description of the principal regions of Spain, the major historical cities and also the influence of Basque on Spanish surnames. This work is useful for genealogical studies.

146. Northrop, Marie E. *Spanish-Mexican Families of Early California: 1769–1850*, Vol. I. New Orleans, LA: Polyanthos, 1976. 386 p. Index.
This genealogical work includes over 4,000 names of early Californians up to 1848. It is based on selected families from Thomas Workman Temple's "Genealogical Tables of Spanish and Mexican Families of California" in the Bancroft Library at Berkeley. The family surnames are arranged alphabetically, and for each individual name the following data are provided: place and date of birth, names of parents, marriage (name, birth, death, and parents of wife), children (names, birthdates, baptismal dates, death or burial dates), death date, and a short biographical sketch of available information from Bancroft's *History of California*. The author hopes this work will help historians "to disentangle the interlaced web of families in northern and southern California" and serve as a useful tool for the understanding of relationships between landowners, for unraveling land litigations and for tracing wills. The author has indicated that this work is the first volume in a series which will identify the earliest known Latin families of the West Coast.

147. Rowland, Leon. *Los Fundadores: Herein Are Listed the First Families of California and also All Other Persons with Family Names that Were in California, 1769–1785, Except Those Who Died at San Diego in 1769.* Fresno: Academy of California Church History, 1951. 46 p. Index.
This is an attempt to list the names of men who came from Mexico to settle in California between 1769 and 1785. Approximately 194 Spanish surnamed soldiers, settlers, servants, and presidial personnel are mentioned. The list excludes names of priests. Most of the data were obtained from the records of the seven central California missions which were complemented by Culleton's *Indians and Pioneers of Old Monterey*, Bancroft's Index in the *History of California*, Bolton's *Anza* and *Fray Juan Crespi*, and Palau's *Noticias*. Each name is followed by the date and place of birth, occupation, year of arrival in California, marriages, spouse, and children, and, in some cases, the racial background. This work is a most useful source of genealogical materials on the early Spanish-Mexican population of California.

148. Woods, Richard D. "Sources for Identification of Spanish Names." *Journal of Ethnic Studies, 4* (Summer, 1976): 91–94.
A concise analysis of ten basic sources for research on Spanish names, published between 1938 and 1968, is presented in this article. As far as can be identified Richard Woods is one of the first to point out the utility of these works for Chicano studies. His bibliographic essay covers five name dictionaries, two works on principles for name formation, a list of Spanish immigrants in the New World and a guide to noble families of Spain. The purpose and content of each work is described.
Although no detailed study is available for research on Spanish names in the United States, these works will serve as a focal point for investigations into the origin, diffusion, and etymology of Hispanic names in the Southwest.

149. _____, and Grace Alvarez-Altman. *Spanish Surnames in the Southwestern United States: A Dictionary*. Boston: G. K. Hall, 1978. 154 p.
In response to the recent upsurge in genealogical research, this work was compiled for those persons interested in tracing Spanish names in the United States. The more than 1,000 names listed were selected from the 1974–75 telephone directories in Los Angeles,

Denver, Albuquerque, Tucson, and San Antonio. Frequency of occurrence was the basis for inclusion. For each entry there is a description of the information derived from five basic philological sources. The descriptions include the meaning of the surname, the geographical origins in Spain, and the etymology. A selected bibliography of additional sources which can be useful in further study of Spanish surnames is also provided.

# Chapter 5

# *Statistical Sources*

Statistical sources on the Mexican American were generated in the early part of the twentieth century by the Bureau of the Census, the Immigration and Naturalization Service, and various Congressional Committees. Later, during the 1960s and 1970s, other government agencies compiled and issued statistical reports on this ethnic group in response to a growing interest in the welfare of various minorities. At the same time, individuals and research centers associated with academic institutions published statistical studies for the purpose of determining the socioeconomic status and problems of Mexican Americans. Together these sources form a sizable body of references useful in all areas of the social sciences, education, and law.

In spite of the existence of many statistical sources pertaining to the Mexican Americans, there is no reference work or bibliography devoted exclusively to this type of material. The library guides and general bibliographies on the Mexican Americans seldom include sections on statistics. Those which contain a few titles cite the most popular, such as the census and immigration reports. Perhaps the reason for the oversight is the difficulty in gathering and selecting sources of data which are usually scattered throughout government publications, books, reports and studies.

There are, however, two excellent reference tools on ethnic statistical materials. The first, *Ethnic Statistics: A Compendium of Reference Sources,* lists sources of data gathered by various bureaus, offices, and divisions of federal agencies. The second, *Directory of Data Sources on Racial and Ethnic Minorities,* includes a separate section on persons of Spanish ancestry with recent demographic, social, and economic data sources published by federal agencies. Both of these reference works are included in this chapter. In addition, the *American Statistical Index; A Comprehensive Guide and Index to the Statistical Publications of the U.S. Government,*[1] is a guide and index to all federal government publications containing statistical data. Sources relating to Mexican Americans are listed under the headings of "Mexicans in the U.S.," "Spanish Heritage Americans," and "Minority Groups". The usefulness of this reference tool is enhanced by the inclusion of an index by categories, race being one of them. This index makes it relatively easy to locate additional sources of statistical data on Mexican Americans.

The statistical sources included in this chapter were chosen because they specifically contain data on Mexican Americans or, in a few cases, on the Spanish-speaking. Frequently these data indicate socioeconomic characteristics: population size, geographical distribution, educational achievement, income levels, employment patterns, unemployment rates, health conditions, housing, and fertility. Some of these statistical sources are national in scope and others are limited to the Southwest or to individual states.

Several statistical sources on Mexican Americans were not included in this chapter because of their extensive coverage of other unrelated groups. The most important of these sources is the U.S. Census.[2] Since 1930, people of Mexican descent have been treated in separate categories. These reports, in spite of their unreliability, lack of comparability because of changing categories, and tendency to undercount, have served as the basis for most statistical studies on Mexican Americans. The annual reports of the Immigration and Naturalization Service are a second source of data on Mexican Americans.[3] From these, interested researchers may obtain data on the immigration, deportation, and naturalization of Mexicans. Another source is the report of the Immigration Commission (also known as the Dillingham Commission),[4] published in 1911. Any economic study of Mexican Americans in the twentieth century must rely on this unique source as a point of departure. Volumes 1, 24, and 25 contain a series of statistical tables detailing Mexican participation in the agricultural labor force and in other industries of the Western states.

Two other statistical sources which should be mentioned are of value to researchers seeking data on Mexican Americans in the field of education. The first is *Racial, Ethnic and Sex Enrollment Data from Institutions of Higher Education*[5] published annually from 1972 to 1976, and the second is the *Directory of Public Elementary and Secondary Schools in Selected Districts: Enrollments and Staff by Racial/Ethnic Group*,[6] published annually from 1967 to 1972. Unfortunately, these two publications have not been kept up to date.

1. *American Statistical Index; A Comprehensive Guide and Index to the Statistical Publications of the U.S. Government* (Washington, DC: Congressional Information Service, 1978).

2. In addition to the decennial population reports also see: U.S. Bureau of the Census, *U.S. Census of Population: 1960, Subject Reports, Persons of Spanish Surname, Final Report* (Washington, DC: Government Printing Office, 1962); *Persons of Spanish Origin in the United States. November 1969* (Washington, DC: Government Printing Office, 1971); *U.S. Census of Population: Special Reports, Mexican Americans, or Population Characteristics, Persons of Spanish Origin in the United States* (Washington, DC: Government Printing Office, 1970); *Persons of Spanish Origin in the United States. March 1972 and 1973* (Washington, DC: Government Printing Office, 1973); *1970 Census of Population: Persons of Spanish Ancestry* (Washington, DC: 1973); *1970 Census of Population. Persons of Spanish Origin* (Washington, DC: Government Printing Office, 1974); *Population Characteristics—Persons of Spanish Origins in the United States*, Series P-20, (March 1973, 1974) (Washington, DC: Government Printing Office, 1974); *Data on the Spanish Ancestry Population; Available from the 1970 Census of Population and Housing* (Washington, DC: Government Printing Office, 1975); *Persons of Spanish Origin in the United States: March 1977* (Washington, DC: Government Printing Office, 1978).

3. U.S. Immigration and Naturalization Service. *Annual Report of the Immigration and Naturalization Service*. Various Issues.

4. U.S. Immigration Commission, *Reports of the Immigration Commission, Immigrants in Industries* (Washington, DC: Government Printing Office, 1911).

5. U.S. Department of Health, Education, and Welfare. Office for Civil Rights. *Racial, Ethnic and Sex Enrollment Data from Institutions of Higher Education* (Washington, DC: Government Printing Office, 1976).

6. U.S. Department of Health, Education, and Welfare. Office for Civil Rights. *Directory of Public Elementary and Secondary Schools in Selected Districts; Enrollments and Staff by Racial/Ethnic Group* (Washington,DC: Government Printing Office, 1972).

150. Belden Associates. *The Mexican American Market in the United States: Market Characteristics from a Personal-Interview Survey in Spanish, City and County Populations from the U.S. Census.* Dallas, TX: Belden Associates, 1962. 37 p.

This is one of the first reports of marketing data on the Spanish-speaking Mexican American population in the United States. It covers the five states with the greatest concentration of Mexican Americans: Arizona, California, Colorado, New Mexico, and Texas. Within these states twelve areas were selected for the survey on the basis of the size of the Mexican American population. The areas are Phoenix, Los Angeles, San Diego, San Francisco Bay Area, Denver, Albuquerque, Corpus Christi, El Paso, Houston, Laredo, San Antonio, and Lower Rio Grande Valley. This report is the result of a personal-interview survey conducted in Spanish in the spring of 1962. Data on home ownership, car ownership, telephone in home, bank accounts, savings, credit, magazine and newspaper reading, etc., are provided. It also contains population figures by city and county taken from the 1960 census of Spanish surnames in Arizona, California, Colorado, New Mexico, and Texas.

151. Broadbent, Elizabeth. *The Distribution of Mexican Populations in the United States.* San Francisco, CA: R & E Research Associates, 1972. 121 p.

A series of tables and maps tracing the growth and changing distribution of the Mexican population in the United States from 1850 to 1930 are contained in this work. The statistical data are all based on U.S. census reports.

152. Browning, Harley L., and S. Dale McLemore. *Statistical Profile of the Spanish-Surname Population of Texas.* Austin: Bureau of Business Research, The University of Texas, 1964. (Population Series, no. 1) 83 p.

This is one of the earliest and best statistical studies of the Spanish-surnamed of Texas. It provides 33 tables of figures on the numbers, growth, geographical distribution, basic population characteristics, education, employment, occupation, and income. Also included are statistical tables comparing the Spanish-surnamed of Texas with those of California, Colorado, Arizona, and New Mexico. The data are based on the 1950 and 1960 U.S. census reports.

153. California. Department of Industrial Relations. Division of Fair Employment Practices. *Californians of Spanish Surname: Population, Education, Income, Employment.* San Francisco: Fair Employment Practices Commission, 1976. 61 p.

This is an excellent concise reference source for statistics on Mexican American population, education, income, and employment covering the years 1960–1970.

This directory reexamines the social, educational and economic status of California's largest ethnic minority and contrasts it in tables and charts with that of the general white population. The data contained in the 23 tables and five charts are based on figures from the U.S. Census of Population.

Information on the population includes birthplace, parentage and mother tongue, area of residence, age, and family size. Employment information covers the labor force participation, weeks of employment in 1969, and the industry and occupation of employed persons of Spanish surname. Data on income are arranged by individual as well as family and categorized by metropolitan area. Educational attainment statistics are provided.

This is the second edition of this title and as such is a follow-up report on the 1964 study which covered the decade from 1950–1960. It provides much the same information as the earlier report but includes more details and elaboration.

154. California. Mexican Fact-Finding Committee. *Mexicans in California: Report of Governor C. C. Young's Mexican Fact-Finding Committee*. San Francisco: R & E Research Associates, 1970. (Reprint of 1930 ed., Sacramento: California State Printing Office.) 214 p.

This is a reprint of the report originally published in 1930 by the State of California. It is one of the earliest works providing statistical data on Mexican Americans in California. It contains 22 tables of figures on immigration, population, and naturalization; 17 tables indicating Mexican participation in industries and nonagricultural occupation; four tables on the labor needs of California with reference to the Mexicans; 35 tables on health, relief, and delinquency among Mexicans; and five tables on the Mexican family, its size, and income. In addition, the report contains 16 charts showing the extent of Mexican population and naturalization in California and 25 other charts illustrating the number of Mexicans in industries and nonagricultural occupations.

155. California State College, San Jose. Department of Economics. *A Racial Profile of California*, by Ernest D. Lampkin, *et al.* San Jose: California State College, 1968. 68 p.

Mexican American, Chinese, Japanese, Black, and Native American population of California are surveyed in this statistical study. It indicates where the various groups settled, their migration patterns, educational characteristics, employment, unemployment, income, housing, health, and organizations. The data are based on U.S. census reports and on a variety of private and public statistical sources in California.

156. Chiavacci, Walter P., and William G. Davey. *The Status of Minorities in the Southwest: A Demographic Profile.* Paper presented at the meeting of the Society of Intercultural Education, Training, and Research held in Chicago, February 24–27, 1977. 30 p. ED 145 993.

This work contains general demographic data on Black Americans, Mexican Americans, and Native Americans of the Southwest. The data were collected by the Bureau of the Census in the states of Arizona, California, New Mexico, Colorado, and Texas. Included are nine tables providing statistical information in the following categories: sex, state of residence, race, head of household, marital status, family size, housing characteristics, percentage of persons in the labor force, family income, income below poverty level, workers 16 years and older, major occupation groups, share of federal salaries, school enrollments, years of school completed, and percentage of high school graduates per state.

157. Choldin, Harvey M., and Grafton D. Trout. *Mexican Americans in Transition: Migration and Employment in Michigan Cities. Final Report.* East Lansing: Agricultural Experiment Station, Michigan State University, 1969. 479 p. ED 079 471.

The U.S. Department of Labor, Office of Manpower Research, conducted this study as part of a larger research project. It was designed to examine the characteristics and social and occupational encounters of Mexican American migrants in their transition from rural to urban society. The target community was the migrant workers in Michigan. The data were obtained by a random sample of heads of household. The following variables were considered: social characteristics, including the composition of household and the educational level attained; migration and community stability; occupational opportunities; employment and income patterns; and income mobility.

158. Colorado. Commission on Spanish-Surnamed Citizens. *The Status of Spanish-Surnamed Citizens in Colorado.* Greeley: Colorado State College, 1967. 125 p.

This work is the result of research conducted on the Spanish-surnamed citizens of Colorado between July 1, 1966, and December 1, 1966. The 47 tables, maps, and charts provide statistical data on population size and distribution, income, family size, employment and unemployment, schooling, crime and delinquency, and health. Some of the information was derived from the 1960 census but much was extracted from the state's statistical reports or compiled by the research staff of the Commission.

159. Elac, John Chala. *The Employment of Mexican Workers in U.S. Agriculture, 1900–1960; A Binational Economic Analysis.* San Francisco: R & E Research Associates, 1972. 152 p.

An economic analysis of the employment of Mexican agriculture workers in the United States from 1900 to 1960 is provided in this study. Included are 29 tables of statistical information on the immigration of Mexicans, production of selected agricultural products, labor force, and wages. The data were obtained from both U.S. and Mexican official sources.

160. Estrada, Leobardo F. "A Demographic Comparison of the Mexican Origin Population in the Midwest and Southwest." *Aztlán,* 7 (Summer, 1976): 203–234.

This statistical analysis compares the Midwestern and Southwestern population of Mexican origin, based on the 1970 census. The comparison was made in the following areas: population distribution in 11 Midwestern states and five Southwestern states, metropolitical residence, native and foreign-born, migration, median age, educational achievement, marital status, employment of wives, income, occupation, and industries where employed.

161. Fellows, Lloyd. *Economic Aspects of the Mexican Rural Population in California with Special Emphasis on the Need for Mexican Labor in Agriculture.* San Francisco: R & E Research Associates, 1971. 95 p.

The appendix of this work contains 37 statistical tables. The first 16 provide data on the level of salaries and wages in various parts of Mexico and the average cost of living for a workingman's family in 13 key states of Mexico. The remaining 21 tables focus on economic aspects of Mexican labor in California. Much of the data were obtained by the author through personal field research. Other sources of data include Mexican government reports; surveys by the University of California; surveys and reports by the Department of Agriculture of the Los Angeles Chamber of Commerce; U.S. government reports from the Departments of Agriculture, Labor, and Commerce; and reports of hearings before the U.S. House of Representatives Committee on Immigration.

162. Friend, Reed E., and Samuel Baum. *Economic, Social, and Demographic Characteristics of Spanish-American Wage Workers on U.S. Farms.* Washington, DC: Economic Research Service, U.S. Department of Agriculture, 1963. (Agricultural Economic Report, no. 27) 21 p.

This report contains 18 tables with figures indicating social and demographic characteristics of Spanish-American farm workers during the year 1960. Among the information provided are birthplace, age and sex, education, wages, unemployment, and employers. The data were compiled by the Bureau of the Census and published in a supplement to the February, 1961 *Current Population Survey.*

163. Gutiérrez, Elizabeth, and Herman D. Luján. *The Kansas Migrant Survey: An Interpretive Profile of the Mexican American Migrant Family.* Lawrence: Institute for Social and Environmental Studies, University of Kansas, 1973. 75 p. ED 107 419.

The results of a survey of 245 migrant families, all Mexican Americans, conducted from June to August, 1972, in ten counties of western Kansas, are reported in this work. The survey produced data on citizenship, family size, education, language facility, religion, settling out, living and working conditions, service availability, and attitudes toward services. The statistical information is presented in 29 tables. The sponsoring agency was the Kansas Council for Agricultural Workers and Low-Income Families.

164. Hill, Susan, and Ronald Jessee. *The Bilingual Education Program: 1972-73 Regular and 1973 Summer School Terms.* Washington, DC: National Center for Education Statistics, U.S. Department of Health, Education, and Welfare, 1976. 9 p.

This source provides a statistical profile of the bilingual education programs for the 1972-73 school term and 1973 summer session. The data indicate federal expenditures, staff training, and pupil participation in all Title VII projects. This information was obtained by the Consolidated Program Information Report (CPIR). Although the data cover all students involved in Bilingual- Bicultural programs, the statistical information is most important for the Spanish-speaking since Spanish was the language of instruction for 88 percent of those enrolled. Furthermore, almost 70 percent of the pupils were from the Southwest.

165. Leonard, Olen E., and Helen W. Johnson. *Low-Income Families in the Spanish-Surname Population of the Southwest.* Washington, DC: Economic Research Service, U.S. Department of Agriculture, 1967. (Agricultural Economic Report, no. 112) 29 p.

Included in this report are 13 tables and eight charts indicating residence, nativity, mobility, fertility, income distribution, labor force participation, industrial composition, occupational pattern, and educational level of low-income Spanish-surname families of the Southwest: Arizona, California, Colorado, New Mexico, and Texas. The statistical data were obtained from the 1950 and 1960 Special Census Reports entitled *Persons of Spanish Surname.*

166. Loosley, Allyn Campbell. *Foreign Born Population of California, 1848–1920*. San Francisco: R & E Research Associates, 1971. 83 p.
This statistical study traces the growth of the foreign population of California from 1848 to 1920. It focuses on nine foreign-born elements: Chinese, English, French, German, Irish, Italian, Japanese, Mexican, and Portuguese. Chapter IV of this work consist of 19 tables with statistical information obtained from reports of the U.S. Census. An appendix includes nine additional tables which indicate the distribution of the foreign-born population as of 1920.

167. Mellor, Earl F. *Directory of Data Sources on Racial and Ethnic Minorities*. Washington DC: U.S. Department of Labor, 1975. (Bureau of Labor Statistics, *Bulletin*, 1879). 83 p. Annotated. Index.
Arranged by minority group, this directory covers a large and diverse number of recent demographic, social, and economic data sources published by federal agencies as of September, 1974. It includes reports from the 1970 census of population and housing, the monthly Current Population Surveys, reports on private industry employment, the Equal Employment Opportunity Commission, the Civil Service Commission, the 1969 Census of Agriculture, a 1969 survey of minority business firms, and selected reports from other agencies of the U.S. government. The introduction mentions that health, arrest, prison, armed forces statistics, and school desegretion data are not included. Sources for this data can be acquired from agencies mentioned in the introduction. Section II is the most relevant to the Mexican Americans; it is entitled "Persons of Spanish Ancestry". Useful appendixes include information on how to find source publications; a locater guide for national level data in the 1970 decennial census; state, area, place and other subnational level data in the 1970 census; and subject and report series indexes.

168. Mexican-American Population Commission of California. *Mexican-American Population in California: October 1970, with Projections to 1980*. San Francisco: The Commission, 1971. 19 p.
This work is a statistical survey of the Mexican American population in California. It was done in response to the failure of the 1970 census to accurately count Mexican Americans in the United States. The Mexican American Population Commission of California has determined that the figures in this report are the most accurate possible. They were obtained by examining unpublished California State Department of Education school statistics for 1970 and then comparing these with the California Cooperative Manpower Plan for fiscal year 1970. The Department of Education figures were further verified with published and unpublished 1966, 1967, and 1969 Spanish-surnamed school statistics; with the 1970 California Parochial school statistics; and with California Human Resources Development statistics on percentage of work force using Department of Labor-funded agencies. More recent surveys may have been conducted by the Commission, but the reports have not been located.

169. "The Mexican American Population of Houston; A Survey in the Field, 1965-1970." by Mary Ellen Goodman, *et al. Rice University Studies, 57* (Summer, 1971): 1-125.
The appendix of this monograph on cultural anthropology contains 12 tables of data pertaining to Mexican American migration into Houston, their age group percentages,

income, employment, participation of women in the labor force, school years, and housing conditions. The data were compiled from the 1960 Final Report of the Census, the 1950 U.S. Census of Population, and *Career Guidance Through Groups,* July 1, 1969–August 15, 1970, a publication of the Vocational Guidance Service of Houston, Texas.

170. Mindiola, Tatcho. *A Demographic Profile of Texas and Selected Cities: Some Recent Trends, 1950–1970.* Houston: Center for Human Resources, University of Houston, 1974. 59 p. ED 097 147.

Analyses of changes within the Black, Anglo and Spanish-surnamed population of Texas from 1950 to 1970 are contained in this report. Three main areas of population changes were examined: growth, components of growth (births, deaths, migration), and distribution. The data were obtained from the 1950, 1960, and 1970 U.S. census reports. Of the 23 statistical tables, 13 include Mexican Americans. This work was sponsored by the Division of Occupational Research and Development of the Texas Education Agency in Austin.

171. Pomerance, Deborah, and Diane Ellis. *Ethnic Statistics: A Compendium of Reference Sources.* Arlington, VA: Data Use and Access Laboratories, 1978. 133 p. Indexes.

This is a most important tool in the search for statistical sources on the Mexican American. It consists of 92 detailed abstracts of federal resources which contain data on Blacks, American Indians, Asians, and the Spanish population. The abstracts represent 11 departments and agencies and they reflect a wide range of federal government activities. Each entry provides information on the purpose of the census or survey producing the data, the geographical coverage, the period, frequency, and racial or ethnic groups for which data are available. To assist the users, this compendium includes three very helpful indexes: racial/ethnic, subject, and title/survey. The authors' companion publication—*Ethnic Statistics: Using National Data Resources for Ethnic Studies*—is intended as a college-level teaching aid and a guide to research in statistical data on ethnic groups.

172. Saunders, Lyle. *The Spanish-Speaking Population of Texas.* Austin: University of Texas Press, 1949. (Inter-American Education Occasional Papers, no. 5) 56 p.

Basically a series of tabulations indicating the number, proportion, and distribution of the Spanish-speaking population of Texas prior to 1949; included are nine tables of figures obtained from census reports and other nonofficial sources.

173. Schmidt, Fred H. *Spanish Surnamed American Employment in the Southwest.* Washington, DC: Government Printing Office, 1960. 247 p.

This work, funded by the Equal Employment Opportunity Commission, provides statistical information on the job patterns of the Spanish-surnamed in the Southwest. The data were based on U.S. government reports since 1940 and they indicate Spanish-surnamed participation in the labor force, fertility, education, housing, income, health and mobility.

174. Talbert, Robert H. *Spanish-Name People in the Southwest and West.* Fort Worth: Leo Potishman Foundation, Texas Christian University, 1955. 90 p.

Data concerning persons of Spanish surname in Texas, Arizona, California, Colorado, and New Mexico are analyzed in this study. The data were obtained from the 1950 U.S. Census of Population and Housing and were used to indicate the geographical distribution of the Spanish-surname population, their urbanization, nativity, age distribution, age pattern in Texas, educational attainment, marital status, income distribution, unemployment, females in the labor force, occupational pattern, and housing conditions.

175. U. S. Civil Service Commission. *Study of Minority Employment in the Federal Government.* Washington, DC: Government Printing Office, 1965. 193 p.

This source contains statistics on full-time minority group employment in the federal government as of June 30, 1965. It covers Blacks, American Indians, Mexican Americans, Orientals, and Puerto Ricans. In the case of the Mexican Americans, the data were obtained from the five states of Arizona, California, Colorado, New Mexico, and Texas and from the metropolitan areas of Los Angeles–Long Beach, San Francisco–Oakland, Denver, Dallas, Fort Worth, Houston, and San Antonio. Tables on the Mexican Americans are found on pages 153-167.

176. U.S. Congress. Joint Economic Committee. Subcommittee on Inter-American Economic Relationships. *Recent Developments in Mexico and Their Economic Implications for the United States: Hearings Before the Subcommittee on Inter-American Economic Relationships of the Joint Economic Committee, Congress of the United States, 95th Congress, 1st Session, January 17 and 24, 1977.* Washington, DC: Government Printing Office, 1977. 401 p.

This is a report of the hearing conducted by the Subcommittee on Inter-American Economic Relationships of the U.S. Congress. Exhibit D of this report (Title V Regional Action Planning Commission, 1976) contains numerous statistical information on legal and illegal immigration from Mexico and other data relevant to Mexican Americans in the four border states of Arizona, California, New Mexico, and Texas.

177. U. S. Department of Agriculture. Economic Research Service. *Spanish-Surname Farm Operators in Southern Texas.* Washington, DC: Government Printing Office, 1969. (Agricultural Economic Report, no. 162) 69 p. ED 055 699.

This is a statistical study and analysis of 3,600 Spanish-surnamed farm operators in 14 Texas counties based on the 1964 agricultural census. It contains information on the type of farming, size of farms, productivity, tenure, production, characteristics of the operators and their households, and income from sources other than the farms operated.

178. Upham, W. Kennedy, and David E. Wright. *Poverty Among Spanish Americans in Texas: Low Income Families in a Minority Group.* College Station: Department of Agricultural Economics and Sociology, Texas A & M University, 1966. 55 p. ED 024 520.

The Spanish-surname population of Texas, based on the 1960 census, is statistically analyzed in this report. The focus is on the extent of poverty; the distribution of poverty; and on education, unemployment and family size as aspects of poverty among the Spanish-speaking population. Comparative data on poverty among the major ethnic groups of Texas are provided and also figures indicating the level of poverty in areas of heavy minority concentration.

# Chapter 6

# *Directories*

The directories in this chapter identify the human resources among Mexican Americans, facilitate communications between different segments of the Mexican population, and indicate sources of assistance and points of contact within governmental agencies. They were compiled by private and public institutions during the 1970s in response to growing interest in the welfare and potential of the Mexican American community. The majority originated in California but a few were published in New Mexico, Arizona, Texas, Kansas, Maryland, and New York. The federal government is one of the main producers of directories for all minorities. Examples of works issued by the Department of Commerce, the Civil Rights Commission, and the Cabinet Committee on Opportunity for the Spanish Speaking are cited in this chapter.

One category of directories lists organizations and agencies which provide services to the Spanish-speaking. The services are generally in the areas of civil rights, health, education, employment, financial assistance, politics, and housing. Nearly half of these directories are specifically for Mexican Americans. Among these only one is national in scope. The remainder are related to local and statewide services in California. Noticeably absent are directories from other states with substantial Mexican American population such as Texas, New Mexico, and Arizona. They may exist but are either unavailable or not well publicized.

A second category of directories lists names of Mexican Americans in various professional fields or those who have achieved a certain level of education or prominence. These include elected and appointed office-holders, scientists, engineers, academicians, librarians, and college graduates. With few exceptions, most of these directories are national in scope. As far as can be determined, there are no directories which identify Mexican Americans in medicine, law, primary and secondary education, business, and other fields. These works facilitate contact and communication between the individuals listed and do not generally provide biographical information.

A third category includes directories which list Chicano faculty and programs in colleges and universities throughout the United States. In the fourth category are directories of educational and bilingual-bicultural programs for Mexican American children. The fifth category includes lists of vendors, publishers, and distributors of materials of interest to the Mexican Americans. These are particularly useful for librarians and educators.

Also cited in this chapter are three directories, published by the Office of Minority

Business Enterprise of the U.S. Department of Commerce, which are not covered by any of the above categories. They include the *National Directory of Minority Manufacturers, 1974,* the *National Roster of Minority Consulting Professional Firms,* and the *Directory of Minority Media.* They were produced to assist minority groups, Mexican Americans included, in achieving fuller participation in the mainstream of American life.

Currency and accuracy are two of the most important criteria for judging the usefulness of directories. The user should be aware that there is a time lag between the collection of data and the publication of particular works. The information contained in the tools cited below may be dated or obsolete. Some of the directories will be updated periodically but others will not and will become useless except for historical purposes.

179. American Political Science Association. Committee on the Status of Chicanos in the Profession. *Roster of Chicanos in Political Science.* 2nd. ed. Washington, DC: The Association, 1976. 31 p.

This is the second edition of a national directory of Chicano political scientists and graduate students; 58 names are included. The entries are arranged alphabetically by surname in two separate listings. For each political scientist the following is given: position and address, degree and fields, and dissertation topic. For each graduate student, address, degree and fields, institutional affiliation, position, dissertation topic, and date of Ph.D. exam are listed. A final section is a list of Chicano graduate students by institution.

A third revised and updated edition of this directory is currently in preparation and scheduled for distribution in the fall of 1979. This work should serve to increase contacts and communication among Chicanos in the field and to assist in the recruitment of others.

180. California. Ethnic Services Task Force. *Ethnic Library Materials: A Preliminary Vendor List,* compiled by Gwendolyn Weaver, Oscar L. Sims, and Rita Torres. Santa Barbara: California Ethnic Services Task Force, 1978. 27 p.

This is a preliminary guide to vendors which supply published materials on the four major ethnic groups in California: American Indian, Asian, Black, and Spanish-speaking. The work is arranged in four parts by ethnic category. The section entitled Chicano/Spanish-speaking lists over 150 publishers, book dealers, distributors, and other agencies in the United States and Mexico which supply material on the Mexican Americans, Latin America, and Spanish language and literature. Each entry includes the vendor's name and address; a few telephone numbers are also given.

The selections were based on recommendations of ethnic services librarians and attempts were made to verify all information provided. A more comprehensive and evaluative list is planned for the future. Works of this type should be revised and updated annually. All medium-sized libraries collecting ethnic studies materials will find this source extremely helpful.

181. California. State Department of Education. Bilingual-Bicultural Task Force. *Directory of Spanish Speaking Organizations in California.* Sacramento: The Department, 1971. 11 p.

Although now out of date, this is the first and only California directory which represents a statewide listing of Spanish-speaking organizations. The list includes 21 organizations, 16 of which directly concern the Mexican Americans. The remaining five organizations are peripherally related. The entries contain name of the organization, the principal officer, address, telephone number, date of establishment, and a statement of objectives.

182. California. State Department of Health. Health and Welfare Agency. *State Directory of Health Agencies Serving the Latino Community. Directorio estatal de agencias de salud serviendo la comunidad latina.* Sacramento: The Department, 1977. 128 p.

This is the first directory of California health agencies serving the Spanish-speaking population in the state. Only those which offer bilingual services in health-related professions are listed. The agencies are arranged alphabetically by county in chart format. Each entry includes the name, address, telephone, contact person, and a list of the professional assistance provided. The chart to the right of each agency indicates the specific services provided among the many types available, e.g., medical, dental, X-ray, laboratory, mental health, drug abuse, alcoholism, VD prophylaxis, family planning, prescriptions, counseling, nutrition, health education, optometry, and physical therapy. Bilingual, full-time, part-time, and volunteer staff are also indicated.

There are approximately 200 local clinics, centers, and other types of agencies listed in this work. The appendix is a directory of all California county health officers, with addresses and telephone numbers.

183. *Chicano Faculty Research Directory: University of California, Academic Year 1971-1972.* Edited by Reynaldo Macias. Los Angeles: Aztlán Publications, 1972. 85 p.

Chicano faculty in the University of California system are listed in this directory, the first of its kind. Coverage includes the 1971-1972 and 1972-1973 academic years. The contents consist of five parts: the introduction, the faculty list, the faculty research directory, samples of letters and questionnaires used to compile the directory, and a list of Aztlán publications. Both the list and the research directory are arranged alphabetically by campus. Among the nine campuses the responses of 82 faculty members are listed. Each faculty entry contains the academic status, home address, list of degrees and institutions where received, publications, papers, teaching interests, courses taught, research interests, areas of specialization, and research in progress.

In recent years several national directories have been compiled which updated this early effort. In 1974 Aztlán Publications issued a *National Directory of Chicano Faculty and Research,* by Renée Mares, and a new edition is in progress. Stanford University also distributes annually a *National List of Chicano Contacts in Higher Education.* All of these sources are helpful in identifying the role and interests of Mexican Americans in higher education.

184. Cole, Katherine W. *Minority Organizations: A National Directory.* Garrett Park, MD: Garrett Park Press, 1978. 385 p. Indexes.

This is the most comprehensive listing of organizations established by minority group members or for the benefit of minority groups. The minority groups covered are Native Americans, Blacks, Hispanics, and Asian Americans. There are 2,705 organizations listed of which 486 are Hispanic-oriented; Puerto Rican and Cuban organizations are included but most are Mexican American. The entries provide, in addition to the official name, and sometimes the logo of the organization, the address, telephone number and a brief description of function. Use of this directory is facilitated by alphabetical, geographical, and functional indexes. A glossary of terms which helps to identify the different types of organizations is also included.

185. El Congreso de California. *California Directory of Agencies and Organizations Serving Latino, Asian and Pacific Island Communities.* San Jose: El Congreso, 1977. 131 p. Indexes.

Statewide and regional agencies and organizations, both public and private, which offer services to several of the major ethnic groups in California are listed in this directory. State Senator Alex P. García initiated the project. A coalition of Latino organizations, El Congreso de California, sponsored and carried out the preparation of the directory.

The work is arranged in eight sections and covers 367 organizations. The first section includes statewide agencies and the others cover the agencies of the seven regions. A map of the state is provided with the regional designations. Each section contains a separate index and descriptions of the agencies and organizations listed, with addresses, telephone numbers, and names of the directors. A list of the U.S. Senators and constitutional officers follows the statewide section. Lists of the county seats and the members of Congress and the State Legislature are included in each of the seven regional sections. Address and telephone numbers are given for all officials.

Among the entries for Mexican Americans are agencies and organizations for legal assistance, migrant housing, Spanish-speaking radio stations, health centers, Educational Opportunity programs, art and cultural centers, unions, family service centers, and many others.

186. Congress of Mexican American Unity (CMAU). *Mexican American Community Directory.* Presented by KRLA Radio. Pasadena, CA: The Congress, [1971]. 38 p.

This is a special directory of 292 local and statewide organizations serving the Mexican American community in the Los Angeles area. It is arranged in the following 16 categories: civic and government-funded organizations, church-affiliated organizations, communication and publicity groups, community centers, county and statewide organizations, educational and scholarship groups, mothers and fathers clubs—CMAU-associated, action-accented groups, political clubs and organizations, service clubs, social clubs and groups, senior citizens groups, sports and recreation, youth and MECHA groups.

Each entry includes the name of the organization or group, address, contact person, and telephone number. Outdated at this point, the directory is useful for historical purposes in identifying the variety of organizations, many of which still exist, that were created to serve the needs of the Mexican American population in the area.

187. Dissemination Center for Bilingual Bicultural Education. *Guide to Title VII ESEA Bilingual-Bicultural Programs, 1974–1975.* Compiled by Joanna F. Chambers. Austin, TX: The Center, 1975. 139 p. Indexes.

This is the third revised edition of the directory to Title VII programs funded as a result of the Elementary and Secondary Education Act of 1965. The previous directories were issued annually in 1972–1973 and 1973–1974. The current guide covers 320 projects in 41 states and territories. These are listed by state and city and subarranged alphabetically. Each entry includes the name of the local education agency, the title of the project, the name of the project director or contact person, the address and telephone number, the funding year and the language of instruction.

Programs in Spanish are included in the listing for Arizona, California, Colorado, Connecticut, Delaware, District of Columbia, Idaho, Florida, Illinois, Indiana, Kansas, Louisiana, Massachusetts, Michigan, Missouri, Nebraska, New Jersey, New Mexico, New York, Ohio, Oregon, Pennsylvania, Puerto Rico, Rhode Island, Texas, Utah, Virgin Islands, Washington, Wisconsin, and Wyoming.

The indexes are to programs by language, name, state coordinators, project directors, and contact persons. There is also a table of the statistical overview by state. The earlier 1973–1974 guide must be consulted for descriptions of the programs and statistical information on the number of students, classes, grades, etc., which are not included in the new edition.

188. Dumaux, Sally. *Ethnic and National Collections in the Los Angeles Area.* Los Angeles: Southern California Answering Network, Los Angeles Public Library, 1978. 61 p. Index.

Arranged by ethnic or national group, this directory provides a guide to the special collections of ethnic resources of Los Angeles and Orange counties. Excluded are a number of integrated collections, medium-sized libraries and parish collections. Of particular interest are the sections on Spanish-Speaking Peoples Collections and the Spanish Bookstores. Each entry gives the address, telephone number, contact person or librarian, hours, size of the collection, and circulation information. The guide was prepared with funds from Title I of the Federal Library Services and Construction Act.

189. Hayes-Bautista, David E., and Eleanor Moreno Kent. *A Resource List of Mexican-American Organizations and Services in the East Bay.* Oakland, CA: The Latin American Library, Oakland Public Library, 1970. 43 p. Index.

This directory covers Mexican American organizations and services in the California counties of Alameda and Contra Costa. It was originally published in 1967 by the International Institute and revised in 1970. Included are national and state organizations, service centers, local organizations, organizations that the authors were unable to contact, agencies offering services to the Spanish-speaking, and churches. The entries give addresses and telephone numbers. The organizations are described in terms of the officers, membership, functions and objectives. It was prepared as a reference and educational guide to the resources available to the Mexican American community in the East Bay area.

190. John, Vera P., and Vivian M. Horner. "Program Description." In *Early Childhood Bilingual Education,* pp. 21–107. New York: Materials Center, MLA-ACTFL, 1971. 187 p.

Bilingual-bicultural programs for Mexican American children are listed in this directory. It was prepared to provide information concerning bilingual education for teachers in predominantly minority communities. Based on a nationwide survey of bilingual-bicultural program for Mexican American children, each program listed is followed by a description of its operation, personnel, teacher training, curriculum, testing, evaluations, financing and resources. The programs are arranged alphabetically by state.

191. Johnson, Willis L. *Directory of Special Programs for Minority Group Members, 1974: Career Information Services, Employment Skills Banks, Financial Aid,* 2nd ed. Garrett Park, MD: Garrett Park Press, 1975. 400 p. Indexes.

This updated edition provides information on programs to assist minorities and women in career planning, employment skills, and financial aid. Approximately 1,500 organizations are included under four general sections: General Employment and Educational Assistance Programs, Federal Assistance Programs, Women's Career Counseling and Job Assistance Programs, and College and University Awards. Information on special programs for Mexican Americans can be found in the Program Index under Spanish-speaking programs and specific fields of study. Each entry generally provides the program name, address, summary of program and activities, titles of any publications, and name of funding source. A glossary of terms used in the work and a bibliography of other sources of information supplement this directory.

192. Jordan, Anne. "Mexican American Publishing Guide." *Journal of Mexican American History,* 3 (1973): 190–208.

Publishers of books and periodicals related to Mexican Americans are found in this directory. The listing was produced in order to facilitate the acquisition of materials that are not accessible through regular trade channels. The guide is arranged in four parts: Book publishers, Periodicals, Addendum of current periodicals, and Defunct periodicals.

The listing of 41 book publishers includes the Spanish-language press, community organizations, ethnic presses, institutions with a concern for social conditions, religious publishers of Spanish-language materials, the Chicano press, and a few political organizations. Excluded are the university presses and governmental agencies. With consistency the address and a short description of the type of material published are given for each book publisher entry. Other information, such as the telephone number and the name of the director, is provided when available.

The listing of approximately 109 periodicals includes with each entry, if available, the title, address, telephone number, date of the first issue, frequency, price, circulation, and content description. The titles in the addendum include current periodicals for which little or no information could be found and those titles which are presumed to be defunct. Although this guide is now outdated, much of the information is still useful. An annual publication of this sort would be extremely helpful to librarians and others seeking publications issued by small and alternative presses.

193. Kniefel, Tanya Suárez. *Programs Available for Strengthening the Education of Spanish-Speaking Students.* Las Cruces: New Mexico State University, 1968. 41 p. Annotated. ED 025 366.

This directory provides information concerning the availability of federal funds for training educational personnel in areas with high concentrations of bilingual students. It lists relevant federal legislation, scholarships for Spanish-speaking students, and bilingual educational programs. It gives information on the availability of the funds, eligibility requirements, and guidelines for writing and evaluating federal grant proposals. In addition, it includes an annotated bibliography of materials concerning federal funding offered by the U.S. Office of Education and grant application procedures.

194. Lemus, Frank C. *National Roster of Spanish Surnamed Elected Officials.* Los Angeles: Aztlán Publications, 1974. 410 p.
This is a national directory of elected officials with Spanish surnames. The ethnic origins of the officials are Chicano, Mexican American, Basque, Puerto Rican, Latin American, Spanish American and Cuban American. The purpose of this roster is to encourage and increase direct communication among the Spanish-surnamed people of the United States and their elected officials. One thousand four hundred thirty-five officials are listed from the federal, state, county, and local levels of government. The information was collected between 1972 and 1973 and includes the title or position, term of office, address, telephone number, party affiliation, and ethnic self-identification. Plans for updating this directory are mentioned.

195. _____. *National Roster, California Portion, Spanish Surnamed Elected Officials.* Sacramento: Urban Affairs Institute, 1973. 50 p.
Spanish-surnamed officials in California who were holding public elected positions at the federal, state and local levels in 1973 are identified in this directory. The categories covered by the directory are Chicanos, Mexican Americans, Puerto Ricans, Latin Americans, Spanish Americans, and Cuban Americans. The names are listed alphabetically according to the political office held. Under each entry is the political affiliation, the term of office, the title of the office, address, and telephone number. This is part of a larger work which covers elected officials throughout the country. A periodic updating was promised for this roster but it has not been produced as yet.

196. Mares, Renée. *The National Directory of Chicano Faculty and Research.* Los Angeles: Aztlán Publications, 1974. 141 p. Index.
Spanish-surnamed faculty and researchers in the United States are listed in this directory, the first of its kind. The purpose is to identify the accomplishments of "Chicanos" in teaching and research as a basis for criticism and evaluation. Although not all individuals listed would be considered Chicanos, most are of Spanish American heritage. More than 1,400 names were included following a two-year survey of four-year institutions in 35 states. The entries, arranged by state and institution, provide information on the academic background of the faculty members, publications, research interests, courses taught, addresses, and research in progress. Plans for periodic updating are mentioned. A new edition is forthcoming in 1979.

197. Martínez, Arthur D. *Who's Who: Chicano Officeholders, 1977-78.* Silver City, NM: The Author, 1978. 61 p.
This is a directory of Chicano officials at the federal, state, and local levels. At the federal level there are names of Mexican Americans listed under Senate Staff Aids, U.S. Representatives, Federal Judiciary System, Executive Office of the President, Cabinet Departments, etc. At the state level there are names listed under Governor, Gubernatorial Cabinets, Gubernatorial Staff Aids, Heads of State Departments, Agencies, etc. At the local level there are names listed for all cities with a population of more than 25,000 in California and Texas, and for cities with more than 15,000 in Arizona, Colorado, and New Mexico. Also provided are names of Democratic and Republican functionaries at the national and local levels and the names of chapter committee members of *La Raza Unida* party in the states of Arizona, California, Colorado, New Mexico, and Texas.

Addresses and telephone numbers are given for most entries and in some cases there are portraits and short biographies.

198. Martínez, J. V. *Directory of Spanish Surnamed and Native Americans in Science and Engineering*. Rochester, NY: The Author, 1972. 33 p.

This is the first identifiable directory of Spanish-surnamed and Native Americans in the various fields of science and engineering in the United States. It was compiled to facilitate communication between those professionals who also indicated a commitment to improving the conditions of their respective ethnic group. An asterisk beside a name indicates a desire to participate in training programs for Spanish-surnamed and Native American students.

Listed are 198 names of individuals who responded to a questionnaire along with the following information for each: business and home address; telephone numbers; birthplace and date; degree, discipline, and date awarded; degree-granting institution; and special research interests. Many of the professionals listed are of Mexican American origin. No new editions of this work have been issued. A copy of this directory is located in the Arizona State University Library, Tempe, Arizona.

199. *National List of Chicano Contacts in Higher Education*. Stanford, CA: Office of Chicano Affairs, Stanford University, 1978. 84 p.

Chicano faculty, administrators, and staff in colleges and universities located in 34 states and the District of Columbia are cited in this directory. The arrangement is alphabetical by state and subarranged by institution. The address, telephone number, and total enrollment are provided for each institution recorded. The faculty are listed separately from the administrators and staff. For each individual mentioned the academic degree, title, discipline or department, and telephone number are given. The accuracy is dependent on the responses from the institutions listed. Annual updates are provided.

200. Romero, J. Christian, Dulce María Manzanilla Ouellette, and Esther Pariente Ahmed. *Directorio de agencias federales y estatales para Americanos de habla española en Kansas. Directory of Federal and State Agencies for Spanish-speaking Americans in Kansas*. Manhattan: Kansas State University, 1977. 20 p. ED 154 964.

This is a directory of public and private agencies and organizations that provide essential services for the Spanish-speaking people in the state of Kansas. The 13 types of agencies listed deal with community development, consumer education, day care, economic development, education grants, housing, nutrition, migrants, publicity, welfare and voter information. Of the 36 agencies listed, a number are federal and would be of interest to the Spanish-speaking in other states. Also provided is a glossary of words in Spanish, with their English equivalents, which are commonly used in dealing with agencies. In addition, the address and function of each agency or organization are included. This directory is particularly useful for those individuals with a limited knowledge of English.

201. Shapiro, Beth J. *A Directory of Ethnic Publishers and Resource Organizations*. Chicago: Office for Library Service to the Disadvantaged, American Library Association, 1976. 89 p. Index.

*The Directory of Minority/Third World Publishers and Dealers,* compiled by Joan Newmann, served as the basis for this new directory of publishers and organizations that produce ethnic materials. Emphasis is on Afro-Americans, Native Americans, Hispanic Americans, and Asian Americans. It is organized in three sections: publishers and organizations, archival and research centers, and distributors. For each institution the address, telephone, description of purpose or emphasis, and a list of publications are provided. The publishers and resource organizations producing materials on the Hispanic American can be located under the following categories: Hispanic American—general, Bilingual, Education/Curriculum development, Health, History, Literature, and Social conditions. This is an essential reference tool for librarians and educators.

202. Southwest Network. *Directorio Chicano: A Listing of Chicano Alternative Schools, Distributing Centers, and Related Publications.* Hayward, CA: Southwest Network, 1974. 16 p.

This list of approximately 13 alternative educational programs and 28 distributing centers of alternative education materials was designed to provide assistance for the development of special Chicano schools. Each entry includes the name and the address of the institution and a list of publications. The 41 entries are arranged under four geographical regions which are in turn subdivided by state. The coverage includes California, Oregon, Arizona, Colorado, New Mexico, Texas, Illinois, Iowa, Michigan, Minnesota, Missouri, Wisconsin, New York, and Washington, DC. Following each subdivision is a list of publications related to alternative Chicano education.

203. _____. *Directorio Chicano: A Resource Listing of Chicano Media, Print and Film.* 3rd. rev. ed. Hayward, CA: Southwest Network, 1976. 28 p. Ed 145 984.

A broad spectrum of special Chicano media are listed in this directory. Included are alternative school and research/distribution center publications, journals, magazines, newsletters, prison inmates' newsletters, newspapers, and films. The listed items were obtained following a survey of 235 independent Chicano publishers and film makers throughout the United States. Entries provide address of publication or organization, frequency, language of publication, price, date of first issue, and geographical focus. The first edition of this work was published in 1973. The compilers hope to continue to update the contents periodically.

204. Trejo, Arnulfo D. *Directory of Spanish-Speaking/Spanish-Surnamed Librarians in the United States.* Tucson: Bureau of School Services, College of Education, University of Arizona, 1973. (Graduate Library School Monograph, no. 4) 21 p.

This is a listing of 320 professional librarians in the United States who are of Indo-, Afro-, or Ibero-American ancestry and whose work or interest involves Spanish-speaking Americans. Name, home address, and ethnic or geographical origins are indicated as well as the institution where degree was obtained, the institution where employed, type of library where employed, area of specialization, and degree of fluency in Spanish. Most of those included are members of the organization REFORMA, the National Association of Spanish-Speaking Librarians in the United States, which was created in Houston in 1971. This directory is a revised and augmented edition of one published in 1972.

205. U.S. Cabinet Committee on Opportunity for the Spanish Speaking. *Directory of Spanish Speaking Organizations in the U.S.* Washington, DC, 1970. 224 p. Index.

Based on a survey of over 800 groups, this list contains approximately 207 nonprofit and nongovernmental Spanish-speaking community organizations in 22 states and the District of Columbia. Six of the organizations are considered national and are listed separately. They are American GI Forum of the U.S., Aspira of America, Inc., Cuban Municipalities in Exile, League of United Latin American Citizens (LULAC), National Latin American Federation, and Southwest Council of La Raza (SWCLR). The information provided under each entry includes the scope of activity (whether national, state, or local), date of establishment, ethnic membership, schedule of meetings (weekly, annual), and objectives of the organization. In the case of the six national organizations the name and address of the state chairmen are also listed.

206. ———. *Spanish Surnamed American College Graduates, 1971-72.* Washington, DC: The Cabinet Committee, 1972. 2 vols.

This is a listing of 1971-72 Spanish-surnamed college graduates. This directory is by no means complete since it only represents 30 percent of the 800 institutions surveyed. The information provided includes the name of the graduate, address, degree obtained, and the discipline in which degree was obtained. A chart at the end of each volume shows the number of Spanish-surnamed graduates, type of degrees obtained, and the schools from which they graduated. It was compiled with the purpose of improving employment opportunities for Spanish-speaking Americans. The first edition was produced in 1970.

207. U.S. Commission on Civil Rights. *Civil Rights Directory.* Washington, DC: Government Printing Office, 1970. 181 p.

Intended for those concerned with civil rights in general, this guide is composed of five different sections; the first lists 39 federal agencies dealing with civil rights matters and the second lists specific federal agencies concerned with Spanish-speaking groups. The names of the civil rights coordinators who serve as liaison with Spanish-speaking groups are also mentioned. The third section lists private national organizations with civil rights programs. Only 13 of the 104 organizations listed are exclusively for the Mexican American but many of the others are relevant. The fourth lists agencies in 38 states, the District of Columbia, and Puerto Rico which have civil rights responsibilities. The fifth section includes official municipal and county agencies in 25 states with civil rights responsibilities along with a description of the type of agency, its jurisdiction, and powers. Also indicated are field offices, total population of each state, and percentage of nonwhite population. Addresses and telephone numbers are provided for all individuals, agencies, and organizations included in the directory.

208. U.S. Department of Justice. *Directory of Organizations Serving Minority Communities.* Washington, DC: Government Printing Office, 1971. 88 p.

This directory was compiled for the purpose of providing Department of Justice employers with names and addresses of organizations throughout the country serving minority communities. It lists names and addresses of many federal agencies, private organizations, colleges, universities, newspapers, and radio and TV broadcasters serving women, Blacks, Spanish-surnamed, American Indians, and Orientals. it is divided into two major sections. One lists the headquarters offices of federal and private agencies and other local organizations by state. The second section is arranged by type of agency and organization under the minority groups they serve. Although broader in scope than the *Directory of Spanish Speaking Organizations in the U.S.*, published by the Cabinet Committee on Opportunity for the Spanish Speaking, this directory lists only 18 organizations related to the Mexican American. Only name and address are provided for each organization or institution.

209. U.S. Office of Minority Business Enterprise. *Directory of Minority Media.* Washington, DC: U.S. Department of Commerce, 1973. 89 p.
The purpose of this work is to offer advertisers and businessmen a tool that will be useful in broadening the scope of advertising campaigns and market research. The directory lists Spanish-language publications (newspapers and periodicals) and Spanish-language broadcasting stations (radio and television) according to the states where they are located. Addresses are included. In addition, comparative tables of income and general characteristics of the Black, white, and Spanish-heritage population are included as reported by the 1970 Census. This source covers areas of Mexican American activities not widely known. Statistical tables allow for easy comparison of Mexican Americans with other racial and ethnic groups.

210. _____. *National Directory of Minority Manufacturers, 1974.* Washington, DC: U.S. Department of Commerce, 1974. 121 p. Index.
The primary thrust of this directory is to "identify viable minority manufacturing firms that are available for contracting purposes." It lists manufacturing firms in which at least 50 percent or more of the stock is owned by a minority individual. Each entry includes the name of the firm, address, name of contact person, date of establishment, annual sales, plant floor space, minority group(s) represented in the enterprise, types of products manufactured, materials used, and number of people employed. Five separate indexes facilitate the use of this directory by company, product, geographical location, standard industrial and federal classification numbers. Many Mexican American-owned businesses are represented. They can be identified by the code number and in the geographical location index.

211. _____. *National Roster of Minority Consulting Professional Firms.* Washington, DC: U.S. Department of Commerce, 1973. 121 p. Index.
The purpose of this directory is to identify minority consulting firms in order to increase the involvement of minority consultants in federal contracts. Listed are 310 professional firms which are believed owned by members of minority groups. The criterion for inclusion is that at least 50 percent of the stock is owned by minorities. The roster is divided into six sections: alphabetical listing of coporations, company capability statements, and four indexes—region, state, functional and general. The individual entries include the name of the firm, address, telephone number, name of contact person, date of establishment, geographical limitations of service, major areas of expertise and capabilities. This is the second edition of the roster. The Office of Minority Business Enterprise plans to update it periodically as new information is collected.

212. University of California, Los Angeles. Chicano Studies Center. *Guide to Chicano Studies Departments, Programs, and Centers*. Los Angeles: The Center, 1975. 56 p.

This is the first and only national directory of Chicano Studies departments, programs, and centers located in universities and four-year colleges throughout the United States. Included are 42 entries, the majority of which are based on direct responses to a questionnaire. The rest were assembled from other sources. The states of California, Colorado, Michigan, Minnesota, New Mexico, Texas, and Washington are represented, with California reporting the largest number of programs.

Although information varies, the standard response includes the name of the institution, the address of the center or program, the director or administrative officer, the statement of purpose, associated faculty, degrees awarded, curricular structure, special programs, and the tuition per quarter. This work was compiled for the use of students, faculty, and others interested in Chicano studies.

213. University of California, Los Angeles. Institute of Industrial Relations. *Directory of Organizations in Greater Los Angeles*. Los Angeles: The Institute, 1973. 196 p. Annotated. Index.

Designed primarily as a directory for those concerned with the social and economic problems of the Los Angeles area; 12 categories of organizations and agencies are listed. The majority are related to the interests of the South-Central and East Los Angeles communities. The categories are Civil and legal rights; Cultural and religious; Community and neighborhood; Training programs; Business assistance; Coordinating, research, and referral; Government; Political; Service; Social and fraternal; Labor; Communications, and legal services. In addition to the name of the organization or agency the entries include the address, telephone, name of the director, branches, a statement of purpose, and a geographical code to indicate the areas that are served. Some of the organizations and agencies listed are exclusively for Mexican Americans but there are many others that are directly or indirectly relevant as they seek to aid and promote the well-being of the underprivileged. This directory revises and updates all previous editions.

214. _____. *Directory of Organizations in South and East Los Angeles*. Los Angeles: The Institute, 1969. 112 p. Annotated. Index.

This directory was compiled by the staff of the Institute of Industrial Relations at UCLA for the purpose of providing information on the organizations and agencies which are based in, or are especially relevant to, the South and East Los Angeles communities. Numerous organizations and agencies are included under the categories of Civil and legal rights; Cultural and religious; Community and neighborhood; Training programs; Business assistance; Coordinating, research and referral; Government; Political; Service; Social and fraternal; Labor; Communications; and legal services. The entries provide, in addition to the name of the organization or agency, the address, telephone number, name of director, and a statement of general purpose and function. Whenever appropriate, the organizations and agencies are listed according to their ethnic focus, Mexican Americans and Blacks being the principal ones. This directory updates the one published in 1966.

215. University of Texas, Austin. Center for Mexican-American Studies. *Mexican-Americanists of Texas: A Chicano Studies Directory*. Austin: The Center, 1971. 17 p.

Mexican Americans in Texas with an interest in Chicano studies are included in this directory. Most of the 170 listed are educators but a few community leaders, government officials, and social workers are mentioned. Following the name of the individual is his/her title or function, address, telephone number if available, and an indication of areas of specialization or interest.

216. Wynar, Lubomyr Roman. *Encyclopedic Directory of Ethnic Organizations in the United States*. Littleton, CO: Libraries Unlimited, 1975. 414 p. Annotated. Index.

This directory, the first comprehensive guide of its kind, was designed as a companion to the author's *Encyclopedic Directory of Ethnic Newspapers and Periodicals in the United States,* published in 1972 and revised in 1976. The purpose of this work is to identify the major national ethnic organizations in terms of their objectives, activities, and publications and to provide a service to scholars and librarians.

The introductory material explains the methodology, scope, and arrangement, and discusses the nature of ethnic organizations. The directory includes 1,475 organizations and is arranged under 73 headings, each representing a separate ethnic group. The 41 organizations that relate specifically to the Mexican American are found under the headings Mexican American and Spanish American. The organizations included are cultural, religious (lay), fraternal, professional, educational, scholarly, and youth. Excluded are seminaries, schools, libraries, museums, and economic institutions.

Each entry includes the address and telephone, principal officers and staff, date founded, branches, membership and dues, scope, special requirements, publications, affiliation, conventions and meetings. The appendix is a selective list of major multi-ethnic and research organizations. An index lists the names of the organizations and the table of contents serves as a subject index.

# Chapter 7

# *Dictionaries*

The Spanish language in the United States as spoken and written by Americans of Mexican heritage is rich in influences from many sources. Regional variations still exist with many examples of early seventeenth- and eighteenth-century Spanish vocabulary, words of indigenous origins and words and expressions of English derivation. Since the late 1600s Spanish-speaking people have inhabited what was to become the United States Southwest. The early Spanish-Mexican settlers brought their language to the region and were the first to leave their European linguistic imprint. As they came into contact with various Indian cultures of the area, new words entered their Spanish vocabulary. In some areas especially northern New Mexico and southern Colorado, traces of early Spanish can be found today. In the nineteenth century the language was further modified through the interaction of Mexicans with English-speaking people who settled in the West and Southwest following the Mexican-American War. By the twentieth century, this contact had effected enduring changes in both the Spanish and the English in the region. Early in the 1900s waves of Mexican immigrants came to the United States, introducing new words and new definitions into the Spanish of the Southwest. Many of these immigrants were from agricultural communities in Mexico where special terms were used to describe activities and customs of *campesinos*, rural Mexicans. Those who came from the Central Plateau region employed words and expressions of Nahuatl origin, or *aztequismos*.

As a result of these influences, Spanish sustains an important role in the life and culture of the Southwest. Particularly since World War II, these influences have gradually spread to other parts of the United States as well. A great many individuals still maintain Spanish as their first language and contact between speakers of English and Spanish along the United States–Mexican border is an everyday occurrence. The Chicano youth in urban barrios have developed various Spanish slang ''dialects,'' sometimes called Tex-Mex, *Caló,* Pachuco or Cali-Mex. Folklore, songs, proverbs, and sayings in Spanish, passed down by earlier generations, are still remembered by many; and the works of Western literature by English-speaking writers are filled with words of Spanish origin. These examples and others, such as the Spanish place names in the region, are ever-present reminders of the historical and linguistic heritage.

Growing recognition of the Spanish language in the United States has encouraged the preparation of many research and reference tools which assist in translating and defining Spanish as used by Mexicans and Mexican Americans. These works, which are described in this chapter, include dictionaries, vocabularies, word lists, glossaries, and the like. Among these, seven general categories are recognized: place names, Western words, regional Spanish vocabularies, Mexicanisms, Chicano Spanish, practical Spanish for health and social service personnel, and Spanish proverbs and sayings from the Southwest.

The sources are arranged in two sections. The first primarily contains published works which have been examined and annotated. The second section is a partial list of master's theses, completed between 1929 and 1973, which are important to linguistic research in the Southwest. The latter are not so readily accessible as the titles in the first section and have not been examined. They are listed here for the convenience of researchers who intend to carry out more in-depth investigations.

Separately published works, in the first category, assist in identifying and locating the Spanish place names in California, Texas, New Mexico, Colorado and Arizona. Several give pronunciation, history, and derivation of the names. Numerous Spanish toponyms listed in these sources belie the historical, legendary, and linguistic past of the region. For additional information researchers may consult the *Bibliography of Place Name Literature: United States and Canada*.[1] This work cites approximately 46 books, articles, and manuscript compilations which contain Spanish place names.

In the second category are works that contain words of the American West, many of which are of Spanish or Mexican origin. Each one presents a slightly different perspective. Two sources list the words commonly used by cowboys, miners, gamblers, and other vocations of the Old West during the nineteenth century; others list Spanish words and variations used by English-speaking people in the Southwest; and another focuses on farm and ranch Spanish in Texas. Together they illustrate Spanish influence on English and the widespread use of Spanish vocabulary and terminology by the English- speaking population in the West.

A third category includes scholarly studies, vocabularies, word lists, and glossaries of Spanish as spoken in various states or locales in Texas, California, Louisiana, New Mexico and southern Colorado. This group contains the largest number of entries and covers over a century of research. Many of these were landmark studies in their time and some continue to be the only research available on the language in particular areas.

The fourth category includes works which list Mexicanisms, or words of common usage in Mexican Spanish. Among these are sources of words of Nahautl origin, of rural Mexican Spanish, and provincialisms and *barbarismos* from the borderlands between the United States and Mexico. These are useful in identifying the origin and meaning of words and expressions employed by many Mexicans and Mexican Americans in the United States. The most comprehensive is the *Diccionario de mejicanismos*, by Francisco Santamaría.

The fifth category includes dictionaries of Chicano Spanish, published between 1973 and 1977. Most of these attempt to identify the slang, or *Caló*, used by contemporary Mexican Americans in the barrios. Many of the words are frequently associated with criminals, the drug culture, and street gangs, which one author refers to as the "language of poverty." With the exception of *El diccionario del español chicano/The Dictionary of Chicano Spanish*, by Roberto A. Galván and Richard V. Teschner, the works are generally superficial and not based on extensive scholarly research.

The sixth category includes vocabularies and guides to Spanish for health service personnel, community and social workers, school personnel, and others who have frequent contact with Spanish-speaking people. Some of the vocabularies are particularly related to the Spanish of the Southwest but most were designed in recent years to facilitate communication with all Spanish-speaking people.

In the final category are several lists of Spanish proverbs and sayings which contain examples of words and expressions used by generations of Spanish-speaking people in the Southwest. These sources are useful in the study of language, psychology, and culture of individuals of Hispanic heritage.

In addition to the works cited in this chapter, the language bibliographies should be consulted for supplementary sources on the Spanish language in the United States.

1. Richard B. Sealock and Pauline A. Seely, *Bibliography of Place-Name Literature: United States and Canada*. 2nd. ed. (Chicago: American Library Association, 1967), 352 p.

# MAJOR WORKS

217. Adams, Ramon F. *Western Words: A Dictionary of the American West.* Norman: University of Oklahoma Press, 1968. 355 p.
This dictionary covers words of the American West in general as they were used by cowboys, sheepherders, miners, mill workers, buffalo hunters, stagecoach drivers, freighters, gamblers and others. Explanations of each word are provided. Many of the words are of Spanish origin and this is indicated as appropriate.

This is a revised and enlarged edition of the author's *Western Words: A Dictionary of the Range, Cow Camp and Trail,* published in 1944. It is useful to those interested in vocations of the West and to students and researchers of Western life and history.

218. Aranda, Charles. *Dichos: Proverbs and Sayings from the Spanish.* Santa Fe, NM: The Sunstone Press, 1977. [32] p.
Nearly 370 proverbs and sayings which are part of the Spanish folklore tradition of the Southwest are listed in this work. The *dichos* are arranged alphabetically by the first word. A literal English translation is provided for each entry. An equivalent English-language proverb or an interpretation is offered for the benefit of the non-Spanish-speaking user. The compiler did not include an introduction and, therefore, no information has been provided on the origin of the expressions nor on the methods used in selecting and identifying them for this work.

219. Barnes, Will C. *Arizona Place Names.* Revised and enlarged by Byrd H. Granger. Tucson: University of Arizona Press, 1960. 519 p. Index.
New and updated information has been added to this revision of the well-known 1935 edition. It hopes to prove a stimulus to the centralization of data on Arizona place names but does not pretend to be complete. Many names still need to be verified before they are added to a future edition. The place names are listed by county. Each entry provides the name of the site, elevation, location on map, references, and variant and associated names. When available, the description, history, and origin of the names are given.

Names of Spanish origin are indicated with their English equivalents. Guides to use and pronunciation are included. Biographies of informants consulted; bibliographies of maps, books, articles and government publications; and 18 pages of maps enhance the usefulness of this new edition. Arizona's place names are a central part of the folk history and culture. They reveal the events, legends, and famous family names of the past.

220. Bentley, Harold W. *A Dictionary of Spanish Terms in English; With Special Reference to the American Southwest.* New York: Octagon Books, 1973. 243 p.

This dictionary is more properly labeled a study and vocabulary of Spanish words used by English-speaking people. Originally the author's thesis, it was first published in 1932 by Columbia University Press and reprinted in 1973.

The introductory study discusses the history and origin of the influence of the Spanish language on English, and describes the written source material from which the words have been selected. The vocabulary lists approximately 500 Spanish words and their variations adapted by English-speakers. Each entry includes pronunciations, definitions, and illustrations of usage, arranged by date. The appendixes contain a list of words of American Indian origin; a list of Spanish place names in 34 states in the United States; bullfight terms and examples of bilingualism. A select bibliography of dictionaries, glossaries, word lists and historical and cultural studies complement this work.

221. Blanco S., Antonio. *La lengua española en la historia de California: Contribución a su estudio.* Madrid: Ediciones Cultura Hispánica, 1971. 827 p.

Five separate listings of words and expressions which have linguistic and historical significance for Mexican American studies are contained in this study of the Spanish language in California. The first list is a vocabulary of "Californianismos." These are expressions in Spanish used in the province of California prior to 1848. They are taken directly from manuscripts in the Bancroft Library, the Archivo General de la Nación (Mexico City), from personal diaries, mission archives, the early bilingual newspapers and older histories of California. The second list is a glossary of Gold Rush terminology in Spanish. During the early history of the state, Spanish words were common in mining terminology.

The third list is the *Vocabulario de términos españoles en el Inglés.* These words indicate the Spanish influences on English language vocabulary. The date of the earliest usage of the words are noted. The fourth is a *Vocabulario de verbos nuevos.* The list demonstrates the influence of English on Spanish verbs. The final list is a *Vocabulario de pachuquismos,* slang words commonly used by the criminal elements in the early history of California. Many of the words relate to drugs and drug use. Most of the vocabulary in this work is extensively analyzed in terms of origin, usage, and meaning. Other chapters of interest relate to the origin of the California population and the Spanish spoken in California up to the end of the nineteenth century.

222. Bomse, Marguerite D., and Julian H. Alfaro. *Practical Spanish for Medical and Hospital Personnel.* 2nd. ed. Elmsford, NY: Pergamon Press, 1978. 203 p.

This is a practical guide to fundamental Spanish for health services personnel. The work is arranged in 16 chapters which include dialogues useful to doctors, nurses, dentists, laboratory technicians and other health related professionals. The situations covered are patients' complaints, doctors' examination, accident, diet, treatment and medication, ambulance, hospital admissions, nurse, laboratory X-rays, obstetrician, pediatrician, optometrist, dentist, and visiting nurse. A list of video tapes, available from Steve Campus

Productions, relates to several of the dialogues. The work concludes with an English/ Spanish vocabulary of the words used in the text.

This work can appropriately be used in a practical Spanish course in conjunction with Bomse's *Practical Spanish Grammar* and *Practical Spanish Dictionary and Phrase Book,* published by Pergamon Press.

223. _____, and Julian H. Alfaro. *Practical Spanish for School Personnel, Firemen, Policemen and Community Agencies.* 2nd. ed. Elmsford, NY: Pergamon Press, 1978. 243 p.

Fundamental Spanish for various social service personnel is provided in this practical guide. The work includes 27 chapters, consisting of dialogues, grammatical notes and sentences to translate, pertinent to school personnel, firemen, policemen, and social workers.

Situations covered by the conversations include the teacher in class, school secretary, illness, school doctor, burglary, accident, drug arrest, family dispute, intoxicated driver, traffic ticket, missing person, family, abandoned wife, food stamps, unemployment, banking, and travel agency. A list of available video tapes for several of the dialogues supplements the text. An English/Spanish vocabulary, covering all words in the dialogues, concludes the work.

This guide can be used in a course on practical Spanish in conjunction with two other Pergamon Press publications by Bomse: *Practical Spanish Grammar* and *Practical Spanish Dictionary and Phrase Book.*

224. Bow, Ernie L. *Chicano Slang: A Short List.* Santa Maria, CA: The Author, 1977. 10 p.

This is a short list of *Caló* or Chicano slang words arranged in two parts. The first is a list of 140 commonly used words and idiomatic expressions and the second is a list of 27 words related to the drug culture. For each word or expression the following information is provided: part of speech, English equivalent (roughly translated and modified), and an example of its use in conversation. Many of the words are of English derivation, most are street language, some are commonly used Spanish words with a variant meaning.

225. Cabrera, Luís. *Diccionario de aztequismos.* México: Ediciones Oasis, 1975. 166 p.

Words of Nahuatl origin which are used frequently in the Spanish of Mexico are included in this work. Listed are 4,100 words arranged alphabetically under 17 consonant and five vowels sounds. Cabrera provides the etymology of the words and distinguishes between what he labels true *aztequismos* and the assumed ones. The words that are assumed to be of Nahautl origin are listed and their true origins described. Many of the listed *aztequismos* have found their way into the language of Mexican Americans and, therefore, this dictionary is a useful reference tool.

226. Cerda, Gilberto, Bertha Cabeza, and María Julieta Farias. *Vocabulario español de Texas.* Austin: University of Texas Press, 1970. 347 p.

This is a regional dictionary of Spanish vocabulary spoken in eight counties of Texas— Cameron, Duval, Edwards, Kinney, Val Verde, Webb, Willacy, and Zapata. It consists of three parts: 1) vocabulary; 2) idioms, locutions, sayings and proverbs; 3) Hispanicisms which are used by the English-speaking people of the area. For each vocabulary word the entry indicates the part of speech, definitions in Spanish, and where it is used in other parts of the Americas. For the idioms, locutions, and saying and proverbs the entry indicates definition and the equivalent, if any, in the *Diccionario de la lengua española*. This work was used extensively by Lurline H. Coltharp in *The Tongue of the Tirilones: A Linguistic Study of a Criminal Argot* and it primarily includes words that are not found in the *Diccionario de la lengua española* or those that the compilers have defined differently. This work was originally published in 1953 as volume 5 in the series University of Texas Hispanic Studies, edited by M. Romera-Navarro and Elmer R. Sims.

227. Cobos, Rubén. *Southwestern Spanish Proverbs; Refranes españoles del Sudoeste*. Los Cerrillos, NM: San Marcos Press, 1973. 144 p. Index.
Spanish proverbs from the states of Texas, Colorado, New Mexico, Arizona and California are listed here. A total of 1,697 proverbs are included with translations and the English equivalents, if any. The *refranes* are listed alphabetically by the first word. A Spanish key word index and an English topical index provide bilingual access to the proverbs. A selected bibliography of works consulted is appended. This work is useful in understanding the psychology, sentiments, attitudes, and values of the Spanish-speaking people in the Southwest.

228. Coltharp, Lurline H. *The Tongue of the Tirilones: A Linguistic Study of a Criminal Argot*. University: University of Alabama Press, 1965. (Alabama Linguistic and Philological Series, no. 7) 313 p.
This is primarily a linguistic study and vocabulary of a Spanish dialect spoken in El Paso, Texas. The dialect is the *Caló* or slang used by the "Tirilones" of the El Paso border area. Approximately 750 words are listed and they were gathered in the course of interviews between 1962 and 1963. Each vocabulary word or phrase is followed by: number of informants who used it; various definitions; part of speech; indication of its presence in the *Diccionario de la lengua española* of the Real Academia; and whether included in the works of other lexicographers. Prior to the actual listing of the vocabulary, the author describes the anthropological background, the methodology used in collecting the words or phrases, and the informants. She also provides a detailed description of the dialect and indicates the phonology. A bibliography at the end of the study lists other sources useful in the research of Spanish slang vocabulary as spoken in certain areas of the United States.

229. Cordasco, Francesco, and Pablo Rivera Alvarez. *Useful Spanish for Medical and Hospital Personnel with a Bibliography on Hispanic Peoples in the United States*. Detroit: Blaine-Ethridge, 1977. 146 p.
Portions of this manual of Spanish vocabulary and expressions were originally developed and used for medical and hospital personnel by the Migration Division of the Department of Labor, Commonwealth of Puerto Rico. The series of constructs, brought together in this publication, are in standard Spanish understood by most Latin Americans and adaptable for Mexican American patients. The work is arranged in four sections. The first contains a pronunciation guide, general expressions, and topics such as admissions, social service, nutrition, medication and other health-related service. The second section includes chapters on each of the special departments in a hospital, e.g., Cardiology, Gynecology, Pediatricts, and Surgery, to name a few. Section three covers language

essentials such as numbers, time, months, days, and verb conjugation, with an extensive glossary of relevant general and medical vocabulary in English and Spanish. The fourth section is a bibliographical compendium originally published in 1974 by the U.S. Department of Housing and Urban Development. Entitled *Hispanic Americans in the United States: A Selective Bibliography, 1963-1974*, it has been expanded and reprinted in this guide.

Technical terminology is reduced to a minimum and space is provided for the user to note additional expressions and vocabulary not included in the manual. This guide can serve as a textbook in a Spanish course for health-related personnel and as a personal handbook.

230. Dawson, John Frank. *Place Names in Colorado; Why 700 Communities Were So Named, 150 of Spanish or Indian Origin*. Denver: The Author, 1954. 52 p.
The 670 place names in this booklet are arranged in alphabetical order. Included are populations of 50 or more people, and certain ghost towns with historical interest. Each name includes a description or definition of the meaning and the origin, when known. For each community the county where it is located and the year it was formed are given. The author collected the names during 24 years of travel in the state. As the title indicates, many of the place names are of Spanish origin.

231. *Diccionario Bilingüe-Cultural/Bilingual-Cultural Dictionary*, by Henry Pascual, Pedro Ribera-Ortega, Grace J. Gutiérrez, and Mariano Romero. Santa Fe, NM: Santa Fe Public Schools, 1974. 50 p.
This Spanish-English dictionary was produced as a cooperative effort of the State Department of Education and the Bilingual Education Staff of the Santa Fe Municipal Schools. As an essential component in the first year of the bilingual-bicultural program, it presents basic vocabulary words and phrases in New Mexican Spanish that are familiar to the Spanish-speaking children in the area. Each example is appropriately illustrated. The work is arranged alphabetically by the Spanish words, with the English equivalents on opposite pages.

The dictionary is supplemented by a workbook/coloring book which is designed to improve language and motor skills at the elementary level. It is unfortunate that a corrected edition has not been issued since so many errors have been identified on the errata sheet at the end of the work.

232. Espinosa, Aurelio Macedonio. "Apuntaciones para un diccionario de nuevomejicanismos: algunas formas verbales raras y curiosas." In *Estudios eruditos in memoriam de Adolfo Bonilla y San Martín (1875-1926)*, pp. 615-625. Madrid: Imprenta Viuda e Hijos de Jaime Rates, 1930. Vol. 2.
Outlined in this article are 14 unusual verb forms of Spanish used in New Mexico. The work was written in preparation for a "diccionario nuevomejicano" which never materialized. Evidently the manuscript for the proposed dictionary has never been located. The following expressions and their variants are analyzed: *a redo vaya; cómo está muncho; desfondingarse; entengas; esmorecerse; esque; jayarse; meramente; ójala; ¿ónde güeno? quése; rejunjuñar; replantigarse; ti albechu.*

The words in the article were selected from his vocabulary—the fourth part of his *Studies in New Mexican Spanish.*

233. Fuentes, Dagoberto, and José A. López. *Barrio Language Dictionary: First Dictionary of Caló.* Los Angeles: Southland Press, 1974. 160 p.

This is a dictionary, or even more appropriately a selective word list, of barrio slang used by certain Mexican Americans in the Southwest. The words and expressions were compiled from interviews with people of the barrios and they reflect, for the most part, contemporary language patterns. Each entry is followed by a short English translation. Many of the words are derived from English. Although this *Caló* dictionary claims to be the first, a similar compilation prepared by Jay B. Rosensweig was published a year earlier.

234. Galván, Roberto A., and Richard V. Teschner. *El diccionario del español chicano; The Dictionary of Chicano Spanish.* Silver Spring, MD: Institute of Modern Languages, 1977. 144 p.

This is a revised and enlarged edition of their previously published *El diccionario del español de Tejas/The Dictionary of the Spanish of Texas,* 1975. The geographical coverage in the new edition is expanded to include California, Arizona, New Mexico, Colorado, Florida, and Texas. Acclaimed as the first comprehensive dictionary of the Spanish of the Southwest, over 1,000 new words and expressions have been added to the 7,000 of the original work.

Like its predecessor this work supplements the traditional Spanish dictionaries. A lengthy bibliography of secondary works on Spanish language is appended. It is an essential reference tool for libraries, bilingual-bicultural programs, social workers, and students in Chicano Studies programs.

235. _____, and Richard V. Teschner. *El diccionario del español de Tejas/The Dictionary of the Spanish of Texas: Spanish-English.* Silver Spring, MD: Institute of Modern Languages, 1975. 102 p.

Approximately 7,000 words and expressions used in Texas Spanish are listed in this "supplementary" dictionary. Included are slang words, proverbs, and sayings not found in most Spanish dictionaries and not considered part of standard Spanish. Whenever possible the words and phrases are categorized according to their level of social use, i.e., slang, colloquialism, criminal, vulgar, rustic, euphemistic, etc. The entries include spelling and definition in English, usage, parts of speech, social designation, gender, and occasional variations. The words in this dictionary, although used in parts of Texas, are not considered unique to Texas. Many of the words in the lexicon can be found in the speech of the Spanish-speaking people throughout the Southwest. A bibliography of secondary sources is included in the appendixes.

236. García Icazbalceta, Joaquín. *Vocabulario de mexicanismos.* México, D.F., 1975. (Facsimile reprint of 1899 ed., México, D.F.: La Europa.) (Ediciones del Centenario de la Academia Mexicana, no. 5) 241 p.

This first scholarly vocabulary of Mexicanisms by the esteemed García Icazbalceta has been reprinted to commemorate his centennial. Approximately 2,000 words covering *abadejo* to *gusto* are listed, defined, and carefully documented. The work remained incomplete until the philologist Francisco J. Santamaría revised and completed the work in 1959. Both of these works (the *Vocabulario* and the *Diccionario*) should be consulted for occasional references to words which relate to border Spanish and to the Spanish spoken by Mexican Americans in the United States.

237. Gerritsen, William D. *An English-Spanish Glossary of Basic Medical Terminology in the Dialect of Northern New Mexico.* Santa Fe, NM: [Santa Fe County Health Department], 1964. 61 p.

Included in this carefully prepared glossary of relevant medical terminology are approximately 500 English words and their Spanish equivalents as used in the northern part of New Mexico. An accurate and simple key to pronunciation precedes the vocabulary. Vowels, consonants, stress, and notes on diacritics are treated separately. Each noun includes the appropriate definite article; the adjectives are given in the masculine singular; and verbs are given in the infinitive form. Sample sentences exemplify usage. An asterisk is used to designate the nonstandard form followed by the standard modern Spanish in parentheses. About 170 items are indicated as nonstandard usage.

This vocabulary is particularly useful for persons employed in medical and health-related services that deal with the Spanish-speaking people of the Southwest.

238. Gómez, Ernesto, and Gilberto Cerda. *The Social Significance and Value Dimensions of Current Mexican American Dialectal Spanish; Part II: A Glossary for the Human Service Professions.* San Antonio, TX: Worden School of Social Service, Our Lady of the Lake University of San Antonio, 1976. 218 p.

The purpose of this glossary of Mexican American Spanish is to offer a listing of vocabulary which will enable the human service professionals to better serve the barrio through an improved understanding of the dialectal Spanish employed. Included in the vocabulary are over 1,000 archaic Spanish terms, terms of Mexican indigenous origin, Spanish terms, invented terms, terms of English origin, English terms, and abbreviated speech. The expressions in the list are mainly found in the barrios of San Antonio, Texas, and the surrounding area.

The work is divided into three sections : Vocabulary; Locutions and idiomatic phrases; and Proverbs, maxims and familiar sayings. Each term is followed by a definition, an example of usage, and the English translation. A guide to pronunciation is included to assist readers unfamiliar with Spanish.

239. Gudde, Erwin G. *California Place Names: The Origin and Etymology of Current Geographical Names.* 3rd ed. Berkeley:University of California Press, 1969. 416 p.

This is a new edition of one of the major works on place names in California. The purpose is to show when, how, and by whom place names of California were applied; to tell their meaning, origin, evolution, their connection with national history and relation to the landscape and people. The names included are of cities, railroad stations, Spanish and Mexican land grants, lakes, rivers, mountain ranges or hills, capes and islands. They were drawn mainly from a composite map made of several official maps. Notable features of this work are the glossary; the bibliography, which lists and describes the sources used in obtaining information about the place names; a pronunciation guide; and a section on obsolete names.

Since numerous place names in California are of Spanish origin this work is useful for cultural, historical and linguistic studies. The first edition was published in 1949. A revised and enlarged second edition appeared in 1960.

240. *The Handbook of Texas*, ed. by Walter Prescott Webb. Austin: Texas State Historical Association, 1952–1976. 3 vols.

The objective of this monumental work was to assemble in one source the most significant information about Texas. The first two volumes contain approximately 16,000 entries dealing with persons (not living), places, events, organizations, enterprises, institutions, industries, agricultural pursuits, flora, fauna, and other significant factors related to Texas, from prehistoric times to the present. Volume III includes the same format and type of information but adds new and revised information and includes all the items mentioned in the other two volumes. As such it serves as a supplement and index to the other two volumes.

Biographical entries are limited to people who have had an impact on Texas history and society. All towns with population of 1,000 or more are included as well as all county seats, regardless of population, and towns associated with important historial events. This is a unique work; it is both a place-name dictionary and an encyclopedia of Texas. No equivalent works exist for other states in the Southwest.

241. Islas Escarcega, Leovigildo. *Vocabulario campesino nacional*. México, D.F.: Editorial Beatríz de Silva, 1945. 287 p.

This vocabulary consists of terms used by the rural population throughout Mexico. The purpose of the work is to rectify and expand Mariano Silva y Aceves' *Vocabulario agrícola nacional*, published in 1935. The revised and updated work is arranged in two parts. Part one is the listing of corrected terms that appeared in the 1935 edition. Part two is a supplement which adds new terms not included in the Silva y Aceves vocabulary. Each word is followed by a definition in Spanish and the regional variations. *Aztequismos* are so identified.

The author has attempted to use orthography that corresponds to the pronunciation. The words in the supplement have been selected because of their close relationship with the various activities and customs of the *campesinos*, particularly in the Central Plateau region. This word list is important to the study of the language of Mexican Americans because a majority of the Mexican immigrants that came to the United States originated in rural communities. One can assume that many of the words and expressions found in this work are closely related to the Spanish spoken in the West and Southwest.

242. Kantrowitz, Martin P., Antonio Mondragón, and William Lord Coleman. *¿Qué Pasó? An English-Spanish Guide for Medical Personnel*. 3rd ed., revised and expanded. Albuquerque: University of New Mexico Press, 1978. 69 p.

This practical guide provides Spanish translations of vocabulary and expressions used routinely by medical personnel and individuals in health-related fields. Although the work is applicable to nearly all Spanish-speaking people, a few Southwestern localisms are included. The contents cover common phrases; everyday questions and answers; 22 workups with questions, answers, and phrases relating to major common complaints; terminology including anatomical terms, numbers, days of the week, months of the year, colors; and a vocabulary of additional useful medical terms.

The first edition of this work, compiled in 1974 by William Lord Coleman and Antonio Mondragón, was entitled *¿Qué Pasó? An English-Spanish Medical Dictionary with Vocabulary of Northern New Mexico and Southern Colorado.* The new edition is considerably expanded and revised with additional sections on family planning, overdose/poisoning, and the unconscious patient, which were not in the previous editions. In general the more than 500 vocabulary words listed in this work are standard Spanish forms.

243. Kelly, George W., and Rex R. Kelly. *Farm and Ranch Spanish. s.1.:* The Authors, 1960. 241 p.

Spanish words and grammar relating to everyday activities of ranchers and farmers in Texas are contained in this vocabulary and phrase book. The work is arranged in three sections: Ranch Section, Farm Section, and Grammer [sic] Section. The first section includes 20 chapters devoted to words and expressions which relate to fence building, rounding up stock, fixing windmills, and other such activities. The second section contains 18 chapters on cotton picking, irrigation, beets, cabbage, and so forth. The third section provides very simplistic, unscholarly and often misleading explanations of the basic rules of Spanish grammar and border vocabulary. Richard V. Teschner, in *Spanish and English of United States Hispanos,* has aptly described this work as containing "mind-blowing hints on morphosyntaxis . . . and lexicon . . ."

The authors have reflected many of their prejudices and paternalistic views toward rural Mexican laborers. Although the concept of the work is a useful and practical one, it should be approached with caution and skepticism.

244. Kercheville, Francis Monroe. *A Preliminary Glossary of New Mexico Spanish.* Albuquerque: University of New Mexico, 1934. (University of New Mexico Bulletin. Language Series, vol. 5, no. 3) pp. 9–69.

This work is a preliminary list of words gathered in New Mexico from newspapers, other printed sources, and interviews. It was compiled in preparation for a dictionary of New Mexico Spanish and it is assumed that the work was never completed. Not all of the words are unique to New Mexico but they do differ from standard or Castilian Spanish. The words are arranged in alphabetical order under the headings of Colloquialisms; Words which suffer phoenetic changes; Archaic or obsolete words; Words of Indian origin; Mexicanisms used in New Mexico; and Hispanicized English words and expressions. Approximately 1,000 terms and expressions are listed. A short bibliography is appended.

This study was published together with G. E. McSpadden's *Some Semantic and Philological Facts of the Spanish Spoken in Chilili, New Mexico.*

245. _____. *A Preliminary Glossary of Southwestern and Rio Grande Spanish including Semantic and Philological Peculiarities.* Kingsville: Texas A and I University, 1967.

The compiler viewed this glossary as "an objective compilation of linguistic facts." The work is arranged in two sections with a one-page bibliography. Section A relates to the Spanish vocabulary employed in the upper Rio Grande area, in particular, southern

Colorado and New Mexico. It is further subdivided into six parts: Colloquialisms, words of peculiar or local usage; Words which suffer phonetic changes; Archaic or obsolete words; Words of Indian origin; Mexicanisms used in New Mexico; and Hispanicized English words and expressions. Part B is less extensive and covers the Lower Rio Grande area including southern New Mexico, southwest Texas and south Texas. The English equivalents are given for the Spanish words and expressions listed. In appropriate parts of the glossary the standard Spanish words are also mentioned.

Many of the dialectal forms recorded in this work are employed throughout the Southwest and in other parts of the Spanish-speaking world. Because of the proximity of the region to Mexico, a large number of Mexicanisms are present in the vocabulary.

246. León, Aurelio de. *Barbarismos comunes en México*. México, D.F.: Imprenta Mundial, 1936–1937. 2 vols., with 1936 supplement.
Words commonly used in parts of Mexico and in the border regions of the United States are found in this curious listing. The compiler has categorized the words as *Anglicismo, Barbarismo, Cursilería, Palabra extranjera, Voz forense, Voz usado en el norte, Provincialismo, Tejanismo*.

The two volumes contain over 500 words and expressions. An eight-page supplement contributes approximately 60 additional entries. Each entry includes an indication of the category to which it is assigned, a definition in Spanish, correct usage, and more appropriate terms. Many of the words are English loan words. The compiler states that these volumes were prepared for laymen and not scholars.

247. Lerner, Isaías. *Arcaismos léxicos del español de América*. Madrid: Insula, 1974. 274 p.
This is one of the most extensive lists of archaic terms used in American Spanish. Most of the words are not currently used in Spain, some are only found in rural areas of the Americas, and many were extant in the literature of sixteenth- and seventeenth-century Spain. For each term listed the following information is provided: a definition in Spanish, synonyms, authorities, and the location where the term is used. The lexicographic content and not the etymological aspects are of primary concern in this work. An extensive supplementary bibliography is included which contains items under such headings as *Bibliografías, Obras generales*, and *Obras especiales por países de America*. A special section is provided for bibliography on New Mexico, Arizona, California, Texas, and the Southwest.

248. MacCurdy, Raymond R. *The Spanish Dialect of St. Bernard Parish, Louisiana*. Albuquerque: University of New Mexico Press, 1950. (University of New Mexico Publications in Language and Literature, no. 7). 88 p.
Included in this work is a study and a word list of the little-known Spanish dialect from St. Bernard Parish, Louisiana. The 650 words, which are largely gallicisms and dialectalisms from the Canary Islands, were gathered between 1941 and 1947. They were selected from the folklore, fauna, flora, and from among domestic and occupational articles of the Louisiana bayous. The entries include English translations of the words, their relation to Spanish and French, and information concerning their use in other parts of the Hispanic world.

The study and vocabulary was based on the author's dissertation at the University of North Carolina in 1948.

249. McSpadden, George E. *Some Semantic and Philological Facts of the Spanish Spoken in Chilili, New Mexico.* Albuquerque: University of New Mexico, 1934. (University of New Mexico Bulletin. Language Series, vol. 5, no. 3) pp. 71–102.
This work consists of a study and vocabulary of the Spanish used in Chilili, New Mexico. Listed and discussed are 79 words. The author points out semantic changes and gives the English equivalents. Also listed are approximately 70 new forms of Spanish words, archaisms, anglicisms, and words of uncertain origin. In addition to the vocabulary, the author includes a useful history of the region studied.
This study was published together with F. M. Kercheville's *A Preliminary Glossary of New Mexico Spanish.*

250. Molera, Frances M. "California Spanish Proverbs." *Western Folklore,* 6 (January, 1947): 65–67.
Proverbs in Spanish which were of common usage in California are recorded here. The list contains 34 proverbs and expressions which the compiler learned from relatives and other Spanish Californians of earlier generations. They are arranged in alphabetical order with the English equivalents or translations provided.

251. Moreno, H. M. *Moreno's Dictionary of Spanish-Named California Cities and Towns.* San Luis Obispo, CA, 1916. 95 p.
This dictionary claims to contain every Spanish-named locale in California. It gives the origins of the name California and of the names of every county in the state. Non-Spanish county names are included. He excludes only those places too remote to be reached easily and, therefore, "not on the map." There are approximately 300 entries which were compiled from the U.S. Postal and Parcel zone guides, the *California Blue Book,* the Velázquez dictionary, the Southern Pacific and Union Pacific maps, and other sources such as Irvine's *History of California.* Each word includes the English definition, pronunciation, and derivations. It was compiled during a period of great interest in Spanish place names, or what Moreno considered "the quaint names" in California.

252. Pearce, Thomas Matthews. *New Mexico Place Names; A Geographical Dictionary.* Albuquerque: University of New Mexico Press, 1965. 187 p.
This dictionary of New Mexico's place names contains more than 5,000 individual names collected between 1936 and 1940 by workers of the New Mexico Writers' Project. The names included are those of all the counties and county seats; all present post offices and those discontinued before 1964; state and national parks; state and national monuments; the more important cities, towns, settlements, and land grants; better-known lakes, creeks, mesas, mountain ranges and peaks. The entries provide location, origins, major highways and railways, and relevant historical and economic information.
The numerous Spanish place names in New Mexico include not only descriptive and incident names, but also many names commemorating personages or places important to Spanish and Mexican history. The place names reveal the historical and linguistic heritage of this state.

253. Rosensweig, Jay B. *Caló; Gutter Spanish.* New York: Dutton, 1973. 123 p.

Words used by Mexican Americans in the barrios of the Southwest, and by other Spanish-speaking groups as well are in this compilation. The words included are slang but the author prefers to call it the "language of poverty." For each word listed, a translation or definition in English is given. An introduction provides a background description of *Caló* and of the usefulness of a list of this type.

Although Rosenweig considers this the only work of its kind, various similar word lists and slang dictionaries have been published. The most recent one was published in 1976 by Librado Keno Vásquez and María Enriqueta Vásquez, entitled *Regional Dictionary of Chicano Slang.*

254. Santamaría, Francisco. *Diccionario de mejicanismos.* México, D.F.: Editorial Porrua, 1959. 1197 p.

This is one of the most complete dictionaries of vocabulary of common usage in Mexico. The author includes the definition of each word, the etymology, and the geographical areas in Mexico where most frequently used. Examples of usage are also provided. This work is a revised and enlarged version of *Vocabulario de mejicanismos,* by Joaquín García Icazbalceta, published in 1899. It is cited here as a possible source for the study of the vocabulary and dialects of Mexican Americans.

255. Stewart, George R. "Two Spanish Word Lists from California in 1857." *American Speech,* 16 (December, 1941): 260–269.

This work reprints two Spanish word lists which were published in the *Alta* during October, 1857. The lists indicate the degree to which Spanish terminology was incorporated into the vocabulary of Americans in the Gold Rush period. The compiler of the lists is unknown but presumed to be one of the editors of the *Alta.* As the compiler indicates, the words "describe things or acts for which there is no name, or no convenient name in English." In addition, the words in the second list were of frequent use in conversation and in newspapers in California.

The first list (October 12, 1857) includes 42 words which relate to cattle ranching, land-tenure, and the Spanish-Mexican social system. The second list (October 19, 1857), of more common terms, includes titles, words of address, foods, flora, and fauna. More important than the words included are those which were excluded even though commonly used at the time; for example, mining terminology. The lists are analyzed in detail by Stewart and have historical value.

256. Tallichet, H. "A Contribution Towards a Vocabulary of Spanish and Mexican Words Used in Texas." *Dialect Notes,* 1 (1890–1896): 185–195.

Spanish words, which the author identified as being used mainly in Texas, are included in this early listing. The 174 words and variations were collected by Prof. Tallichet in the 1880s from his associations with surveyors, cattlemen, prospectors, land agents and settlers during nine years in Texas. The majority of the words that appear in this list were used in the western part of the state. Each entry includes pronunciations, definitions, examples of usage, and symbols indicating references cited in other dictionaries or glossaries of the period.

257. Tireman, Loyd S. *Spanish Vocabulary of Four Native Spanish-Speaking Pre-First-Grade Children.* Albuquerque: University of New Mexico Press, 1948. (Publications in Education, no. 2) 64 p.

This is a vocabulary of 3,437 words or forms of words used by four native Spanish-speaking children in New Mexico. The purpose of the study was to analyze the extent of oral Spanish vocabulary of children from Hispanic heritage. It was assumed in the early part of the century that the Spanish-speaking child was not as well equipped with a significant vocabulary in Spanish or in English as the average English-speaking child.

The conclusion of the study demonstrated that the Spanish-speaking children possessed about the same size vocabulary as the English-speaking children of similar age. The words listed relate to clothing, schools, family, food, music, occupations, religion, sports, transportation, stories, etc. Symbols are used to designate the anglicisms, archaism or New Mexicanism, misuse in meaning, and substitutions or made-up forms. No definitions are provided.

258. Utley, John Herbert. "A Mexican Word List." *Hispania,* 23 (December, 1940): 357–361.

The purpose of this work was to prepare a list of vocabulary words found in Mexican books, literature, and newspapers which are unique to the Spanish of Mexico. These words are called "Mexicanismos." One hundred are listed along with the English equivalents. This list is included for its historical value and for its usefulness to students and teachers.

259. Vásquez, Librado Keno, and María Enriqueta Vásquez. *Regional Dictionary of Chicano Slang.* Austin, TX: Jenkins Publishing Co., 1975. 111 p.

Regional slang used by the Chicanos of the Southwest is found in this compilation. The expressions are from the "dialects" called Tex-Mex, *Caló, Pachuquismo,* and Cali-Mex. Over 1,200 words and phrases are listed in alphabetical order with their appropriate English translation and meaning. Symbols are provided to indicate regions where the words are used most extensively. This dictionary also includes a pronunciation guide, a list of proverbs and sayings, riddles, folk medicine, and folk songs (six songs with lyrics) which are identified with the Spanish-speaking people of the Southwest. Knowledge of Spanish is essential to a proper use of this work since no translation nor explanation in English is given for certain sections of the dictionary (e.g., the proverbs and sayings, the riddles, and the folk medicine and songs).

260. Watts, Peter. *A Dictionary of the Old West, 1850–1900.* New York: Alfred A. Knopf, 1977. 399 p.

This dictionary is a guide to words and phrases of the Old West found in books and written records from the period of 1850–1900. The compiler has attempted to identify the authentic words from those invented during the twentieth century by writers of Western stories and novels. Pronunciation has not been included since it is nearly impossible to verify. As can be noted, the influence of Spanish and Mexican-Spanish was indeed very pronounced, particularly in regard to terminology of the cattle-range and stockman.

For each entry the definition and usage are provided as well as variant forms, cross references and quotes from references where the words or phrases were located. The various origins and locations of the words are identified. The origins include French,

Mexican-Spanish, and Spanish and the locations include Northwest, Southwest and Western. Many charming illustrations accompany the definitions. Separate bibliographies of works cited and works consulted are appended.

261. Wells, Harry L. *California Names.* Los Angeles: Kellaway, Ide, Jones, 1934. 94 p.

Over 2,500 place names, individual names, words, and phrases commonly used in California are incorporated in this small dictionary. It was compiled for residents and tourists to help them understand the pronunciation and meaning of the numerous place names with a "foreign" origin. The entries include pronunciation, definition, and linguistic derivation.

This work is included for its historical interest since it is one of the early attempts to identify the origin of California place names, most of which are derived from Spanish and Indian words.

## MINOR WORKS—THESES AND DISSERTATIONS

262. Carlisle, Rose Jeanne. *A Southwestern Dictionary.* Master's thesis, University of New Mexico, 1939. 398 p.

263. Cervantes, Alfonso. *A Selected Vocabulary of Anglicisms Used by the Spanish-Speaking First Grade Students of the Elementary Schools of Del Rio, Texas.* Master's thesis, Southwest Texas State University, 1973. 68 p.

264. Días, Rosario Simón. *A Vocabulary of California Spanish Words of English Origin Used by the First Generation Spaniards of California.* Master's thesis, Stanford University, 1941. 131 p.

265. Farias, María Julieta. *The Spanish Language in Texas. Duval, Webb, and Zapata Counties.* Master's thesis, University of Texas, Austin, 1950. 122 p.

266. Fody III, Michael. *A Glossary of Non-Standard Spanish Words and Idioms Found in Selected Newspapers of South Texas during 1968.* Master's thesis, Southern Illinois University, 1969. 154 p.

267. Frausto, Manuel H. *Vocabulario español de San Marcos, Texas.* Master's thesis, Southwest Texas State University, 1969. 55 p.

268. Galván, Roberto A. *El dialecto español de San Antonio, Tejas.* Ph.D. dissertation, Tulane University, 1954. 314 p.

269. _____. *Un estudio geográfico de algunos vocablos usados por los habitantes de habla española de San Antonio, Texas.* Master's thesis, University of Texas, 1949.

270. García, Lucy. *Vocabulario selecto del español de Brownsville, Texas.* Master's thesis, Southwest Texas State University, 1972. 64 p.

271. García, Trinidad. *A Vocabulary of New Mexican Spanish Words of English Origin from Southwestern New Mexico*. Master's thesis, Stanford University, 1939. 96 p.

272. Gross, Stuart Murray. *A Vocabulary of New Mexican Spanish*. Master's thesis, Stanford University, 1935. 78 p.

273. Ivey, Alfred Joe. *A Study of the Vocabulary of Newspapers Printed in the Spanish Language in Texas*. Master's thesis, University of Texas, Austin, 1927. 137 p.

274. Kelly, Rex R. *Vocabulary as Used on the Mexican Border*. Master's thesis, Baylor University, 1938. 39 p.

275. Luna, Juanita J. *A Selected Vocabulary of the Spanish Spoken in Sabinal, Texas*. Master's thesis, Southwest Texas State University, 1970. 101 p.

276. McKee, Okla Markham. *Five-Hundred Non-Dictionary Words Found in the El Paso-Juárez Press*. Master's thesis, Texas Western College, 1955.

277. Marambio, John L. *Vocabulario español de Temple, Texas*. Master's thesis, Southwest Texas State University, 1970. 109 p.

278. Ramón, Simón Rene. *Vocabulario selecto del español regional de Del Río, Tejas*. Master's thesis. Southwest Texas State University, 1974. 70 p.

279. Reséndez, Víctor, Jr. *Vocabulario español de Seguín, Texas*. Master's thesis, Southwest Texas State University, 1970. 81 p.

280. Sorvig, Ralph W. *A Topical Analysis of Spanish Loan-Words in Written American English of the American Southwest*. Ph.D. dissertation, University of Denver, 1952. 295 p.

281. Trejo, Arnulfo D. *Vocablos y modismos del español de Arizona*. Master's thesis, Universidad de las Americas, 1951. 92 p.

282. Trujillo, Luís M. *Diccionario del español del Valle de San Luís de Colorado y del Norte de Nuevo México*. Master's thesis, Adams State College, 1961. 41 p.

# Chapter 8

# *Newspaper and Periodical Sources*

This chapter contains bibliographies, lists, directories, and indexes of Mexican American serials. These tools provide information on journals, newspapers, newsletters, bulletins and the like, both in Spanish and English, which have served or are serving as principal means of communication for Mexican Americans throughout the United States. As outlets for public opinion, creative and artistic expression, and academic research, these serial publications are rich sources of primary and secondary research material.

Mexicans and Mexican Americans have published newspapers in Texas, New Mexico, and California since the early nineteenth century. Today many Mexican American communities continue to have their own daily or weekly newspapers. They report political developments, legal problems, economic conditions, social events, and religious activities, often emphasizing the concerns of the immediate community.

Aside from newspapers, all other periodical publications on Mexican Americans generally date from the 1960s and 1970s. Some of these are clearly political, others are social, and a few are scholarly. But most were published to give voice to the diverse elements that emerged among Mexican Americans in the course of their growing cultural consciousness and pride. Many of these publications have gone through changes in character reflecting the shifting ideologies of American society and Mexican Americans themselves.

In general, Mexican American newspapers and periodicals have been plagued by irregular or intermittent publication. Many titles have completely ceased after only a few issues. These problems have been caused by inadequate financial support and a limited circulation base. Under the circumstances, it has been difficult for libraries and research center collections to maintain complete and accurate holdings of Mexican American serials.

Access to the various serial publications on the Mexican American is facilitated by the works listed in this chapter. The sources on newspapers are the most numerous. They include lists of newspapers published in particular regions and states, comprehensive listings of Mexican American newspapers since 1848, and checklists of current titles associated with the Chicano Movement. Because Mexican Americans concentrate in the Southwest, the guides to newspapers in Texas, New Mexico, and California are especially useful. These usually indicate location of newspaper files, extent of holdings, and dates of publication. Other helpful sources are the comprehensive listings which are not limited geographically but are part of an overall effort by scholars and bibliographers to identify the largest number of titles relevant to Mexican Americans. Such works are valuable tools for historians and other social scientists, although file locations are not frequently provided. The checklists are generally short bibliographies of alternative publications which express the social and political views of Mexican American activist groups. It is virtually impossible to obtain information on many of these newspapers in the standard directories, guides, and indexes.

The remaining sources are guides and union lists which include newspapers and periodicals in major Mexican American collections; general lists of Mexican American serials, not associated with any particular library; and directories of ethnic serials which contain Mexican American or Spanish American newspapers and periodicals. These works are more important to current research because, together, they cover most of the contemporary serial publications on the Mexican Americans. Furthermore, the majority of the titles listed in these works are either still in publication or were published up to a short time ago. This increases their accessibility through subscriptions or from libraries with substantial Mexican American collections.

Three unique works included in this chapter are not actual listings of serial publications but they provide information about newspapers and periodicals. The first is a bibliography of sources that discuss or list Chicano serials. This work, entitled *A Bibliography of References of Chicano/Raza Serials,* was produced in 1976 by the Chicano Research Library at the University of California, Berkeley. The second, *Apuntes Tejanos,* by Arnoldo De León, is an index to several nineteenth-century Texas newspapers. This two-volume work identifies news items which reported activities or incidents involving Mexican Americans. The third is a clipping and indexing service by Comité de México y Aztlán. It specializes in current news about Mexico and Chicanos appearing in seven major Southwestern newspapers.

As many of the current Mexican American periodicals become well established publications, the standard periodical indexes in the social sciences and the humanities will begin to include them in their coverage. *The Hispanic American Periodicals Index,* edited by Barbara Cox (University of California, Los Angeles) has already indexed several Mexican American journals. In addition, a number of major Chicano research centers with strong Mexican American collections have formed a consortium for the purpose of indexing their holdings of Mexican American serials. Richard Chabrán (Chicano Studies Library, University of California, Berkeley) is director of the project. As the first stage in the project, the consortium developed a thesaurus of indexing terms more appropriate to Mexican American studies than those found in many standard indexes. The index, with retrospective coverage up to 1978, will be completed in 1979, according to projections.

283. Cabello-Argandoña, Roberto, Juan Gómez-Quiñones, and William Tamayo. "Library Services and Chicano Periodicals; A Critical Look at Librarianship." *Aztlán,* 2 (Fall, 1971): 151–172. Annotated.
This extensive listing of 206 Chicano periodicals published in Mexican American communities throughout the Southwest was compiled for the purpose of assisting libraries in identifying Chicano publications and in improving their services to Chicano communities. Each entry includes name and address of the publisher, language of publication, frequency, location, and holdings statement. Most of the titles are in the Los Angeles Library system, the University of California Libraries, or the Chicano Research Library at UCLA.

In 1971 this was one of the most complete listings of periodicals relating to Mexican

American studies. Since then several other sources have been published that supersede this one.

284. Comité de México y Aztlán. *News Monitoring Service for Chicanos.* Oakland, CA: COMEXAZ, May, 1972+ Index.
Issued monthly, this collection of clippings, reports, political, educational, economic, and editorial news on Mexico and Mexican Americans from seven major Southwestern newspapers. In addition to the general categories of coverage, this collection also includes selective items in the areas of sports, archeology and anthropology, natural disasters and accidents, travel, book reviews, obituaries, social and cultural events, letters to the editor, advertisements, marriages, etc. The newspapers (*Arizona Republic,* Denver *Post,* Los Angeles *Times,* San Antonio *Express,* El Paso *Times,* San Francisco *Chronicle,* and Albuquerque *Journal*) were selected to provide a balanced geographical coverage of the area with respect to the distribution of the Mexican American population. The monthly index is divided into four parts: Bylines, Geographics, Personal Names, and Subjects.

285. Dawson, Muir. *History and Bibliography of Southern California Newspapers, 1851–1876.* Los Angeles: Dawson's Book Shop, 1950. (Originally issued in Historical Society of Southern California, Los Angeles. *Quarterly,* 32 (March, 1950): 5–44; 32 (June, 1950): 139–174) 86 p. Annotated.
This work is a guide to early southern California newspapers. The titles of 76 newspapers from 18 cities and towns are listed with a description, history, name of the editor, size of the publication, any title changes, circulation when known, and locations of some issues. The arrangement is by city or town. Several of the papers were published in Spanish and circulated among Spanish-speaking residents. Many of the other papers also carried news items related to the cultural, historical, and social life of the local Spanish-speaking population in southern California. A bibliography of 37 items on the history of early printing and newspapers in California is appended.

286. De León, Arnoldo. *Apuntes Tejanos: An Index of Items Related to Mexican Americans in Nineteenth Century Texas.* Ann Arbor, MI: University Microfilms International, 1978. 2 vols.
Items related to Mexican American history in several nineteenth-century Texas newspapers are indexed in this two-volume work, sponsored by the Texas State Historical Association. The first volume contains an introduction and the indexing for the San Antonio *Express* (1869–1900) and the San Antonio *Herald* (1855–1878). The second volume includes a separate introduction and the indexing for the Corpus Christi *Weekly Caller* (1833–1899), the Corpus Christi (Matamoros and Brownsville) *Ranchero* (1859–1870), El Paso *Times* (1883–1899), El Paso *Daily Herald* (1881–1899) and the Austin *Statesman* (1871–1899). The indexes are arranged chronologically. Each entry includes date, page, column number, and a short description of the article cited. Also furnished are the places and dates for wire-service and correspondent reports. Excluded from the index are the letter lists of general delivery mail which mentioned many Spanish-surnamed individuals and appeared on a weeklybasis.

The indexes contain approximately 3,000 citations which mention court cases, arrests, historical articles, sports events, publishing activity, political and economic news, social events, and stories of human interest related to the Mexican Americans in Texas. This work is a unique reference tool. It provides access to primary source information for research in the social history of Mexican Americans in the nineteenth century.

287. "Directory of Raza Magazines." *La Luz,* 2 (April, 1973): 55.
A very limited listing of ten Hispanic American magazines published in the United States; titles from Texas, California, Illinois, Missouri, and Washington, D.C., are mentioned. The addresses of publishers are included. The majority focus on the Mexican American.

288. "Directory of Raza Newspapers." *La Luz,* 2 (April, 1973): 54–55.
A short alphabetical listing of 21 current Mexican American newspapers; this list is located in the Literary Section of *La Luz.* Each title includes the address of the publisher. Newspapers from Colorado, Texas, California, New Mexico, Michigan, Minnesota, and New York are listed.

289. *Ethnic Serials at Selected University of California Libraries: A Union List.* Compiled by Ethnic Materials Librarians at Participating Libraries. Edited by Barbara Kuhn Al-Bayti, *et al.* Los Angeles: University of California, 1977. 368 p. Indexes.
This guide to some of the ethnic resources in the University of California Libraries is the result of several years of cooperative efforts of librarians from all of the University of California campuses except Berkeley. The list covers Multi-Ethnic Studies, Chicano Studies, Asian American Studies, Afro-American Studies, and American Indian Studies.
The section on Chicano serials includes 234 titles of newspapers and other serials ranging from academic to popular. Each entry includes as much information as was available: place of publication, dates, most current address of the publisher, variant titles, language and library symbols, and holdings statements. Current and retrospective titles are cited. There is a separate index for each ethnic group, with a listing of the appropriate titles from the Multi-Ethnic Section.

290. Gonzáles, John E. *A Bibliography of References to Chicano/Raza Serials.* Berkeley: Chicano Studies Library, University of California, 1976. (Chicano Studies Library. Publication Series, no. 1) 19 p.
This is the most comprehensive guide to published and unpublished articles, parts or chapters of books, and documents that list or discuss serial publications relating to Mexican Americans. All of the 150 items in the list are available in the Chicano Studies Library at Berkeley. Call numbers and location symbols are provided. Coverage includes newspapers, journals, magazines, and other serials. Approximately 29 are unpublished items, authored by John E. Gonzáles. Most of the entries are not included in the standard general bibliographies. Particular emphasis is on those lists of titles held at Berkeley.
This is a very handy tool for researchers and librarians who need to identify sources which can provide verification and location of Mexican American serials.

291. Gregory, Winifred. *American Newspapers 1821–1936: A Union List of Files Available in the United States and Canada.* New York: Kraus Reprint, 1967. (Reprint of 1937 ed., New York: Bibliographical Society of America.) 791 p.
Newspapers that were published in the United States and Canada between 1821 and 1936 are cited in this extensive union list. Its purpose is to identify the location of existing files

and render more effective the resources of American libraries. Some of the files are in libraries and others are preserved in county courthouses, in newspaper offices, and in private collections. The newspapers published in states with large Mexican American populations, and Spanish-language newspapers, are easily located with this reference work. The arrangement is alphabetical by state or province and city. The entries include title, frequency, period of publication, name changes, and location. A bibliography of union lists of newspapers is appended, which is helpful in locating other titles possibly not in this work.

This tool is particularly useful for historians, genealogists, and social scientists.

292. Grove, Pearce S., Becky J. Barnett, and Sandra J. Hansen. *New Mexico Newspapers: A Comprehensive Guide to Bibliographical Entries and Locations.* Albuquerque: University of New Mexico Press, 1975. Index.
The purpose of this guide was to compile the most complete directory of newspapers published in New Mexico between 1835 to 1974. Many of the titles are in Spanish or at least include a section in Spanish. Emphasis has been placed on comprehensiveness rather than accuracy since complete bibliographic data are not available for some of the older unlocated titles. The guide is arranged by county, subarranged by town and by the titles of the newspapers. Indexes provide access through an alphabetical listing by town, by title, and a chronological list by date of first issue.

This work supersedes the *Check List of New Mexico Newspapers,* published in 1935, by Wilma Loy Shelton and the University of New Mexico Library.

293. Kennedy, Diane. "Underground Newspapers: The Chicano Press." *Missouri Library Association Quarterly,* 30 (Sept., 1969): 221–224.
This is an early alphabetical listing of now familiar publications by the Chicano Press across the United States. No purpose is mentioned and no criteria are given. Presumably it was compiled to familiarize librarians with the increasing number of Chicano serial publications. The newspapers, periodicals, and magazines cited are all quite relevant to the study of Mexican Americans. Each entry includes the address of the publisher and the price. Since the publication of this basic list many new Chicano serial titles have appeared.

294. MacCurdy, Raymond R. *A History and Bibliography of Spanish-Language Newspapers and Magazines in Louisiana, 1808–1949.* Albuquerque: University of New Mexico Press, 1951. (University of New Mexico Publications. Language and Literature Series, no. 8). 43 p.
As the title indicates, this is a history of Spanish-language printing in Louisiana between 1808 and 1949, with a bibliography. The intent of the author and compiler was to identify the previously undiscovered Spanish-language titles in Louisiana, both those which have been preserved as well as those which have not, and to present a chronological history of the publishing activity during the period. The bibliography, covering pages 34 to 40, lists in alphabetical order the commercial newspapers and magazines which have been preserved. Excluded are the fraternal and private publications. Each entry includes subtitle, dates of establishment and termination (if known), frequency of publication, names of the publisher and the editor, address of the publisher, and location of the preserved issues.

This work is useful for historians and students of Hispanic culture in that the titles shed light on the social, political, and historical events in Louisiana.

295. Randall, Michael H. *Chicano Studies: Serials Holdings at UCLA.* Los Angeles: Library, University of California, 1976. 21 p. Index.

This is a fairly comprehensive record of UCLA's holdings of 224 serial publications dealing with Chicano studies. The list was compiled from the holdings of eight campus units and it includes some titles dating back to the early 1800s. The largest number of entries are from California, Texas, and New Mexico, but there are titles from 11 other states, the District of Columbia, and Baja California. The arrangement is alphabetical by title with a geographical index. Each entry includes title, place of publication and a brief holdings statement. The initiative for the production of the list was provided by an ad hoc committee on Chicano studies serials at UCLA.

296. *Retrospective Newspaper Collection, 1844–1943.* Berkeley: Chicano Studies Library, University of California, 1974. (Selected Collections of the Chicano Studies Library, no. 1) 40 p.

In 1970, under the direction of Herminio Rios, this collection of microfilmed newspapers was added to the holdings of the Chicano Studies Library at the University of California, Berkeley. Although a number of years have elapsed since then and other titles may have been added, this list of 177 titles represents the state of the early newspaper files up to that time. The work is arranged in three sections: Title list, Location list, and Chronological list. The most useful and complete listing is the first which, in addition to title and place of publication, gives the span of dates and the reel number. Detailed holdings are available in the library's newspaper title catalog.

The majority of the newspapers are from New Mexico, a sizable number are from Texas, seven are from California, and one is from Arizona. Most of the titles appear to be in Spanish but this information is not provided.

297. Rios, Herminio, and Lupe Castillo. "Toward a True Chicano Bibliography; Mexican-American Newspapers: 1848–1942." *El Grito,* 3 (Summer, 1970): 17–24.

This bibliography of Mexican American newspapers contains sources of social, economic, and political information useful for historical research. The 193 newspapers listed cover the period from 1848 to 1942. Most of the papers were published in Arizona, Texas, California, Colorado, and New Mexico, the states with the largest concentration of Mexican American population. Each entry gives the newspaper's title, frequency, and dates of publication. The arrangement is alphabetical by state and city.

298. _____, and Lupe Castillo. "Toward a True Chicano Bibliography—Part II." *El Grito,* 5 (Summer, 1972): 38–47.

Mexican American newspapers, published between 1881 and 1958, are found in this list. It supplements the earlier one published by the same authors in *El Grito* in the summer of 1970. The combined lists include a total of 378 newspaper titles, published since the end of the Mexican-American War, which relate to the study of the Chicano. This part contains 185 titles.

299. Rojas, Guillermo. "Chicano/Raza Newspaper and Periodical Serials Listing." *Hispania,* 58 (December, 1975): 851–863.

Chicano/Raza newspapers and periodicals located in 20 selected Southwestern institutions are listed here. The titles include bulletins, journals, newspapers, and newsletters from the

1960s and 1970s that provide information on issues related to Spanish-speaking communities throughout the United States. The nearly 200 serials, many of which have ceased to exist, were and are published by all sectors of the Chicano population, i.e., student organizations, prison groups, Chicano Studies centers, school districts, community groups, labor groups, and offices sponsored by the Economic Opportunity Program. Each entry includes title, type of publication, sponsoring group, address, pertinent notes, and location of extant files. Those titles which have ceased or which have been superseded are also identified.

This listing was first published in *El Grito* in 1973 under the title ''Serials Listing: Chicano/Raza Newspapers and Periodicals, 1965-1972.'' This version was reprinted in *Hispania* with minor revisions and an enlarged introductory statement.

300. Shelton, Wilma Loy. *A Check List of New Mexico Newspapers.* Albuquerque: University of New Mexico Press, 1935. (University of New Mexico Bulletin, Sociological Series, vol. 2, no. 2) 31 p.

This is one of the earliest attempts to record and locate files of New Mexico newspapers. The list, prepared by the University of New Mexico Library, contains 575 titles, 115 of which were published all or partially in Spanish. The earliest recorded newspaper published in the state, the *New Mexican Review,* was established in 1848. The titles are arranged in alphabetical order under the place of publication. Files were located for 201 of the titles. Information provided includes frequency, language, dates of publication, location of files and holdings. The checklist was compiled to aid historians and others with an interest in these materials and to encourage their preservation by libraries in the state.

This work has been superseded by *New Mexico Newspapers: A Comprehensive Guide to the Bibliographical Entries and Locations,* compiled by Pearse S. Grove, Becky J. Barnett, and Sandra J. Hansen.

301. Wallace, William Swilling. ''A Checklist of Western Newspapers in the Mills Collection.'' *New Mexico Historical Review,* 30 (1955): 136-152.

Newspapers in the Mills Collection of the Rodgers Library, New Mexico Highlands University, are cited in this guide. The newspapers are primarily from the late nineteenth century and for the most part from the State of New Mexico. A few are from Texas and Mexico while others are from Arizona, California, Colorado, and Kansas. Many are English-language publications, but some are in Spanish. The entries indicate frequency and dates of publication. Also indicated are the number of issues of each newspaper in the Mills Collection. Arrangement is alphabetical by state and city.

302. Wheeler, Jean French. *Historical Directory of Santa Clara County Newspapers, 1850-1972.* San Jose: Sourisseau Academy for California State and Local History, San Jose State University, 1973. (Occasional Paper, no. 1) 37 p.

This is a guide to the location and holdings of the county's newspapers in libraries, museums, historical societies, and newspaper publishing companies in Santa Clara County. The work includes an introduction; a directory of selected institutions in Santa Clara County which have holdings of county newspapers; a list of a few selected libraries outside the county which also have a substantial number of the county's newspapers; and the listing of the newspapers. Of particular interest to Mexican American studies are both the college/alternative press publications, usually in Spanish and English and the early local newspapers which date back to the mid and late 1800s.

The alternative press publications and newsletters reflect the current interests and concerns of Chicano student groups in the area. These frequently include artistic and literary efforts as well as political essays. The early newspapers contain valuable data for social, economic, and historical research on life in California following the signing of the Treaty of Guadalupe Hidalgo. The list is arranged geographically by city and subarranged alphabetically by title. A few titles are identified for which no holdings could be located.

303. Work Projects Administration of Texas. Division of Professional and Service Projects, Historical Records Survey Program. *Texas Newspapers, 1813-1939: A Union List of Newspaper Files Available in Offices of Publishers, Libraries, and a Number of Private Collections.* Houston: San Jacinto Museum of History Association, 1941. 293 p. Indexes.

The goal of the compilers was to prepare an updated and comprehensive list of Texas newspapers. They uncovered 3,212 titles of newspapers published in 738 towns and cities of Texas between 1813 and 1939, many of which were not in the *Union List of Newspapers,* published in 1937. Arrangement is alphabetical by city and subarranged by title. Each entry includes frequency of publication, date of the first issue, location of depositories, and contents. A chronological index indicates those depositories having files of Texas newspapers that appeared prior to 1877.

This is a rich source of titles with historical information on Mexican Americans, particularly of those newspapers from the border counties and towns of Texas.

304. Wynar, Lubomyr Roman, and Anna T. Wynar. *Encyclopedic Directory of Ethnic Newspapers and Periodicals in the United States.* 2nd ed. Littleton, CO: Libraries Unlimited, 1976. 248 p. Annotated. Index.

The second edition of this directory is completely revised although the format remains much the same. The purpose also remains the same: to serve scholars involved in research of American social and ethnic groups and to provide librarians with a useful reference tool and a guide to building their ethnic collections. The directory identifies newspapers and periodicals published by 63 ethnic groups in the United States. There is a special section of Chicano materials on pages 180-190 and another section on the Spanish Press which includes titles published by Puerto Ricans, Cubans, Argentinians, and Mexican Americans.

Each entry in this edition of the directory includes the title, address of the publisher, editor, sponsor, language, circulation statistics, frequency and price. Short annotations provide descriptions of the content, scope, and purpose. An introductory chapter offers a discussion on the ethnic press and the appendix provides statistical analysis of each individual press. Although the coverage for Mexican American titles is not as broad as in other publications, the selection is basic and the data and bibliographical information are current.

The first edition, by the same title, was published in 1972.

# Chapter 9

# *Audiovisual Sources*

Separately published sources of audiovisual materials which relate to the study of the Mexican American are cited in this chapter. It is difficult to generalize about their characteristics because there are so few. Some of the works are restricted to particular collections, several are limited to a certain type of media, and others cover all forms of nonbook materials. A few works cite titles on various ethnic minorities, among which the Mexican American or Spanish-speaking are included.

Agencies of the federal government were among the first to issue guides to media for and about the Mexican American. In the 1960s the U.S. Public Health Service published two of the first film lists on Mexican migrant workers, in a continuing effort to identify communication aids for Spanish-speaking Americans. In 1971, the U.S. Cabinet Committee on Opportunities for the Spanish Speaking included audiovisual materials in their bibliography entitled *The Spanish Speaking in the United States: A Guide to Materials.* And more recently, in 1973, the Department of Health, Education, and Welfare issued a guide to film, filmstrips, and slide collections in Spanish on health-related topics, entitled *Guide to Audiovisual Aids for Spanish-Speaking Americans.*

Between 1970 and 1976, the University of Utah, the University of Houston, the University of Texas at El Paso, and several major research institutions in California began to include audiovisual resources in their library guides and bibliographies of Mexican American materials. As media collections developed, some institutions prepared separate listings of their holdings on the Mexican American. One of the best examples is the *Chicano Film Guide*, by Emma González Stupp, issued by the Mexican American Library Project at the University of Texas at Austin.

During the same period a variety of organizations and institutions issued media catalogs and indexes that did not pertain to any particular collection. The American Library Association, the Institute for Communication Research, and the Southern Folklore Center were among the sponsors of publications on films, filmstrips and videotapes related to the Mexican American. One of the listings, *Ethnic Studies and Audiovisual Media: A Listing and Discussion*, by Harold A Layer has been reproduced on microfiche by Educational Resources Information Center (ERIC) and is available in many libraries.

Several lists in this chapter contain audiovisual materials which may be of particular interest to public and junior college libraries, and social service organizations. The titles in these sources are generally of a practical nature and pertain to health education, crafts, travel, and general culture for adult audiences. The works issued by the Public Health Service and the American Library Association are examples of sources in this category.

Some of the audiovisual sources are more appropriate for use in primary and secondary schools. These sources offer selections which enhance the understanding and appreciation for Mexican American culture. Grade level, content description, availability, and rental or purchase options are usually given.

Several of the media lists and guides were designed to assist academic librarians or faculty in ethnic studies programs in selecting resources for college and university media collections. The use of audiovisual materials for research and teaching at this level is more recent and controversial. Although public libraries and junior colleges have actively collected audiovisual resources for a number of years, academic libraries have only seriously acknowledged the value of nonprint media in the past decade or so. Major academic libraries in the West and Southwest began building Mexican American media collections concurrently with the selection of books and periodicals on this ethnic group. The audiovisual materials on the Mexican American collected by these institutions were often the only items available in certain subject areas or served to substitute for the lack of written resources. These media collections generally include materials which document aspects of the culture, such as the history, music, literature, folklore and drama, or the political, social, and economic conditions associated with the contemporary Mexican American experience. Some of the listings indicate that various academic libraries and Chicano research centers are producing their own recordings and videotapes of speeches, conferences, oral history, and other unpublished materials in order to preserve and document information for researchers.

In spite of the increasing recognition given to the use of media for the study of the Mexican American, many institutions have not produced guides to their collections. Others have issued only ephemeral lists for local use and distribution. A recent publication by Martin H. Sable, entitled *A Guide to Nonprint Materials for Latin American Studies,* will assist in locating references to materials on Mexico and Mexican Americans.[1] In this work Sable lists all the important general reference tools which contain entries for Hispanic American topics. There is still no major reference source which can be relied upon to provide a comprehensive listing of all available audiovisual resources, and publications about these resources, on the Mexican American.

In addition to the titles cited in this chapter, it is advisable to consult the Index for references to other bibliographies and guides which also contain audiovisual materials and directories of audiovisual producers and distributors.

1. Martin H. Sable, *A Guide to Nonprint Materials for Latin American Studies* (Detroit, MI: Blaine-Ethridge, 1979), 141 p.

305. **American Library Association. Adult Services Division. Subcommittee on Spanish Materials.** *Films for Spanish-Speaking and Spanish-Culture Groups.* Flushing, NY: Department of Library Science, Library Materials for Minority Groups Institute, Queens College, 1971. 16 p. Annotated.

A committee of the American Library Association prepared this listing of films and filmstrips for librarians and community groups that provide services to adults of Spanish heritage. The films range in date from 1937 to 1971, but many of the items are not dated. The five criteria used in the compilation of the list include: adult level, currency of information, relevance to the audience, educational and/or recreational value, and timeliness. Films in Spanish and English are cited. Each entry gives title, language, length, color, date, and producer or distributor. A list of distributors is provided at the end of the work.

Of the 68 films and five filmstrips, 13 relate specifically to the Mexican American and 26 are of general interest. The rest concern Puerto Ricans and other Hispanic groups. Films marked with an asterisk may appeal to children or young adults. The selection is balanced in terms of educational and recreational interest, and many of the titles would be appropriate for courses in Mexican American studies.

306. Arizona State University. Hayden Library. *Cassettes and Phonotapes on the Chicano: A List of Cassettes and Phonotapes in the Microforms Services Department.* Tempe, AZ: The Library, 1974. (Chicano Studies Library Projects) 7 p.

This is a short list of recordings held by the library of Arizona State University. Included in the collection are tapes by Alurista, José Angel Gutiérrez, Julian Nava, Octavio Romano, Reíes López Tijerina, César Chávez, and other Chicano activists on such topics as poetry, bilingual education, literary criticism, history, philosophy, politics, and economics. The list was produced to provide a guide for library patrons interested in Mexican American studies.

307. Baird, Cynthia. *La Raza in Films: A List of Films and Filmstrips.* Oakland, CA: Latin American Library, Oakland Public Library, 1972. 68 p. Annotated.

As one of the few lists of films and filmstrips which are directly related to Mexican American studies, this work provides a special service. The films listed have been selected for content rather than quality and deal with background materials on Mexico and Latin America in general, with themes of the third world in Latin America, and the Spanish-speaking in the United States. Nearly half of the list covers topics of current interest. Each entry indicates color, length, language, price, and distributor of the film or filmstrip in order to facilitate purchase or rental. Each film is annotated with short content description. Some of the annotations were taken from other sources since the compiler was not able to preview all the titles. Those not previewed are so indicated. This compilation fills a gap in the area of media resource bibliographies on the Spanish-speaking in the United States, although somewhat dated now. A *Supplement to La Raza in Films,* published in 1976, updates the first edition. The supplement is six pages in length and adds 19 new titles.

308. Center for Southern Folklore. *American Folklore Films and Videotapes: An Index.* Memphis, TN: The Center, 1976. 338 p. Annotated. Index.

This is the first complete index of American folklore films and videotapes. The materials in this catalog cover the folk experience, the history and background of folk culture, and folk traditions such as music, lore, crafts, and foods. Of the more than 1,800 titles, approximately 35 which relate to the Mexican American can be found in the subject index under The Minority Experience—Mexican American; The Minority Experience—Spanish American; The West; Missions; Folk Music—Mariachi; State—California; and several others.

Separate film annotations, video annotations, and special collections follow the subject index. The films and video tapes are arranged alphabetically by title. Each entry includes length, size, color, date, producer, distributor, and a concise description of the contents. An appendix contains a listing of titles by distributor, a directory of distributors, and the photo credits. A supplement to be published in 1980 will update the original index.

309. Chávez, Alex J. "Recommended Sources for Commercially Available Discs and Field Tape Collections of Chicano Music." Music Library Association *Newsletter,* 14 (September–October, 1973): 1–2.
Among the 54 recordings and five field collections are numerous selections relating to the Spanish folk music of the Southwest and Mexico. The works are listed by the distributor or producer with addresses. Included are children's songs, *corridos, rancheras, boleros,* and popular tunes in Spanish and English. In most instances the performers or groups are mentioned with each title. Some of the songs, although familiar to Mexican Americans in the Southwest, are known throughout the Spanish-speaking world. A few of the recordings are representative of contemporary Chicano music.
The bibliography was first produced for and distributed at the Las Vegas Conference of the Music Library Association, June, 1973.

310. Cine-Aztlán. *La Raza Film Bibliography,* by Rubén García, *et al.* Santa Barbara, CA: La Causa Press, 1975. 99 p. Annotated. Indexes.
This compilation of 267 films, of interest to Mexican American studies, presents those works available up to 1975. The films include, in addition to those depicting the Mexican American experience, a few titles on the historical background of Latin America, Brazil, Cuba and Bolivia. Instructional films on health topics and crafts as well as documentaries are among the selections. Short annotations, with a leftist bias, describe the content of each film and identify those which the compilers feel reinforce racist stereotypes. Films in English and Spanish are so identified. The citation for each film does not include price, length, nor recommend level of usage. A list of 75 film distributors and title and subject indexes are included. Appended are the results of the Treviño/AHORA Survey: an historical profile of the Chicano and Latino in Hollywood film productions.

311. González Stupp, Emma. *Chicano Film Guide.* Austin: Mexican American Library Project, Benson Latin American Collection, The General Libraries, University of Texas, 1978. 16 p. Annotated. Index.
The Mexican American Library Project was organized to insure the acquisition and preservation of films and other materials related to Chicano studies. The selection of 52 films in this guide were made during 1974–1977. The subjects covered include education, migratory labor, health, fine arts and music, social life, and customs. The color, language, length, price, address of the distributor, and a content summary are provided for each film. The guide is useful for other libraries or instructors considering purchase or rental of a particular film.

312. Johnson, Harry A. *Ethnic American Minorities: A Guide to Media and Materials.* New York: R. R. Bowker, 1976. 304 p. Annotated. Indexes.
This is one of the most recent and complete guides to instructional materials and media on the four major minority groups in the United States: Afro-American, Asian American, Native American, and Spanish-speaking American. The purpose of the guide is to en-

hance the understanding and appreciation for American minorities through selected audiovisual materials. Chapter IV, pp. 189–239, covers the Spanish-speaking American which includes Mexican Americans. The subjects covered by the instructional items are art, culture, history, social problems, crafts, music, education, theater, poetry, economic situation, politics, and children's literature. Among the media items listed are films, filmstrips, slides, transparencies, audio recordings, cassettes, video cassettes, study prints, pictures, posters, and graphics. The annotations for each source include grade level, release date, rental and purchase price at time of publication. A directory of producers and distributors is appended.

313. Layer, Harold A. *Ethnic Studies and Audiovisual Media: A Listing and Discussion.* Stanford, CA: Institute for Communication Research, Stanford University, 1969. 11 p. ED 031 091.
Audiovisual resources for general ethnic studies are covered in this work: Asian American, Black, Mexican, Spanish American, and Native American studies. The selections are directed toward senior high school and college-level ethnic studies programs. Arranged alphabetically by title under broad subject areas are approximately 270 films, filmstrips, audiotapes, records, videotapes, and transparencies. Each entry includes title, medium, distributor, availability, and a short description of content. An index of distributors is included at the end of the work.
Among the 270 items, 15 deal directly with the Mexican American and 36 relate to general ethnic studies. The latter provide a broad perspective of various groups, including Mexican Americans, through a comparative approach. The selections exclude art and the ''mother country'' and emphasize the history and present reality of non-Anglo minorities.

314. Mandell, Gerry. *Spanish Language Film Catalog.* Austin, TX: Dissemination and Assessment Center for Bilingual Bicultural Education, 1975. 315 p. Annotated. Index.
This is one of the most complete listings of 16 mm films in Spanish suitable for children and adults; over 1,900 titles are annotated. Although the majority of the films were produced nearly 30–40 years ago, a few titles of recent vintage are listed. The items are arranged in one alphabetical list by the English translation. All of the films are still available for rental or purchase. The prices for both options are given with a list of producers and distributors. Many of the titles in this catalog are useful for courses in Chicano studies and for libraries building film collections on the Mexican American.

315. Robertson, Carol E. *Catalog of Latin American Recordings of Music and Oral Data.* Bloomington: Archives of Traditional Music, Indiana University, 1971. 17 p.
This is a catalog of sound recordings pertaining to Latin America that are part of the Archives of Traditional Music at Indiana University. Although the list is outdated now, it indicates the areas and types of materials that are collected. The Archive broadly defines Latin America as South America, the Caribbean, Central America, and Spanish-speakers in the United States. The catalog entries for the last-named category are quite minimal. Selections include music from Texas and New Mexico, primarily popular vocal and instrumental music. There is a more lengthy section on Mexico with some items, such as *corridos,* which are relevant to a study of Mexican American music and folklore.

The catalog is arranged geographically. The general Latin American materials are listed first. This is followed by general South American items, Caribbean materials, and the Central American section. Music from Mexico and the United States is listed at the end of the catalog. The Archive's accession number, name of the individual who recorded or edited the collection, date recorded or issued commercially, size of the collection, and a concise description of the type of music are provided for each collection listed.

316. U.S. Health Services Administration. *Guide to Audiovisual Aids for Spanish-Speaking Americans; Health Related Films, Filmstrips, and Slides: Description and Sources.* Rockville, MD: Department of Health, Education, and Welfare, 1973. (DHEW Publication, no. (HSA) 74-30) 37 p. Annotated.

As part of the continuing effort by the Health Services Administration, in the Department of Health, Education, and Welfare to provide information for Spanish-speaking Americans, this guide was prepared. Films, filmstrips, and multimedia kits in Spanish and English are listed under the following health-related categories: accident prevention, aging, community health, dental health, diseases, emergency health care, family planning, human body, mental health, migrant health, nutrition, personal hygiene, physical fitness, prenatal and infant care, and smoking.

The entries are arranged alphabetically by title under each topical division. Included are size, color, length, date, purchase or rental price, distributor code, and a short annotation. The descriptions are those of the distributors since none of the films were previewed before inclusion in the guide. The titles listed in this filmography are particularly useful for public and school libraries in Spanish-speaking communities or health and welfare agencies that serve Spanish-speaking people.

This listing is a companion to the bibliography entitled *Spanish-Language Health Communication Teaching Aids: A List of Printed Materials and their Sources* (DHEW Publication, no. (HSM) 73-19) issued in 1972.

317. U.S. Public Health Service. *Selected Films for Migrant Workers.* Washington, DC: U. S. Department of Health, Education, and Welfare, 1964. (PHS Publication, no. 869) 16 p. Annotated.

This is a listing of 45 films on health and nutrition of migrant workers, arranged in two sections: health education, and films to broaden community understanding of migrants and their way of life. Some of the films are to be used in acquainting community groups with the plight of migrants while others are to aid Spanish-speaking migrants and their families in improving their health and living conditions. Many of the films are available in both English and Spanish. Each entry indicates the location, language, and distributor. It is difficult to tell the age of the films since no dates are given.

This listing is a revised edition of *Agricultural Migrants—Selected Films,* published by the Department of Health, Education, and Welfare in 1961. *Health Leaflets for Spanish-speaking Migrant Families* (PHS Publications, no. 795) is a companion piece to this film list.

318. University of California, Los Angeles. Chicano Studies Center. *The Chicano Studies Film Program.* Los Angeles: University of California, n.d. 14 p. Annotated.

This is a small but useful alphabetical listing of 49 films, video cassettes, and multimedia kits pertaining to Chicano schooling, labor, art, and history. Thirty-eight of the films deal exclusively with Mexican Americans while the remainder cover peripheral matters of some interest to their experiences. The collection includes most of the classic and award-winning films produced about the Mexican American. The entries indicate title, length, color, and rental fees. The annotations give short content summaries and recommended usage.

The film collection was first established in 1969 as part of the Chicano Library Unit's efforts "to develop a strong collection of print and audiovisual material documenting all aspects of the Chicano experience." In 1972 the film program developed as a cooperative effort between the Chicano Studies Research Library and the UCLA Media Center Film Library. It is regarded as one of the first programs of its kind.

319.  Yanniello, William, and Helen Johnston. *Agricultural Migrants; Selected Films*. Washington, DC: U.S. Public Health Service, 1961. (PHS Publication, no. 869) 12 p. Annotated.

Selected films for and about agricultural migrants are cited in this publication. Most of the films are particularly suitable for Spanish-speaking laborers and their families. The work is arranged in two parts: films for the education of migrants and films designed to improve an understanding of migrants and their problems. Many of the films, although now dated, are excellent historical documentaries depicting an early period in the life of Mexican Americans. Part one includes 30 films in the field of education. The films concern various health problems such as tuberculosis, oral hygiene, and nutrition. Part two lists ten films on agricultural migrants in general and were produced to promote an understanding of their problems. Entries include title, color, length, language, size, and distributor. Annotations provide useful content summaries.

This list was updated in 1964 by the Public Health Service. The new publication is entitled *Selected Films for Migrant Workers* (PHS Publication, no. 869).

# Part 2

## SUBJECT BIBLIOGRAPHIES

# Chapter 10

# *Education*

Interest in Mexican American education increased in the early twentieth century when schools were confronted with the children of newly arrived Mexican immigrants. This interest continued intermittently up to the 1960s but at local levels. Since the 1960s research has expanded substantially, motivated by the demands of activist groups within the Mexican American community and the support from federal agencies. Presently, Mexican American education is a widely recognized field of study and one of the most expansive and prolific areas of research. The concepts, methodologies, materials, and programs, proposed as necessary for the educational progress of Mexican American students, have not ceased to stir debate and discussion.

Over the years, a number of issues and problems in this field have encouraged sociologists, psychologists, and educators to produce an immense volume of literature on the Mexican Americans. Most early works, published prior to World War II, established rationales for the failures of Mexican Americans in the schools by pointing to their cultural values, attitudes, and intellectual deficiencies. These factors, described and analyzed in the literature, were used to formulate policies that were detrimental to the educational achievement of students of Mexican heritage.

Dramatic changes took place in the 1960s. Old assumptions concerning the Mexican American students were questioned and the direction of research and criticism shifted radically to the educational institutions. Education became the focus of most efforts to improve the status of the Mexican Americans and as such attracted the attention of educational theorists and strategists. Two basic themes were expressed in the publications of the last decade and a half. One concerned socioeconomic circumstances and barriers within the traditional system of education—arbitrary testing, language difficulties, racial discrimination, segregation, ineffective methods, and insensitive teachers. The second theme concerned innovative approaches to the education of Mexican Americans—new teaching techniques, bilingual-bicultural education, teacher preparation, and special materials for students of Mexican background.

Research in the field of Mexican American education is supported by a large number of bibliographies. These were compiled by both Mexican Americans and others from 1933 to the present, but the majority were issued since 1968. These bibliographies appeared in books, articles, and numerous unpublished sources. Their primary emphasis has been on the elementary and secondary levels of education; only a handful refer to sources on higher education. Many were prepared by public school systems, schools of education, and state departments of education. Others were compiled by research institutes such as the Center for Applied Linguistics, Educational Systems Corporation, and Integrated Education Associates, or by public and academic libraries. Although many of the bibliographies are unpublished, most of these are readily available through the Educational Resources Information Center (ERIC). Nearly three-quarters of the bibliographies in this chapter are part of the ERIC collection.

The Educational Resources Information Center, established in 1964 by the U.S. Office of Education, is maintained by the National Institute of Education. Through several of its clearinghouses (Early Childhood Education, Rural Education and Small Schools, Urban Disadvantage, and Teacher Education) a great many bibliographies on Mexican American education have been preserved. Each document obtained by ERIC is assigned an ED number, microfilmed, and made available to the public. All new acquisitions are listed in their monthly journal, *Resources in Education (RIE),* and in the annual *Educational Documents Index* which brings together all the documents cited in *RIE* during the previous calender year.

The bibliographies in this chapter fall within four broad categories: general bibliographies on Mexican American and/or Spanish-speaking education; sources on curriculum materials; bibliographies on bilingual-bicultural education; and bibliographies on the teaching of minorities and ethnic groups.

The general bibliographies cover all aspects of the education of the Mexican Americans and/or the Spanish-speaking and list sources related to educational concepts, policies, and methods. With these sources researchers may trace the evolutionary perception of Mexican Americans within the American system of education.

The second category of bibliographies relates to curriculum materials. These include books in Spanish or on the Hispanic heritage for children, resources for bilingual-bicultural programs, materials for high school and college-level programs in Chicano studies, and general curriculum materials on the Mexican American for teachers, librarians, and children. Bibliographies of this type represent the largest number of works in this chapter.

The third category includes bibliographies on bilingual-bicultural education. The continuing debate over the effectiveness of bilingual-bicultural education has generated a great deal of literature. Sources cited in these bibliographies cover teacher preparation, counseling, program development, research findings and reports, and general works on various aspects of bilingual-biculturalism. Although the bibliographies in this category refer to several non-English-speaking minorities, most of these sources are on the Mexican American or the Spanish-speaking. The overwhelming majority of the bilingual-bicultural programs in the country have been established for Mexican Americans.

The final category of bibliographies in this chapter pertain to the teaching of minorities and ethnic groups. These were not compiled specifically for the Mexican Americans but the issues and problems discussed in the sources are significant to research on Mexican American education. Included are works on rural and migrant education, poor or disadvantaged children, early childhood education, and the training of teachers who instruct minorities.

For additional sources on Mexican American education researchers should consult the chapters on General Bibliographies, Library Guides, Literature, Directories, and Statistics, as well as recent issues of *Resources in Education, Educational Documents Index,* and *Education Index* for more current information.

320. Altus, David. *Bilingual Education: A Selected Bibliography*. Las Cruces: New Mexico State University, 1970. 228 p. Annotated. Indexes. ED 047 853.
This bibliography provides access to research findings and developments in bilingualism and bilingual education. Part I contains 176 citations which appeared in *Research in Education* up to June, 1970. Part II contains 28 items cited in *Current Index to Journals in Education* for the period January, 1969, to July, 1970. Although the selected references deal with the subject of bilingual education in general, specific entries on the Mexican American are included. Subject indexes based on the ERIC *Thesaurus* are provided.

321. Andersson, Theodore, and Mildred Boyer. *Bilingual Schooling in the United States*. Austin, TX: Southwest Educational Development Lab, 1970. 2 vols. Annotated. Indexes. ED 039 527.
Sponsored by the Office of Education of the Department of Health, Education, and Welfare, this major work serves as a guideline for planners of bilingual programs and a basic survey of information on bilingualism. In Volume I (pp. 149–292) there is an extensive bibliography of 870 items on bilingual education. Listed are books, articles, bibliographies, official documents, bulletins, theses, dissertations, manuals, papers, and pamphlets. Many of these are found under the heading of Spanish-speakers in the United States. In addition, this work provides demographic data; a list of bilingual programs in the United States; a directory of persons and organizations involved in bilingual education; sources of teaching materials; and the names and addresses of U.S. Office of Education, Bilingual Design Project Advisory Committee members. A new edition, issued by Blaine-Ethridge Books in 1976, includes a supplemental bibliography by Francesco Cordasco. This was not available for examination by the reviewers.

322. Babin, Patrick. *Bilingualism; A Bibliography*. Cambridge, MA: Harvard Graduate School of Education, 1968. 30 p. ED 023 097.
Designed to assist school systems with planned or established bilingual programs, this work provides a list of only the most significant works published prior to 1968. The 412 entries include selected books, journal articles, unpublished papers, and bibliographies. Many of the selections are appropriate for use in Spanish-English programs and are relevant to Mexican American education. In addition, the sources are suitable for a comparative view of the problems of bilingualism.

323. Barnes, Regina. *A Selected ERIC Bibliography on Teaching Ethnic Minority Group Children in the United States of America*. New York: Columbia University, 1969. 22 p. Annotated. ED 027 360.
This bibliography is designed to acquaint educators with ERIC materials which provide information on teaching minority group children. It covers selected documents and books from the first ERIC collection up to the January, 1969, issue of *Research in Education*. The materials are arranged in five sections: the first is a general bibliography and the following four each relates to a specific minority group, including the Mexican Americans. Lengthy abstracts are provided.

324. Barrios, Ernest. *A Resource Guide for Teaching Chicano Studies in Junior and Senior High Schools.* San Diego, CA: San Diego City Schools, 1969. 222 p. Annotated.

A resource guide and bibliography for junior and senior high school teachers, it is divided into four units: History, Chicano cultural characteristics, Chicano cultural contributions, and Chicanos on the move. It covers the history, sociology, anthropology, literature, art, and music of Mexican Americans. The bibliography contains books, periodical and newspaper articles, and reports, arranged by subject. Following this are the sources of instructional aids and a list of Spanish-language radio and television stations.

325. Bengelsdorf, Winnie. *Ethnic Studies in Higher Education: State of the Art and Bibliography.* Washington, DC: American Association of State Colleges and Universities, 1972. 260 p. Annotated. Indexes.

The purpose of this work is to identify and summarize recent materials on ethnic studies in higher education. A discussion on the state of the art and trends in ethnic studies is included. Of interest to the Mexican American is the section of articles and reports dealing with the survey and research in Chicano higher education arranged chronologically; general information sources; historical and sociological materials; and a list of institutions offering degree programs or courses in Chicano studies.

326. *Bibliography of Spanish Materials for Children: Kindergarten through Grade Six,* by Julia Gonsálves, *et al.* Sacramento: California State Department of Education, 1971. 48 p. Annotated. ED 048 797.

Instructional materials for students, teachers, and native Spanish-speakers in kindergarten through the sixth-grade level are covered in this bibliography. The selections are intended to serve the needs of both native speakers and children who are studying Spanish as a foreign language. Contained in the list are more than 400 items that emphasize both language and culture. Materials are arranged under headings by type of publication: Children's literature; Dictionaries and encyclopedias; Dramatization, rhymes and poetry; Games, puzzles, and activities; Health; Science; Mathematics; Music; Reading and language arts; and Social science. This is one of the more recent bibliographies that can be used with elementary and preschool children in bilingual bicultural classroom situations.

327. Blatt, Gloria T. ''Mexican Americans in Children's Literature.'' *Elementary English,* 45 (April, 1968): 446–451.

This article includes a bibliographical essay on the treatment of the Mexican American in children's literature. The article reviews 32 children's books about Mexican Americans in an effort to determine if prejudicial attitudes are projected by the authors. The selected books actually deal with Mexicans as well as Mexican Americans since so few children's works could be found dealing with the Mexican American alone. A list of the children's books discussed in the essay is appended with the references from which the books were selected. An invaluable list, although somewhat dated, for teachers, librarians, and concerned parents.

328. Bolner, James. *Racial Imbalance in Public Schools: A Basic Annotated Bibliography.* Baton Rouge: Louisiana State University, 1968. 73 p. Annotated. Index.
Literature on the debate over racial imbalance in public schools is listed in this bibliography. Included are important articles, legislative and executive actions, and judicial decisions dealing with the topic up to 1967. While some of the entries focus primarily on Blacks, the entire issue of racial imbalance in public education and the legal principles involved are of great significance to Mexican Americans. The material listed is crucial to research on school integration and civil rights.

329. Brady, Agnes Marie. *"Materials for Teaching Spanish in Elementary and Junior High Schools." Hispania,* 42 (September, 1959): 385–405. Annotated.
This list offers an array of materials useful in teaching Spanish in elementary and junior high schools. Included are general works, audio aids, maps, charts, filmstrips, films, slides, syllabi and guides, language lab equipment, songs, verse, plays, dances, games, books, readers, foreign books for children, miscellaneous teaching aids, and bibliographies. Each entry includes price, source, appropriate grade level and rating. This is a revised edition of a previously published bibliography that appeared in the September, 1955, issue of *Hispania.* Further revisions or supplements may appear in later issues of this journal.

330. Cahir, Stephen, Rosa Montes, and Brad Jeffries. *A Selected Bibliography on Mexican American and Native American Bilingual Education in the Southwest.* Las Cruces: New Mexico State University, 1975. 299 p. Annotated. Index. ED 103 148.
The latest findings or developments in bilingual education which specifically relate to Mexican Americans and/or American Indians in the Southwest are provided by this bibliography. It contains 263 entries compiled from abstracts appearing in *Research in Education* from January, 1971, until June, 1974. The topics most emphasized are biculturalism, bilingualism, content analysis, English as a second language, program evaluation, and Spanish. The ERIC document numbers are provided for each entry to facilitate use.

331. California State Polytechnic College, San Luis Obispo. Library. *The Education of Mexican-American Children and Teaching English as a Second Language.* San Luis Obispo: The Library, 1969. 18 p.
This list of materials, available at the California State Polytechnic College Library, focuses on the education of Mexican American children and teaching English as a second language. It covers an extensive collection of books and periodical articles, curriculum guides, teaching aids, textbooks, state and federal publications, juvenile literature, and numerous selections from the ERIC files. The entries are arranged in sections according to their physical location, e.g., Main Library, Curriculum Library, etc. This is a useful tool for students in teacher preparation courses, for teachers in bilingual classrooms, and for librarians in developing Educational Service collections.

332. *CARTEL: Annotations and Analyses of Bilingual Multicultural Materials.*
Austin, TX: Dissemination Center for Bilingual Bicultural Education,
1973+ Annotated. Indexes.

Resources for bilingual-bicultural programs are cited in this quarterly publication. The
materials are primarily directed at educators and librarians and are heavily oriented toward
Spanish language and learning. Although contents vary considerably, depending on the
sources available, topics covered include classroom resources, ESL materials, bibliographies, professional literature for teacher education, Spanish language sources, early
childhood education, and vocational education. The works listed are restricted to those
available in the United States, or the territories, which are appropriate for bilingual
children or for staff training in bilingual multicultural programs. Each entry provides title,
author(s), name and address of the publisher/distributor, date, pages, language, and
audience or level.

Volumes I through III were published on a monthly basis under the title *CARTEL:
Annotated Bibliography of Bilingual-Bicultural Materials*. Annual cumulations are available; the early cumulations contained author, title, subject and publisher indexes, lists of
distributors, and titles in series.

333. Caskey, Owen, and Jimmy Hodges. *A Resource and Reference Bibliography on Teaching and Counseling the Bilingual Student*. Lubbock: Texas
Technological College, 1968. 45 p.

This resource and reference bibliography on teaching and counseling bilingual students is
pertinent to all minority groups and covers a wide range of topics in education. More than
700 entries are arranged in one alphabetical list with no subject divisions. Without an
index it is cumbersome to use and browsing is required to find the desired titles. The
citations range from ca. 1920 to 1967 and include journal articles, dissertations, and
government publications. Many of the items can be utilized successfully by teachers and
counselors of Mexican American students.

334. Charles, Edgar B. *Mexican-American Education: A Bibliography*. University Park: New Mexico State University, 1968. 28 p. Annotated. Index. ED
016 562.

This is a selected bibliography that contains 90 books, monographs, journal articles, and
unpublished papers on the education of Mexican Americans. The materials included were
published between 1958 and 1967. They cover preschool, elementary, secondary, adult,
higher, and migrant education. Topics relating to each of these levels include curriculum
content, counseling, language arts, reading, and innovative programs. The entries are
arranged by ERIC code numbers with subject access provided in the index. The list was
originally prepared for a meeting of the National Conference on Educational Opportunities
for Mexican Americans in April, 1968.

335. Ching, Doris C. "Reading, Language Development, and the Bilingual
Child: An Annotated Bibliography." *Elementary English*, 46 (May,
1969): 622–628. Annotated.

This bibliography was compiled to help educators understand the needs of bilingual
children and to identify publications that present various methods, approaches, and ideas
that can be used in teaching.

Included are articles, mainly from journals of education, on the teaching of Blacks, whites, and Spanish-speaking. Many of the articles stress the negative aspects of bilingualism. The annotations are concise, analytical, and content oriented. Many of the items are quite dated but may contain useful methods and ideas. Nevertheless, the material is important for its historical perspective on reading instruction and language development.

336. Conley, Howard K. *An Annotated Bibliography of Dissertations on American Indian, Mexican American, Migrant, and Rural Education, 1964–1972.* Las Cruces: New Mexico State University, 1973. 46 p. Annotated. Index. ED 080 251.
Dissertations on Native Americans, Mexican Americans, migrants and rural education in general are found in this bibliography. It claims to be comprehensive. Listed are 103 doctoral dissertations written between 1964 and 1972. A section comprising 26 entries deals directly with all aspects of Mexican American eduation. The studies are selected from *Dissertation Abstracts.* Each dissertation is available on microfilm or bound xerographic copy. Order numbers are given for the benefit of the researcher. The index provides subject access to the materials.

337. Conwell, Mary, and Pura Belpré. *Libros en Español: An Annotated List of Children's Books in Spanish.* New York: New York Public Library, 1971. 52 p. Annotated. Index.
This is a superb list of children's books in Spanish located in the New York Public Library. Included are picture books, books for the very young, books for the beginning reader, and books for the young adult. Also included are books on folklore, myths and legends, songs, games, bilingual books, books for learning Spanish, and anthologies of Spanish and Spanish American literature. Only titles still in print and available from the publishers are listed. Annotations are in both English and Spanish. This is an excellent guide for teachers in bilingual-bicultural programs. Teachers and librarians would benefit by an updated edition of this work, as well as patrons of the New York Public Library.

338. Cooperative Children's Book Center. *Materials for Those with a Spanish-Speaking Background.* Madison, WI: The Center, 1969. 10 p. ED 036 371.
Materials available at the Center that are considered appropriate for children of Hispanic heritage are in this list. It was compiled to meet the needs of their patrons. Over 150 books and audiovisual aids, all in English, are listed. The entries are arranged alphabetically under appropriate geographical areas or national origins and subgrouped by grade level. The section on Mexico contains the largest number of items. This bibliography is useful for teachers and children's librarians.

339. Copenhaver, Christina, and Joanne Boelke. *Library Service to the Disadvantaged; A Bibliography.* Minneapolis: ERIC Clearinghouse for Library and Information Sciences, University of Minnesota, 1968. (Bibliographic Series, no. 1). 19 p. ED 026 103.
This is one of the few bibliographies designed to provide a listing of materials on library services for the culturally, educationally, or economically disadvantaged in the United States and Canada. Cited are 365 journal and periodical articles, reports, books, bibliographies, and pamphlets published from 1960 to 1968. They cover such areas as federal

legislation and programs, minority groups, rural disadvantaged literacy problems, and school library services. Although the references do not deal specifically with Mexican Americans, the materials are generally applicable to this and other minority groups. Many of the items are available in the ERIC collection.

340. Cordasco, Francesco. "Poor Children and Schools: A Bibliography." *Choice,* 7 (April, 1970): 202–212; 7 (May, 1970): 355–356.
These guides provide selected references dealing with "the education of the children of the poor." Each contains a bibliographic essay describing the materials listed. Included are works on the role of the school, dropouts and delinquents, characteristics of the disadvantaged student, teaching and teacher education, programs, and materials. An additional list of general works on poverty provides a wider range of sources. A number of entries relate directly to Mexican American children. The entries are accurate but incomplete; place and publisher are lacking for most citations. This is a useful background work on disadvantaged children.

341. Cotera, Martha. *Education: Guide to Chicano Resources.* Crystal City, TX: Crystal City Memorial Library, 1971. 58 p. Annotated.
A variety of Chicano resources available and useful to librarians, teachers, and students are listed in this guide. The selections are arranged in 11 categories by type of material: History and social sciences books; Literary works; Reports and pamphlets; Bibliographies; Journals; Newspapers; Theater groups; Films and filmstrips; Tapes; Records; Publishers, and distributors of posters, pins, and buttons. An appendix lists additional sources of Chicano and Spanish language materials for young people, books for high school students and adults, and 16 mm films. The entries generally provide information on availability and price. All items relate to the Mexican American.

342. Croft, Kenneth. *TESOL, 1967–68: A Survey.* Washington, DC: TESOL, Georgetown University, 1970. 32 p.
This list is the result of a survey which attempted to locate materials published in 1967 and part of 1968 on the subject of teaching English to speakers of other languages. Listed are textbooks, monographs, and articles. Most of the 535 entries are articles from 35 foreign and domestic journals. The section on bilingual education is of particular interest to teachers who work with Spanish-speaking children. Although cross references are used extensively, a subject index would be desirable.

343. *Culturally Disadvantaged: A Bibliography and Keyword-out-of-Context (KWOC) Index,* by Robert E. Booth, *et al.* Detroit: Wayne State University Press, 1967. 803 p. Index.
This computer-produced bibliography and index to the literature on the education of the culturally and economically disadvantaged lists 1,400 items chosen from a variety of sources. Each item has been identified by 20 to 25 keywords. Those relevant to Mexican American studies are grouped under such headings as Mexican American, Spanish-speaking, Migrant, Bilingual, Southwest, etc. The work is arranged in two parts: the first is the keyword index and the second is the bibliography of complete citations. Books, monographs, reports, articles, theses, and ERIC documents are among the materials listed. This project was a cooperative effort of Wayne State University, College of

Education, and the Grand Rapids, Michigan, Board of Education. A preliminary first edition was issued in 1966.

344. Dabbs, Jack A. "Bilingualism: Programs, Methods, and Materials." In *Bilingualism,* reports of the Annual Conference of the Southwest Council of Foreign Language Teachers (3rd, El Paso, November 4–6, 1966), pp. 27–30. Edited by Charles Stubing. El Paso, TX: The Council, 1966. 64 p. Annotated. ED 016 435.
The bibliography in this work forms part of the second report on bilingualism by Jack Dabbs. A chronological listing of 32 selected items, mostly periodical articles from 1922 to 1966, focuses on programs and methods of bilingual education for Mexican Americans. The materials supplement the report and indicate new trends and developments in the field. The annotations are brief one-line descriptions of content with a justification for inclusion in the list. This listing is one of the first that recognizes and relates to the topic of bilingualism, incorporating selections from the literature over a period of four decades.

345. Detroit Public Schools. *Bibliography of Literature Books Related to Spanish History and Culture.* Detroit: Detroit Public Schools, 1969. 14 p. Annotated. ED 032 958.
This list is intended as a concise guide for schools selecting literature that depicts the history and the culture of Spanish-speaking people; materials are for elementary level education. Approximately 90 books are cited which were published between 1946 and 1969. The items are arranged by language in separate sections: Spanish, English or Bilingual. Although they are recommended for all Spanish-speaking groups in the United States, most are relevant to the Mexican Americans and to bilingual-bicultural programs. This work is indicative of the efforts made by school districts throughout the United States to integrate their curriculum with appropriate bilingual-bicultural materials.

346. Díaz, Carmen. *Bilingual-Bilcultural Materials.* Lawrence, KS: Special Education Instructional Materials Center, 1973. 93 p. Annotated. ED 084 915.
This list recommends educational materials which are both bilingual and bicultural. The 68 books and audiovisual materials are arranged under the headings of English as a foreign language, Mathematics, Music, Reading, Science, Social Studies, and Spanish as a for-eign language. Included also are evaluative instruments for assessments of children from Spanish-speaking families. A final section contains reference sources and bibliographies for English as a second language. This is a fairly current tool that can be helpful to teachers in TESOL and bilingual-bicultural programs.

347. "Easy Materials for the Spanish-Speaking." *Booklist and Subscription Books Bulletin,* 64 (July 15, 1968): 1266–1277. Annotated.
Devoted to materials in Spanish, this unique bibliography is for disadvantaged Spanish-speaking adults with reading problems. Most of the materials are evaluated at the fourth-grade level or below with content appropriate for more mature readers. Among the list of materials are works of fiction, newspapers, magazines, and records for learning English. Additional resources can be found in the list of government agencies which publish pamphlets in Spanish, the list of distributors of Spanish materials in the United States, and

the list of distributors of audiovisual materials. Although somewhat dated, this guide can be used by teachers in adult education programs, community centers, and public libraries.

348. Edington, Everett, and Lewis Tamblyn. *Research Abstracts in Rural Education; Rural, Small Schools, Indian Education, Migrant Education, Mexican American Education, Outdoor Education.* Las Cruces: Clearinghouse on Rural Education and Small Schools, New Mexico State University, 1968. 75 p. Annotated. Index. ED 025 357.
This bibliography includes the latest research and development findings on rural education, published between 1959 and 1968. The 98 items are cited from the ERIC files. Of the six sections described in the title, two focus on the Mexican American: Migrant Education and Mexican American Education. The entries are arranged according to the ERIC document numbers. The majority of the materials are devoted to specific problems and needs, administrative organization, innovations, and planning for educators in rural settings.

349. Fahrer, Kimber, and Robert Vivolo. "Doctoral Dissertations on Urban and Minority Education." *Equal Opportunity Review* (August, 1976): 1–11. Index. ED 128 493.
Educational problems of urban minorities is the focus of this bibiography of 245 dissertations. The materials pertaining to the Mexican American can be approached in the index through such headings as Mexican American, academic achievement, alternative schools, bilingual education, biculturalism, community involvement, counseling, curriculum development, early childhood education, school integration, racial attitudes, reading, and self-concept. The titles were drawn from *Dissertation Abstracts* between January, 1975, and May, 1976. This work provides increased accessibility to many unpublished sources on minority education.

350. Fifield, Ruth. *English as a Second Language: Bibliography.* El Centro, CA: Imperial County Education Center, 1968. 19 p. ED 024 513.
This bibliography is a selection of ERIC materials for teachers in bilingual classrooms and in programs teaching English as a second language. The materials are arranged in five sections: Professional materials, Instructional materials, Curriculum resource room, Audio-visual materials, and Spanish-language curriculum materials. Approximately 250 documents from 1946 to 1967 are listed. The selections are useful for school districts with large Mexican American enrollments.

351. Flaxman, Erwin, and Victor Zinn. *The Education of Teachers of the Disadvantaged: A Selected Bibliography.* New York: ERIC Information Center on the Disadvantaged, Yeshiva University, 1969. 10 p. ED 011 907.
A selection of materials on the education of the teachers of socially disadvantaged children and youth is provided by this bibliography. The items represent the current thinking of the period. An estimated 110 items are part of the collection of the ERIC Information Center on the Disadvantaged. Most of the materials were prepared in the 1960s. Included are books, articles, speeches, dissertations, conference proceedings, and reports of teacher education programs, OEO and NDEA Teacher Institutes. Many of the materials are

relevant to the education of Mexican Americans, as a recognized disadvantaged group, although the items are not exclusively about this group.

352. Forbes, Jack D. *Mexican-Americans: A Handbook for Educators*. Berkeley, CA: Far West Laboratory, 1968. 34 p.

This guide, for elementary and secondary school teachers, suggests book and nonbook materials for use in the classroom. The work is arranged in seven sections. The first five cover the Significance of the Mexican American people, the Mexican heritage, the Mexican American way of life, Assets which Mexican Americans bring to the school, Suggestions for teachers and administrators. The last two sections consist of a Guide to further readings and a Bibliography of books and audiovisual materials for classroom instruction. The first bibliography is a general selection of materials in history, culture, language, health, literature, and folklore for teacher-preparation in working with children in a bicultural classroom environment. The second bibliography lists materials to be presented to students in grades K-12. The section on audiovisual materials (transparencies, art reproductions, postcards, recordings, and films) does not actually list the various titles and items; information is given on where and how to obtain the materials that are outlined.

353. Gerez, Toni de. "'Books for Miguel.'" *Library Journal*, 92 (December 15, 1967): 45-47, 51.

Listed in this article is a core selection of children's books in Spanish for an elementary school library. Included are United States and foreign publications arranged in the following categories: Dictionaries and encyclopedias; Picture books, Easy reading and bilingual materials; Legends, heroes and folklore; Classics and fairy tales; Biography; Science and nature; Stories. The 80 titles listed were published between 1936 and 1964. Information on ordering the materials is provided. This list is of interest to public and school librarians and educators in bilingual-bicultural programs.

354. Gómez-Quiñones, Juan. "Selected Bibliographies on Chicanos in Higher Education." In *Chicanos in Higher Education: Status and Issues*, prepared by Ronald W. Lopez, Arturo Madrid-Barela, and Reynaldo Flores Macías for the National Chicano Commission on Higher Education, pp. 171-199. Los Angeles: Chicano Studies Center, University of California, 1976. (Monograph, no. 7) 199 p.

This bibliography has a selection of very specialized materials on the subject of Chicanos in higher education. It supplements the text. One hundred ninety-one items are arranged in five categories: Reference sources; Periodicals; Books and monographs; Articles and periodical literature; Government publications, unpublished documents, and papers. It was compiled by scanning several bibliographies and by conducting computer literature searches. The items include major bibliographies; directories on education; Chicano journals, books, and articles relating to job discrimination and educational opportunities; student surveys; analyses of problems for Chicanos in achieving higher education; and materials on Chicano Studies programs; and Chicanos in professional education.

Much of the cited material is not readily available unless collected by libraries and special Chicano studies collections. Many items are in the form of dissertations, master's theses, unpublished reports, and student papers. Nevertheless, this bibliography indicates a slight increase in research activity on Chicanos in higher education but the published materials are still limited.

355. Harrigan, Joan. *Materiales tocante los latinos: A Bibliography of Materials on the Spanish-Americans.* Denver: Colorado State Department of Education, 1967. 36 p. ED 018 292.

356. _____. *More Materials tocante los latinos: A Bibliography of Materials on the Spanish-American.* Denver: Colorado State Department of Education, 1969. 28 p. Annotated. ED 031 344.

The central theme of the first work is the spreading of knowledge of people of Hispanic origin. It appeals to a wide range of users and levels of interest. Materials are arranged in sections that include books for general reading (for adults, young people, and preschool to third grade); bilingual materials; bibliography of bibliographies; professional education materials; newsletters and periodicals. A directory of publishers is appended. The intentions that motivated this bibliography are admirable but the scope is too broad and many of the selections are inappropriate or irrelevant to the education and study of Spanish Americans.

The Supplement suffers from the same lack of focus as the previous work. The guidelines for selection are too broad. Included are sources published between 1964 and 1969 on Spanish Americans. The 120 entries are listed under five categories: Audiovisual aids; Reading materials for students; Professional materials for educators and librarians; ERIC materials on Mexican Americans; and New or forthcoming materials. The items, according to the compiler, are limited to titles not usually found in the standard sources for print and nonprint resources. Many entries relate to the Mexican American. The acquisition and grade-level information make this source useful in spite of other shortcomings.

357. Heathman, James E. *Migrant Education: A Selected Bibliography.* Las Cruces: New Mexico State University, 1969. 70 p. Annotated. Index. ED 028 011.

358. _____. Supplement no. 1, by James E. Heathman and Alyce J. Nafziger. Las Cruces: New Mexico State University, 1970. 44 p. Annotated. Index. ED 040 002.

359. _____. Supplement no. 2, by David M. Altus. Las Cruces: New Mexico State University, 1971. 140 p. Annotated. Index. ED 055 706.

360. _____. Supplement no. 3. Las Cruces: New Mexico State University, 1973. 159 p. Annotated. Index. ED 075 162.

361. _____. Supplement no. 4. Las Cruces: New Mexico State University, 1974. 134 p. Annotated. Index. ED 087 599.

362. _____. Supplement no. 5, Las Cruces: New Mexico State University, 1975. 123 p. Annotated. Index. ED 101 909.

363. _____. Supplement no. 6. Las Cruces: New Mexico State University, 1976. 131 p. Annotated. Index. ED 118 292.

364. _____. Supplement no. 7. Las Cruces: New Mexico State University, 1977. 213 p. Annotated. Index. ED 139 549.

The original Heathman bibliography and the various supplements provide access to some of the latest research findings on the education of migrants, with emphasis on Mexican and Mexican American children. Over 1,000 publications are listed by ERIC document number. Among the topics covered are curriculum, program evaluation, compensatory education, bilingual education, English as a second language, outreach programs, health services, agricultural laborers, rural population, and adult education. Included are works on Texas, the Southwest, the Midwest, Florida, and New Jersey which have a majority of the migrant population. The selections are from issues of *Research in Education* and the *Current Index to Journals in Education*. Most of the documents were published from the early 1960s to 1976 and are readily available from the ERIC Document Reproduction Service.

365. Heathman, James E., and Cecilia J. Martínez. *Mexican-American Education: A Selected Bibliography*. Las Cruces: New Mexico State University, 1969. 58 p. Index. ED 031 352.

366. _____. Supplement, no. 1, by David M. Altus. Las Cruces: New Mexico State University, 1971. Annotated. Index. ED 048 961.

367. _____. Supplement, no. 2, by Albert D. Link. Las Cruces: New Mexico State University, 1972. 345 p. Annotated. Index. ED 065 217.

368. _____. Supplement, no. 3. Las Cruces: New Mexico State University, 1973. 294 p. Annotated. Index. ED 082 881.

369. _____. Supplement, no. 4. Las Cruces: New Mexico State University, 1974. 360 p. Annotated. Index. ED 097 187.

370. _____. Supplement, no. 5. Las Cruces: New Mexico State University, 1975. 252 p. Annotated. Index. ED 107 428.

371. _____. Supplement, no. 6. Las Cruces: New Mexico State University, 1976. 293 p. Annotated. Index. ED 127 053.

372. _____. Supplement, no. 7. Las Cruces: New Mexico State University, 1977. 344 p. Annotated. Index. ED 144 778.

The primary bibliography by Heathman and Martínez and the numerous supplements cover all aspects of education of the Mexican Americans, with an emphasis on bilingual education and English as a second language. The more than 2,000 items cited include speeches, conference papers, reports, pamphlets, theses, articles and other types of materials found in *Research in Education* and the *Current Index to Journals in Education*. Other topics covered by the selections include cultural pluralism, early childhood education, educational television, ethnic studies, health education, reading achievement, and teacher education. The entries are arranged by ERIC document number. Access to the items is achieved by use of the descriptor terms in the indexes. These bibliographies contain material published between 1965 and 1977, thus updating a similar work by Edgar B. Charles, *Mexican American Education: A Bibliography,* published in 1968 (ED 016 562).

373. Holland, Nora. *A Selected ERIC Bibliography on the Education of Urban American Indian and Mexican American Children.* New York: Columbia University Teachers College, 1969. 19 p. Annotated. ED 029 935.

This ERIC bibliography contains 36 documents dealing with Native American and Mexican American children in urban schools. The documents are arranged under the headings of multi-ethnic and general, Mexican Americans, and American Indians. The listed materials relate to two themes: assimilation and acculturation, and bilingual schooling. The majority of the items concern Mexican Americans. Each entry contains the ERIC number for ease in locating the item in the ERIC microfiche file.

374. Ibarra, Herb. *Bibliography of ESL/Bilingual Teaching Materials.* San Diego, CA: San Diego City Schools, 1969. 29 p. ED 028 002.

Completed as part of a project funded by the Elementary and Secondary Education Act, Title III, this bibliography contains materials collected for use in ESL and bilingual classes. The 406 books, articles, and instructional materials were published between 1945 and 1968 for teachers and Spanish-speaking or bilingual students. Emphasis is placed on English as a second language textual materials from the primary to the adult level. Also included are kits and audiovisual aids for music and science instruction. A separate section is devoted to teacher preparation materials, cultural information, and curriculum guides. This list is of obvious usefulness to Mexican American students since it was prepared by a school district with a large Mexican American community.

375. *Information Services and Mexican Americans: A Selected Topics Bibliography of ERIC Documents.* Las Cruces: New Mexico State University, 1977. 22 p. Annotated. ED 152 476.

This is a chronological guide to resource materials, research findings, and developments in the area of information services and the Mexican Americans. The 21 items cited are from *Research in Education* and *Current Index to Journals in Education.* Most of the selections were published from 1964 to 1974. Entries cover such topics as bilingual education, English as a second language, information systems, library services, information dissemination, resource centers, educational improvements, international education, and educational legislation. A majority of the items are in Spanish. Twelve of the entries are from the *Boletín de información educativa,* published by the Ministerio de Educación in Argentina.

376. Jablonsky, Adelaide. *Mexican Americans: An Annotated Bibliography of Doctoral Dissertations.* New York: ERIC Clearinghouse on the Urban Disadvantaged, Columbia University, 1973. (ERIC-IRCD Doctoral Research Series, no. 1) 88 p. Annotated. Indexes. ED 076 714.

This guide to dissertations on the education of Mexican Americans was compiled for the purpose of identifying recent unpublished sources of information. The 62 entries were obtained from a search of *Dissertation Abstracts* and the holdings of selected university libraries. The items span the years 1965–1973 and generally deal with academic achievement, bilingual education, disadvantaged youth, economically disadvantaged, and school integration. The entries are arranged under nine subject headings: Bilingual, Verbal, Reading, Self-concept, Cultural, Parental influences, Comparisons with other groups, Jensen Theory, Mathematics. Lengthy descriptions of content define the areas of research emphasis. Author, subject, and institutional indexes provide access to the entries.

377. John, Vera P., and Vivian M. Horner. "Curriculum Materials." In *Early Childhood Bilingual Education*, pp. 120–133. New York: Materials Center, MLA-ACTFL, 1971. 187 p. Annotated.
Prepared for use in Spanish-English and American Indian–English bilingual programs, this guide lists sources of foreign and domestic curriculum materials. The arrangement is in three parts: imported, domestic, and teacher-made materials. Within each section there are sources for books, magazines, charts, posters, and maps. The four main subject areas covered are social studies, math, health, songs and games. Only a few of the sources publish science and language arts materials. Complete addresses are given for the 54 professionally printed and teacher prepared sources. Two additional bibliographies are recommended which cite storybooks and children's literature in Spanish published in the United States.

378. Karr, Ken. *A Selected Bibliography Concerning the Education of Mexican-American Migrant Children*. San Luis Obispo: California State Polytechnic College, 1969. 10 p. ED 028 014.
This bibliography concentrates on materials for the education of Mexican American migrant children in the Southwest. It was prepared for a meeting of the American Personnel and Guidance Association, Las Vegas, Nevada, April 2, 1969. The 94 items cited were published between 1960 and 1969 and were selected to assist in developing compensatory education programs. An addendum of 52 related items, some of which were published before 1960, is also included. Many facets of the topic are brought together in one alphabetical listing and the titles are very relevant to Mexican American education.

379. Kramer, Debora. *Mexican Americans: Selected References*. Washington, DC: Legislative Reference Service, Library of Congress, 1964. 2 p.
Mainly on the educational problems of Mexican Americans, this short list of 19 items is arranged in three parts under the headings of Statistical, Books, and Periodicals. Although no indication is given of the purpose and scope, most of the titles focus on Mexican Americans in California. Within the list, a broad range of topics is covered: health, discrimination, migrant labor, academic achievement, language barriers, minority group education, educational philosophy and racial diversity in the public schools. This is just a sampling of the numerous materials that are available on the social, psychological, and economic aspects of Mexican American education.

380. Leyba, Charles. *A Brief Bibliography on Teacher Education and Chicanos*. Washington, DC: ERIC Clearinghouse on Teacher Education, 1974. 11 p. Annotated. ED 090 147.
This work provides a selection of recent materials dealing with teacher education and the needs of Chicano students. The resources are designed to improve educators' understanding of the problems in teaching children of Mexican heritage and to offer new approaches and solutions to these problems. Twenty-five documents from *Research in Education,* arranged in one alphabetical list, cover the topics of bilingual education, migrants, early

childhood education, recruitment of Mexican Americans to higher education, and cultural understanding. This bibliography is a useful tool in the preparation and training of teachers who plan to work in areas with a concentration of Mexican American students.

381. *Library Services and Materials for Mexican Americans: A Selected Topics Bibliography of ERIC Documents*. Las Cruces: New Mexico State University, 1977. 57 p. Annotated. ED 152 477.
Items relating to library services for Mexican Americans are cited in this bibliography. The materials, published between 1946 and 1976, are drawn from *Research in Education* and *Current Index to Journals in Education*. Topics covered by the 93 sources include librarians, library services, public libraries, reference materials, library collections, children's literature, newsletters, educational resources, library programs, Spanish American literature, information services, and foreign language periodicals. The majority of the selections are all quite timely and relevant, and indicate a small but growing recognition of the role of libraries in the education of Mexican Americans.

382. Morrow, Judith C. *An Annotated Bibliography of Spanish Readers for Levels I–IV*. Bloomington: Indiana Language Program, Indiana University, 1971. 60 p. Annotated.
This list was compiled in response to requests from Spanish teachers for information on the availability of Spanish textbooks and readers. The works listed are arranged by grade level. Each entry includes a description of the cultural application, vocabulary, grammar, format and projected teaching use. The readers cover the literature and vocabulary in Spanish from all parts of the Spanish-speaking world, including Mexico. This list gives educators a starting point from which to make their own evaluations and selections.

383. New Mexico State Department of Education. Cross-Cultural Education Unit. *Materials for Bilingual-Bicultural Instruction*. Santa Fe: The Unit, 197? 37 p.
This is a partial list of the collection of multicultural materials available in the Cross-Cultural Education Unit of the New Mexico State Department of Education. Included are materials for multicultural and bilingual-bicultural instruction, bilingual education textbooks, children's books about Mexican Americans, Southwest literature for grades 7–12, easy-to-read fiction and drama, and a list of publishers of Spanish materials. This is a revised and updated version of a bibliography published in 1971 under the title *Spanish Bibliography: A Bibliography of Spanish Materials for Use in the Classroom*, by Henry Pascual. The recent edition is available in the New Mexico State Library.

384. New York State Department of Education. *Annotated Bibliography: Educating the Disadvantaged Child*. Albany, NY: The Department, 1968. 90 p. Annotated.

385. _____. *Annotated Bibliography: Educating the Disadvantaged Child*. Supplement, no. 1. Albany, NY: The Department, 1969. 88 p. Annotated. Index.
Publications pertinent to the education of disadvantaged children are identified in these bibliographies. Included are works dealing with problems that confront school districts,

administrators, and educators in their efforts to provide for the needs of such students. While the overall focus is on the disadvantaged child, there are references under headings such as Migrant children, Parent and community involvement, Pre-school programs, Pupil personnel services, Dropouts, and Developmental and remedial reading, which are related to the education of Mexican Americans.

The supplement includes works available through September, 1969, and covers child development and socioeconomic factors, not included in the original edition. The same format is followed, but an author index, with a key to subject headings, is added to this work.

386. Nichols, Margaret S., and Margaret N. O'Neill. *Multicultural Bibliography for Preschool Through Second Grade in the Areas of Black, Spanish-Speaking, Asian American, and Native American Cultures.* Stanford, CA: Multicultural Resources, 1972. 40 p. Index.

The early-childhood sections of a widely recognized collection of multicultural materials for all ages and reading abilities are listed here. The collection has been exhibited throughout the United States and has works on Blacks, Mexican Americans, Asian Americans and American Indians. Appropriate references for the Spanish-speaking are found on pages 5-10 and in the multi-ethnic section. Included are materials for teachers and parents, materials in Spanish and English, folktales and legends, and curriculum guides. A list of publishers and distributors is another special feature. It has been acclaimed as one of the best bibliographies for preschool to third grade minority materials.

387. O'Donnell, Carolyn. "Selected Résumés of Early Childhood Research Reports." *Head Start CRIB—Childhood Research Information Bulletin,* 1 (1969): 1-55. Annotated. Index. ED 025 318.

This is a compilation of 57 résumés of current research reports on children in Head Start programs. The reports, covering 1965 to 1967, are concerned with ethnic factors, evaluation of programs, community influence, teacher effectiveness, bilingual concentration, and audiovisual equipment. Six of the résumés relate specifically to Mexican Americans and many of the others are useful in working with disadvantaged children of Hispanic heritage. The *CRIB Bulletins* are published biannually and present, rather than evaluate, new research findings.

388. Ohnnessian, Sirarfi, and Dorothy A. Pedtke. *Selected List of Materials for Teachers of English to Speakers of Other Languages.* Washington, DC: Center for Applied Linguistics, 1967. 17 p. Annotated. ED 019 675.

Textbooks and cultural background materials in this list were prepared initially to assist Americans going overseas to teach English. The materials are relevant for teachers in the United States who teach English as a second language and participate in bilingual-bicultural programs. The works cited provide an indication of the variety of background and instructional materials available to teachers for the various age and achievement levels of students of English from foreign countries. The selections are arranged in two parts: Background materials in linguistics, and Methodology and instruction materials. For more comprehensive coverage the compilers recommend: *Reference List of Materials for English as a Second Language.* Part I (ED 014 723), Part II (ED 014 724), and the 1964–1968 Supplement: (ED 025 773)—all published by the Center for Applied Linguistics.

389. Poliakoff, Lorraine. *Ethnic Groups: Negroes, Spanish-Speaking, American Indians, and Eskimos.* Washington, DC: ERIC Clearinghouse on Teacher Education, 1970. 22 p. ED 044 384.

This bibliography focuses on the various kinds of preparation programs available for school personnel serving special ethnic groups. The work is arranged in three sections: Negroes, Spanish-speaking, and American Indians and Eskimos. Cited are a total of 117 documents, 33 of which are on the Spanish-speaking in the United States. Among the documents are bibliographies, manuals, programs, research reports, and reviews. The items listed were acquired and processed by the ERIC Clearinghouse on Teacher Education between July, 1968, and December, 1969. Topics of the materials for all of the groups tend to stress problems of race relations, ethnic conflicts, education of the culturally disadvantaged, curriculum, and programs. This listing serves as an introductory source and is useful for comparative studies.

390. Potts, Alfred M. *Knowing and Educating the Disadvantaged: An Annotated Bibliography.* Alamosa, CO: Center for Cultural Studies, Adams State College, 1965. 460 p. Annotated. Index.

Prepared for those who work with and teach the culturally disadvantaged, this guide focuses on the agricultural migrants. In the first section, books, articles, government publications, and audiovisual materials are arranged under selected topics which reflect major problems and issues relevant to the education of culturally disadvantaged persons. Among the topics covered are the following: Agriculture, Education, Health, Labor, Poverty, Psychology, and Testing. In the second section, complete bibliographical entries are provided, in one alphabetical list, for the 2,457 items.

In the third section there are three addenda. Addendum I is a directory of the publishers of materials listed in the bibliography. Addendum II is a list of agencies, associations, institutes, and committees with a degree of interest in the education of the culturally disadvantaged (i.e., have issued studies, field surveys, research reports, and recommendations). Addendum III lists producers and distributors of audiovisual materials included in the bibliography. The overall emphasis of this work is on education, and numerous items concern the Mexican American.

391. Prichard, Michael Thomas. *A Resource Guide for Grant Union High School Teachers Seeking to Promote an Understanding of Mexican-American Culture.* Master's thesis, Sacramento State College, 1968. 106 p. Annotated.

This guide was developed to provide local high school teachers with current resources which promote cultural understanding of the Mexican American. Included are books and articles about the Mexican American, Mexican American literature, books by Anglo-Americans which depict the Mexican Americans, and books on Mexico. The first section is the most extensive and valuable for teachers in bicultural programs. Annotations are lengthy descriptions and evaluations of the content. Appended is a directory of sources for the material listed, community resource agencies, and recommended publishers.

392. *Public Libraries and Mexican Americans: A Selected Topics Bibliography of ERIC Documents.* Las Cruces: New Mexico State University, 1977. 16 p. Annotated. ED 152 473.

Items in this bibliography are devoted to the topic of public libraries and the services they provide to Mexican Americans. The selections were published between 1970 and 1976 and were taken solely from issues of *Research in Education* and *Current Index to Journals in Education*. All of the items are specifically related to the general topic of current library service to the Mexican American community. The small number of items in this listing indicates a scarcity of research and published sources, and a general lack of attention to the subject, compared to other areas of study concerning Mexican American education.

393. Reilly, Robert P. *A Selected and Annotated Bibliography of Bicultural Classroom Materials for Mexican American Studies.* San Francisco: R & E Research Associates, 1977. 89 p. Annotated.

This bibliography attempts to list the best of the available bicultural reading and audiovisual aids for the study of the Mexican American. The materials are recommended for elementary to high school level. Most of the 258 printed sources and 49 audiovisual aids were published or produced in the 1970s. The topics covered are as follows: art, drama, history, literature, music, social studies, professional teacher resources, and bibliographies. Specifically excluded are dictionaries, histories of Mexico, and ESL material with no bicultural content. These latter items are all rather abundant and can be found in other bibliographies.

The selections in this bibliography were carefully made based on rigid guidelines. The appendixes include helpful lists of journals and newspapers, publishers and distributors—all with addresses. An additional one-page bibliography of sources consulted lists materials on the educational needs of Mexican Americans and articles on cultural pluralism.

394. Reindorp, Reginald D., Bernice M. Boswell, and George I. Sánchez. *References for Teachers of English as a Foreign Language: A Bibliography.* Austin: University of Texas Press, 1949. (Inter-American Education, Occasional Papers, no. 4). 30 p.

The emphasis in this bibliography is on resources for the teaching of English to students whose primary language is Spanish. Part I lists basic references for teachers, i.e., research monographs dealing with the subject of teaching English to foreign-language speakers. Part II lists textbooks and other instructional materials useful to the non-English speaker. Many of these include textbooks regularly used by elementary and secondary Spanish-speaking students in the United States. The third part lists firms in the United States that produce teaching materials related to the subject of the bibliography. It is outdated now but reflects the state of the literature up to 1949.

395. Reynolds, Annie. ''The Education of Spanish-Speaking Children in Five Southwestern States.'' U.S. Office of Education. *Bulletin,* 11 (1933): 61–64. Annotated.

This is one of the earliest works on the problems of ''Mexican education'' in the Southwest. The states covered are Arizona, California, Colorado, New Mexico, and Texas. Listed are journal articles and master's theses which supplement the references cited in the accompanying textual evaluation. The items appeared between 1925 and 1930. They are indicative of prevailing attitudes and prejudices of the times. Particularly noteworthy are the number of studies which discuss "retardation" among Spanish-speaking children. This study and bibliography are useful in research which compares the changing approaches to the educational development of Mexican American children in the Southwest.

396. Rosen, Carl L. *"Bibliography." In Some Needed Research Regarding the Language and Reading Instructional Problems of Spanish-Speaking Children*, pp. 14–18. (Paper presented at International Reading Association Conference, Kansas City, MO., April 30–May 3, 1969) 18 p. ED 031 384.

This short bibliography is devoted to 60 items on language and reading instruction for Spanish-speaking children. The listing includes mainly periodical articles which relate to three major areas of concern. The first area covers normative and descriptive studies of prelearning processes; in particular, analyses of home language and language base which describe bilingual style. The second area contains works on compensatory educational programs. The third area includes research in curriculum and curriculum materials modifications.

Most of the titles are relevant to the study of reading instruction for Mexican Americans since they constitute the majority of Spanish-speaking students in the United States. With a few exceptions the items were published during the 1960s.

397. _____, and Philip D. Ortego. "Language and Reading Problems of Spanish Speaking Children in the Southwest." *Journal of Reading Behavior*, 1 (Winter, 1969): 51–70.

Literature dealing with the language and reading problems of Spanish-speaking children in the Southwest is reviewed in this bibliographical essay. Mentioned and discussed are 70 books and articles published in the 1950s and 1960s. They are, for the most part, directly related to the educational achievement of Mexican American children. The two divisions of the review are subdivided into categories which relate to bilingualism, second-language instruction, language equivalence on a bilingual scale, environmental factors, reading instruction in a common curriculum, preparation for the common curriculum, and adjustments to special needs of the Spanish-speaking child.

The materials presented are useful for teacher training in bilingual-bicultural programs.

398. Rosen, Pamela, and Eleanor V. Horne. *Tests for Spanish-Speaking Children: An Annotated Bibliography*. Princeton, NJ: Educational Testing Service, 1971. 14 p. Annotated. Index. ED 056 084.

This bibliography lists and evaluates currently available testing instruments appropriate for use with Spanish-speaking children. Included are 21 tests which measure intelligence, personality, ability, and achievement. These tests were extracted from *Research in Education, Current Index of Journals in Education,* and from documents held by the Educational Testing Service. The annotations provide information concerning the purpose of each test; groups for which the tests are intended; test subdivisions or tested skills, behaviors, or competencies; administration; scoring interpretations; and standardization. This bibliography is useful in building a sample test collection and in acquainting in-service and pre-service teachers with tests for Spanish-speaking children.

399 Rugh, Patricia A., and Marlene L. Scardamalia. *An Annotated Bibliography on the Education of the Migrant Child.* Lewisburg, PA: Bucknell University, 1968. 87 p. Annotated.
This bibliography was initially prepared for the 1967 Bucknell Conference on Learning Problems of the Migrant Child and Facilitating Learning of the Migrant Child. The cited works are concerned with the migrant laborer's economic position, learning characteristics, and educational problems. They include articles, books, government reports, and pamphlets describing conditions, needs, problems; federal and state legislation on the problem; description of instructional techniques and school programs; and analysis of learning difficulties. While the selections are not all directly concerned with the Mexican migrant, many are of obvious relevancy, particularly for comparative purposes.
    This is an enlarged edition of the author's bibliography entitled *Interdisciplinary Approach to Education for Migrant Children: A Selected Bibliography,* published in 1967 (ED 036 380).

400. Sánchez, George I., and Howard Putman. *Materials Relating to the Education of Spanish-Speaking People in the United States: An Annotated Bibliography.* Austin: Institute of Latin American Studies, University of Texas, 1959. 76 p. Annotated. Index.
This is one of the better early bibliographies on the Spanish-speaking people. It covers books, articles, monographs, bulletins, pamphlets, bibliographies, and unpublished theses and dissertations on various aspects of Mexican American life in the United States. Some of the entries are of interest to other Hispanic groups too. Educational materials are emphasized although sociology, literature, and cultural works are included. A total of 882 items, published between 1931 and 1958, are listed. This bibliography is also available as a reprint from Arno Press in *Mexican American Bibliographies,* edited by Carlos Cortés.

401. Scarth, Peter, and Timothy Regan. *Bibliography for Migrant Education Programs.* Washington, DC: Educational Systems Corp., 1968. 108 p. Annotated. ED 030 052.
Consultants and project directors for migrant education programs sponsored by the Office of Economic Opportunity are assisted in selecting materials by this specially designed bibliography. The arrangement covers curriculum materials (reading, ESL, social studies, mathematics, and vocational guidance), testing instruments (reading, intelligence, achievement and vocational), cultural materials, education and career opportunities, social-personal improvement, audiovisual materials (films and filmstrips), bibliographies, catalogs, and a list of publishers. Many of the items focus on the Mexican American migrant as well as disadvantaged groups in a migrant environment.

402. Social Science Education Consortium. *Materials and Human Resources for Teaching Ethnic Studies: An Annotated Bibliography.* Boulder, CO: SSEC, 1975. (SSEC Publication, no. 184) 275 p. Annotated.
This is a recent survey of selected ethnic curriculum materials. A special section devoted to Mexican American materials is arranged in the following categories: curriculum materials, student resources, teacher resources, and films. Approximately 90 entries are directly related to the Mexican American. The grade level of the material is indicated and rated on the basis of format, realism and accuracy, intercultural understanding, and

educational quality. A list of ethnic organizations and human resources and a directory of ethnic publishers are included. This bibliography is useful for teachers and school districts in planning ethnic studies programs.

403. Spencer, Mima. *Bilingual Education for Spanish-Speaking Children: An Abstract Bibliography*. Urbana, IL: ERIC Clearinghouse on Early Childhood Education, 1974. 45 p. Annotated. ED 091 075.

Current and timely references to materials on bilingual education are provided in this bibliography. It contains 86 documents and journal articles that are listed in *Research in Education* and in *Current Index to Journals in Education*. The works are arranged in one alphabetical list without subject divisions. The selections refer to programs, issues, materials, and methodology involved in bilingual teaching. Although there is no introduction, no statement of purpose, nor criteria for the selections, the level of focus appears to be on the primary grades.

404. Suárez, Cecilia, and Roberto Cabello-Argandoña. *Early Childhood Education: A Selected Bibliography*. Los Angeles: Chicano Studies Center, University of California, 1972. 30 p.

This is a preliminary compilation of sources on the subject of early childhood education selected on the basis of their relevancy to Mexican American children. The arrangement of the material is by format: Books and monographs, Articles, ERIC documents, Theses and dissertations, Unpublished papers, and Bibliographies. More than 200 items are cited and many of these relate to other ethnic groups and minorities as well. The materials range from teacher preparation and educational psychology to curriculum aids and children's literature. This is one of the most recent and up-to-date listings on the subject.

405. Texas Education Agency. *Books on the Mexican American: A Selected Listing*. Austin: The Agency, 1972. 13 p. Annotated. ED 080 445.

Prepared for social studies teachers, young adults, and librarians, this listing was designed to assist them in obtaining appropriate books about the Mexican American. It contains three lists: books for students, books for teachers, and a directory of publishers from which the cited books can be obtained. The selections are of a general nature and date mainly from the late 1960s and early 1970s. Many of the selections focus on the life and culture of Mexican Americans, a few of the titles are more specifically about Mexico, and all are considered useful for students in the seventh to twelfth grades. The 79 titles are well annotated with content descriptions, suggested use, and occasionally the reading level.

406. Turner, Pearl, Ken Karr, and Gloria Jameson. *The Education of Mexican-American Children and Teaching English as a Second Language*. San Luis Obispo: Library, California State Polytechnic College, 1969. 18 p.

This is a sampling of materials concerning the education of Mexican American children and teaching English as a second language. The materials are located in the main library and the curriculum library of California State Polytechnic College. The items listed include children's books, curriculum materials, textbooks, and teaching aids. Also included are children's books about Mexican Americans, periodicals, documents, and ERIC materials. No statement of purpose is given nor any guidelines for the selection. Presumably it was compiled for the students and faculty in the education program at the College.

407. Tuttle, Lester, and Dennis Hooker. *An Annotated Bibliography of Migrant Related Materials.* Boca Raton: Migrant Education Center, Florida Atlantic University, 1969. 123 p. Annotated. ED 032 171.

Instructional and reference materials appropriate for use with migratory children and youth are listed in this third revised edition. The more than 800 entries have been assembled by the Migrant Education Center at Florida Atlantic University. The materials cited include articles, periodicals, pamphlets, brochures, books, films, audio tapes, curriculum aids, and research data. They are arranged in the following six categories: Health, Information on migrants and culturally disadvantaged, Curriculum materials, Guidance, Occupational, Supplementary information. Although there is no index, a coding system assists the user in identifying the content area, form, reading or interest level, and availability of each item. This work contains a great deal of material that is relevant to the study of the Mexican American.

408. University of New Mexico. Learning Materials Center. *Anita Osuna Carr Bilingual-Bicultural Collection Bibliography.* Albuquerque: The Center, 1973. 90 p.

Bilingual-bicultural materials housed in the Learning Materials Center of the College of Education at the University of New Mexico are covered in this bibliography. Part I of the collection of over 2,000 items contains materials, mostly in Spanish, in some of the following areas: Reference, Media, Art, Foreign language, Guidance, Physical education, Home economics, Language arts, Social studies, Science, Music, Mathematics, Bicultural education, and Early childhood education. Part II lists children's literature. The largest number of entries are under the category of Language arts—reading. The lengthy table of contents serves in place of an index. The arrangement is rather disorganized and the annotations are very brief content statements.

409. Villa, José. *A Preliminary Annotated Bibliography with Selected Articles about the Chicano.* San Jose, CA: San Jose Unified School District and Mexican-American Graduate Studies Department, San Jose State College, 1971. 92 p. Annotated.

This bibliography was prepared to provide teachers with useful information for the development of classroom units about Chicanos. It is arranged in the following categories: General bibliography, Readings for elementary K-6 level, Junior high, High school, and Resource guide. The Resource guide includes a list of teachers and the school district's manuals. Most of the items cited are the traditional ones but they are followed by lengthy descriptive annotations and an indication of the grade level.

The bibliography is not well prepared, even for a preliminary list. The pagination does not correlate with the table of contents and half of the work is devoted to four papers on the educational problems of Mexican Americans. Several superior sourcebooks and bibliographies have been published since 1971 and are now available to teachers. For references to some of these professional sources see *Latino Materials: A Multicultural Guide for Children and Young Adults,* by Daniel Flores Durán (Santa Barbara: ABC-Clio, 1979).

410. Watt, Lois, Myra H. Thomas, and Harriet L. Horner. *The Education of Disadvantaged Children: A Bibliography.* Washington, DC: Office of Education, U.S. Department of Health, Education, and Welfare, 1966. 32 p. Annotated. ED 011 898.

Books in the Education Materials Center of the Office of Education that are related to education and the disadvantaged child are cited in this work. The selections include all works on the topic received by the Center between 1963 and 1966. Three categories of books are mentioned: Professional resources, Elementary and secondary school textbooks, and Children's literature. Only a few of the items relate directly to Mexican Americans but, as a disadvantaged group, many are indirectly relevant. The bibliography was prepared in order to highlight new acquisitions available for examination and research at the Center.

411. Weinberg, Meyer. *The Education of the Minority Child: A Comprehensive Bibliography of 10,000 Selected Entries.* Chicago: Integrated Education Associates, 1970. 530 p. Index.

This vast compilation brings together works on the education of minority children in the United States, with a special section devoted to Spanish Americans (pp. 179–200). This section contains materials published since the 1920s and a good many articles from the Chicano press and established journals. While the education of Black children is stressed throughout most of the work, there are numerous items of interest to the Mexican American in the sections on School organization, Teachers in the classroom, Law and government, the Community, and Minorities in foreign countries—Mexico. This bibliography is scholarly in orientation and supports a broad definition of education.

412. Whittenburg, Clarice T., and George I. Sánchez. *Materials Relating to the Education of Spanish-Speaking People: A Bibliography.* Austin: University of Texas Press, 1948. (Inter-American Education, Occasional Papers, no. 2) 39 p.

Education and the Mexican American are the subjects of this early compilation which offers an historical perspective of the literature. The compilers have included a cross section of materials from the social sciences and humanities: books, articles, monographs, bulletins and pamphlets, courses of study, bibliographies, and unpublished theses. Most of the theses were completed at the University of Texas, Austin. Designed for students in the field, this work was a precursor to the 1959 edition by George I. Sánchez and Howard Putman, entitled *Materials Relating to the Education of Spanish-Speaking People in the United States: An Annotated Bibliography.*

413. Whittier College. Bilingual-Bicultural Education Program. *Bibliography of Materials.* Whittier, CA: The Program, 1971. 26 p.

This bibliography of bilingual-bicultural materials lists audiovisual materials, bilingual linguistics, Chicano studies materials, reports, journals, socio-anthropological studies, items on child development, general education, and children's books. Many items, although not directly related to the Mexican American, cover the general subjects of bilingualism and biculturalism. On the basis of this list Whittier College organized its special collection, which was later transferred to the library at California State University, Fullerton, where it is presently housed.

414. Yamamura, Sam. *An Annotated Bibliography of Books About Mexico for Use with Sixth Grade Students.* Master's thesis, Sacramento State College, 1969. 71 p. Annotated. Indexes.

The primary purpose of this bibliography is to facilitate the study of Mexico in the early grades. The selections are limited to 50 children's books on Mexico for use in the third through the ninth grades. Titles were selected from over 100 tradebooks; textbooks were excluded. They cover such topics as family life, folktales, humor, religion, science, Indians, and art. With the exception of the general, animal, and civilization books, many are stories about young Mexican boys. There are almost no selections about young girls nor biographies of famous Mexican men and women. Special features include useful annotations, suggested reading levels, and locations of titles.

# Chapter 11

# *Folklore*

Mexican American folklore, a branch of American ethnic folklore, offers a great challenge to modern scholars. The field has not been neglected but it has been viewed more in terms of the relationship with either Mexican or European culture. Although it cannot be denied that the folklore and culture of the Mexican American people, the majority of whom live in the Southwest, are intimately related to Spanish and Mexican traditions, the uniquely Mexican American aspects of the various genre and materials have not received as much attention. Differences in the folklore from the point of view of language usage, religious practices, artistic expressions, music, predominant forms, and other features, as influenced by the conflicts and contact with the American society in the United States, have not been fully explored. For a deeper understanding of these influences, it is important to have knowledge of the history of the Mexican American people in the Southwest, their religious heritage, their artistic expression, their social context in American society, and their language.

In selecting bibliographic sources for the study of the Mexican American folklore, a broad interpretation of folklore and folk culture, embracing all the material and literary forms of both the rural and urban settings, has been accepted.[1] The bibliographies in this chapter date from the 1930s to 1977 and contain published and unpublished resources from the mid-1800s to the present. They cover not only oral transmissions such as legends, tales, proverbs, riddles, jokes, and *corridos,* but also the instrumental music, dance, drama, arts, crafts, religious beliefs, festivals, foods, folk medicine, and material artifacts which have been described as "the sap and savor of a people."[2]

Two basic categories of bibliographies are available for research on Mexican American folklore: the general sources which cover all forms and genre mentioned above and the specialized sources which related to one particular aspect such as music, dance, or oral traditions.

Among the general folklore bibliographies are works which cover Mexican, Latin American, and Chicano materials. Since folklore and folk culture, similar to language, cannot be restricted by political boundaries, the sources that relate to Mexican and Latin American folklore research are essential to a full appreciation and understanding of Chicano culture, particularly in the borderlands of the Southwest. This region, although part of the United States, continues to maintain cultural ties with Mexico and Mexican folklore forms. The American folk traditions have had little influence on the folkways of

135

the people of Mexican heritage living in the Southwest. As Leo Grebler and others have pointed out, "the traditional isolation of Mexican Americans greatly limited their chances to learn about the society in which they lived."[3] This same isolation, particularly in rural areas of New Mexico or in the urban barrios of Los Angeles, has permitted the preservation or survival of traditional culture for some Chicanos. Proximity to Mexico and contact with continuous waves of immigrants has further reinforced the Mexican influence.

The second category includes specialized bibliographic sources which again emphasize the literature on the surviving traditions of the pre-urban culture: the Spanish ballads and Hispanic elements in the folk dances, drama, music, and art. Most of the books and articles found in these bibliographies focus on the Southwest or New Mexico. Two of these sources, nevertheless, deal with more contemporary research on Chicano theater and Chicano dance, drama, and music.

Certain aspects of early Mexican American culture, which some have considered "quaint and picturesque," have been a fascination to both scholars and laymen throughout the twentieth century and have dominated the literature. Relatively few sources, however, are available on the contemporary folklore of the urban barrios, such as the mural art and graffiti, the health and healing practices, the lore of school children, the protest songs of the labor unions, and the modern folk heroes. Social scientists rather than folklorists have devoted attention to these aspects of the folklore in recent years. They have learned that the character of the Mexican American people (their psychology, values, prejudices, and attitudes) has been shaped to a great extent by their customs, traditions, and folk practices. Michael Heisley's *An Annotated Bibliography of Chicano Folklore from the Southwestern United States* is one of the few sources in this chapter which provide access to the literature on the contemporary folk culture.

Over the past century most of the research relating to Mexican American folklore has been carried out by scholars located in such major institutions as the University of California, Los Angeles; Indiana University; and the University of Texas at Austin. Their research has been published in such long-standing publications as the *Journal of American Folklore*, the *American Anthopologist*, and the *Southern Folklore Quarterly*. Articles on Mexican American folklore have also appeared in newer journals such as *New Mexican Folklore Record*, *California Folklore Quarterly*, *Journal of the Folklore Institute*, *Aztlán: International Journal of Chicano Studies Research*, and *El Grito: A Journal of Contemporary Mexican American Thought*, just to cite a few. The short-lived *Abstracts of Folklore Studies*, published from 1963 to 1975, and the newer *Abstracts in Anthropology*, published since 1970, provide additional current sources on Mexican American folklore.

For other references to folklore consult the Index. The chapters on General Bibliographies, Library Guides, Audiovisual Materials, Dictionaries, and Linguistics contain related resources.

1. Américo Paredes, "Concepts About Folklore in Latin America and the United States," *Journal of the Folklore Institute*, 8 (June, 1969): 20–38.
2. Radoslav A. Tsanoff, "Folklore and Tradition in a Growing Society," in *In the Shadow of History*, Texas Folk-Lore Society Publications, no. 15, edited by J. Frank Dobie, *et al.* (Hatboro, PA: Folklore Associates, c 1939. 1966).
3. *The Mexican–American People: The Nation's Second Largest Minority*, by Leo Grebler, *et al.* (New York: The Free Press, 1970), p. 6.

415. Boggs, Ralph Steele. *Bibliografía del folklore mexicano.* México: Instituto Pan Americano de Geografía e Historia, 1939. 121 p. Annotated.
This bibliography was published to stimulate interest in Mexican folklore. It includes 1,323 items from the mid-1800s to 1939. The books and articles are listed under subjects according to the following arrangement: *Obras generales y misceláneas; Mitología; Leyendas y tradiciones; Cuentos populares; Poesía; Música, danzas y juegos; Fiestas y costumbres; Drama; Ritos y oficios, vestidos y adornos, y arquitectura; Comidas y bebidas; Creencias, brujería, medicina popular y magia; El habla popular; Refranes; Adivinanzas.* The works are in Spanish, German, French, and English from the Biblioteca Nacional, Museo Nacional, Sociedad Antonio Alzate, and private collections of Mexican folklorists.
This work is a reprint from the *Boletín Bibliográfico de Antropología Americana.* It is supplemented and updated by the annual "Folklore Bibliography," in *Southern Folklore Quarterly,* published from 1938 to 1973. Folklore and culture in the Southwest are intimately related to Mexican traditions; therefore, many of the items in this work are of interest to research on Mexican Americans.

416. _____. *Bibliography of Latin American Folklore; Tales, Festivals, Customs, Arts, Magic, Music.* Detroit: Blaine-Ethridge, 1971. (Reprint of 1940 ed., New York: H. W. Wilson.) (Inter-American Bibliographical and Library Association Publications. Series I, vol. 5) 109 p. Annotated. Indexes.
Folklore literature of all the Latin American countries is covered in this work. Over 650 entries are listed, of which 205 relate directly to Mexico. The arrangement and coverage is similar to that of Boggs's earlier bibliography on Mexico. Works in Spanish, English, French, and German published between 1880 and 1940 are cited. Topics relating to Mexico include Mythology; Legends and traditions; Folktales; Poetry, music, dance, games; Festivals and customs, Drama; Arts and crafts; Food and drink; Beliefs, witchcraft, medicine, and magic; Folk speech; Proverbs. This work is crucial for comparative studies in Hispanic folklore.

417. Campa, Arthur L. *A Bibliography of Spanish Folklore in New Mexico.* Albuquerque: University of New Mexico, 1930. (University of New Mexico Bulletin. Language Series, vol. 2, no. 3) 28 p.
Despite the title this is actually a catalog of representative types of Hispanic folklore found in the Southwest. It is the result of an attempt to identify titles of materials collected in southern Colorado and northern New Mexico. The work is divided into the following 12 forms: *Décima, Indita, Cuando, Romance, Corrido,* Folksong, *Alabado, Verso popular,* Riddles and sayings, Religious drama, Secular drama, and Folktale. Each list is preceded by a description and explanation of the genre.
This is one of Campa's earliest publications. In the following years he devoted other publications to in-depth research on the various aspects of folklore in Colorado, New Mexico, and California. His numerous studies and lists, including this one, are essential tools for research on Mexican American folklore in the Southwest.

418. Chabrán, Richard. *Folklore del Chicano*. Berkeley: Chicano Studies Library, University of California, 1974. (Selected Collections of the Chicano Studies Library, no. 3) 14 p.

Selected folklore materials relating to Mexico and the Mexican American which are located in the Chicano Studies Library at the University of California, Berkeley, are cited in this bibliography. The contents are arranged in two parts: Chicano folklore and Selected Mexican folklore. The 139 items date from 1894 to 1974. A broad definition of folklore was used in compiling this work; items from various related disciplines including anthropology, education, history, literature, linguistics, music, and medicine are listed with an emphasis on oral and literary traditions and folk medicine. Among the entries are books, articles from major American folklore journals, and unpublished student papers. The important dissertations in the field have not been included.

This is a useful source for undergraduate students and nonspecialists with an interest in the Spanish American folkways of Mexico and the Southwest.

419. Chase, Gilbert. *A Guide to the Music of Latin America*. Washington, DC: Pan American Union and Library of Congress, 1962. 411 p. Annotated. Index.

This general bibliography on Latin American music provides the framework for an historical survey. Included also are selections on folk music. The work is arranged by country and subdivided chronologically and topically. The section on Mexico is 68 pages in length. In addition, a total of ten pages are devoted to Hispanic elements in the music of the United States. This latter section deals primarily with music in the Southwest from the mission period to the present. Topics covered include Mission music; Religious folk theater; Spanish American folk songs in California, New Mexico, and Texas; Spanish American folk dances; and Biography. The extensive section on Mexico contains material that dates from the pre-Columbian period to the contemporary period. Most of the items listed are located in the Library of Congress.

In 1942 Chase published a work entitled *Bibliography of Latin American Folk Music*. Later, in 1945, he published the first edition of this guide. The second edition incorporates the findings of the earlier works and adds 1,000 more entries.

420. Córdova, Gilbert Benito. *Bibliography of Unpublished Materials Pertaining to Hispanic Culture in the New Mexico WPA Writers' Files*. Santa Fe: Bilingual-Bicultural Communicative Arts Unit, New Mexico State Department of Education, 1972. 44 p. Annotated. Indexes. ED 086 439.

Access to the collection of folklore materials in the Work Projects Administration (WPA) Writers' Project on the Hispanic Culture of New Mexico is provided in this bibliography. Included are 581 manuscripts which are now deposited in the State Record Center and Archives or at the History Library of the Museum of New Mexico. The items are arranged alphabetically in one list. Each entry includes author, title, date, contributors, number of pages or words, location, and content summaries. The documents cover all aspects of Hispanic folklore. The author and subject indexes are helpful. Topics covered include art, dance, drama, dress, customs, music and stories. This work uncovers for researchers unpublished material that has not been included in most other bibliographies.

421. Espinosa, Aurelio M., Jr. "The Field of Spanish Folklore in America."
*Southern Folklore Quarterly*, 5 (1941): 29–35.
This short bibliographical essay focuses on various branches of Spanish folklore in
America. As a state-of-the-art address it discusses sources of folktales, traditional ballads,
proverbs, riddles and *coplas*, folk music and folk drama. Works in Spanish and English
are cited under each of the above categories. In addition, Espinosa names many notable
folklorists who have made contributions in each of the areas covered. He praises the work
done by his predecessors in collecting and compiling works on folklore and claims that the
materials are of interest to anthropologists and historians as well. This paper was read
before the Popular Literature Section of the Modern Language Association in Boston,
December, 1940.

422. _____. "Spanish-American Folklore." *Journal of American Folklore*, 60
(October–December, 1947): 373–377.
A brief survey of the bibliography in the field of Spanish American folklore in the United
States from 1910 to 1947 is provided in this essay. The discussion is arranged geographically and covers New Mexico–Colorado, Puerto Rico, California, and Arizona in detail
and Texas, Louisiana, and Florida in brief. Espinosa mentions the institutions and individuals actively involved in research as well as the locations of special folklore collections. The article is particularly useful in pointing out the areas in need of research at that
time and the lack of bibliographic tools and publication outlets comparable to the *Language Dissertations* published by the Linguistic Society of America.

423. Espinosa, José E. "Bibliography." In *Saints in the Valleys: Christian
Sacred Images in the History, Life and Folk Art of Spanish New Mexico*,
p. 101–108. Albuquerque: University of New Mexico Press, 1967. 122 p.
This specialized bibliography contains primary and secondary sources for the study of
Spanish religious folk art of New Mexico. The list is arranged in three parts with subdivi-
sions. Part one consists of the Principal Archives which contain resources on the topic.
Part two is the Manuscript Sources from the archives listed. Part three is a list of Printed
Works, both books and articles. This final section is the most extensive and is arranged in
the following categories: Spanish and Mexican backgrounds; New Mexican history; Mexican colonial sacred art in New Mexico; Christian iconography and hagiography selected;
Encyclopedias; and Reviews of the 1960 edition. Two hundred twenty-eight entries are
included among the printed works. One reviewer has pointed out that the bibliography
contains no mention of the Archives of the Archdiocese of Santa Fe which contains
valuable manuscripts on sacred folk art.

424. Haywood, Charles. *Bibliography of North American Folklore and
Folksong*. 2nd rev. ed. New York: Dover Publications, 1961. 2 vols.
Annotated. Index.
Folklore and folksong studies in North America are cited in this bibliography. Volume I is
an alphabetically arranged list covering bibliographies, general studies, collections of
folklore and folk dance, folktales, legends, customs, beliefs, superstitions, folk medicine,
proverbs, riddles, speech, place names, dances, children's rhymes, games, arrangements,
and records. Of interest to Mexican American Studies is the Spanish American section
(pp. 593–606). Volume II includes a comprehensive index and an index supplement of

composers, arrangers, and performers. This work is a revised edition of a previous one published in 1951 by Greenberg, Publisher. The section on Spanish American folklore contains no substantive changes or additions.

425. Heisley, Michael. *An Annotated Bibliography of Chicano Folklore from the Southwestern United States.* Los Angeles: Center for the Study of Comparative Folklore and Mythology, University of California, 1977. 188 p. Annotated. Indexes.

This is the first bibliography that refers specifically to Chicano folklore. Included are 1,028 books, articles, theses, and dissertations from 1937 to the present. The compiler has limited the scope to the Southwestern states: California, Arizona, Colorado, New Mexico, and Texas. The first eight sections cover Bibliographies, indexes, and general works; Narrating traditions; Traditional speech; Traditional customs, rituals, healing practices, and beliefs; Traditional drama and *teatro;* Traditional games, play, and play rituals; Traditional art, architecture, technology, foodways, and clothing. Published and unpublished works are listed separately under each category. A final section on Mexican folklore and customs presents an overview of related and relevant materials. Author, geographical and subject indexes contribute to the overall excellence of this work.

426. Herzog, George. "Research in Primitive and Folk Music in the United States." American Council of Learned Societies. *Bulletin,* 24 (April, 1936): 45–97. Annotated.

Folk music in the United States is discussed in this survey and guide to special collections. Following the introductory note is a section on facilities and materials arranged in four parts: a list of folk music collections, a descriptive list of the contents of those collections, a list of unpublished manuscript melodies, and a bibliography of the most important works on folk music. Various collections that contain materials relevant to Mexican Americans are cited, such as those of the New Mexico Folklore Society and the Texas Folklore Society. Items from these and other collections that pertain to Hispanic American folklore are described under the heading Spanish-American, U. S.

The bibliography is subdivided in the following categories: United States, White; Latin American, U. S.; United States, Negro; Creole; Nova Scotia and Newfoundland; West Indian Negro. The Latin American listing includes only 13 major books and articles published between 1893 and 1934. These selections are devoted strictly to folksongs and music in New Mexico, Texas, California, and the Southwest.

427. Huerta, Jorge A. *A Bibliography of Chicano and Mexican Dance, Drama, and Music.* Oxnard, CA: Colegio Quetzalcoatl, 1972. 59 p.

This is perhaps the most current bibliography on Mexican American dance, drama, and music. The publications are from the 1930s to the early 1970s. Its preparation was motivated by a desire to recognize the efforts of Chicanos in the performing arts. Each art form (dance, drama, music) is subdivided by time periods: Pre-Columbian, Mexican, and Aztlán. Books, journal articles, recordings, and plays are listed separately in each period. Nearly 700 works that describe the dance, rhythms, legends, plays, and musical instruments of pre-conquest Indians to present-day Chicanos are cited. Location symbols or call numbers for works in the University of Santa Barbara Library are provided. This selective reference work is one of the few sources available on Chicanos in the creative arts.

428. \_\_\_\_\_. "Chicano Teatro: A Background." *Aztlán*, 2 (Fall, 1971): 63–78.
A bibliographical essay and a selected listing of works on the development and roots of the Chicano theater movement are included in this article. Particular emphasis is on the Southwest. The bibliography contains books and articles listed under Pre-Columbian drama, Mexican drama, Latin American drama, Drama in the Southwest, *Teatro campesino*, Other *teatros*, and Sources consulted. The titles cited present the historical development of Mexican dramatic art as it relates to the regions of the Southwest. Works in Spanish and English are among the sources listed. This is the only bibliography found that relates exclusively to Chicano theater.

429. Igo, John. *Los Pastores: An Annotated Bibliography with an Introduction*. San Antonio, TX: San Antonio College Library, 1967. Annotated.
The primary aim of this bibliography is to list the manuscript sources and related materials of *Los Pastores*, the Spanish-language Christmas drama of Mexico and the American Southwest. Most of the 200 items cited are available in the San Antonio College Library or at the University of Texas, Austin. The collection contains romanticized folklore about *Los Pastores*, literature and criticism concerning the performances, and texts of the drama. The materials are arranged in eleven categories: Manuscripts and typescripts, Books containing texts, Theses and dissertations, Books, Parts of books, Periodical articles, Unpublished articles, Manuscript and printed music, *Las Posadas*, and other cycle materials, Nonbook materials, and Materials in Spanish.

*Los Pastores* is an integral part of the social life and customs of the Hispanic people in certain parts of the Southwest and an important part of the folkdrama tradition of Mexican Americans. As the most comprehensive list available on the topic, it is a valuable contribution to the folklore bibliography of the Southwest.

430. Lomax, Alan, and Sidney R. Cowell. *American Folksong and Folklore; A Regional Bibliography*. New York: Progressive Education Association, 1942. 59 p. Annotated.
This bibliography focuses on the regional folkmusic and lore of the North, West, and South. The works included date from 1907 to 1940. Books, pamphlets, and a few articles are arranged under 13 topical and geographical headings. Material relating to Spanish Americans is in Section X. This portion contains music, songs, lyrics, dance, drama, and a few works on the folklore and social setting, particularly of California and New Mexico. Annotations indicate the number and type of songs, the language (English or Spanish), and whether musical notations or accompaniments are included.

The years of research and extensive use of the material by the compilers are reflected in the careful selection of titles and in the complete and accurate entries.

431. Miller, Margaret A. *Ethnic Dance: A Selected Bibliography*. Sacramento: Library, California State College, 1970. (Bibliographic Series, no. 6) 9 p.
Prepared to assist the library's patrons in making more effective use of the collection, this selected bibliography consist of works on ethnic dance. Ethnic dance is defined and contrasted with other types such as folk dance. Call numbers are given. Most of the materials are from the late 1930s and early 1940s. Books and periodical articles are listed under the following headings: Bibliographies, General references, Afro-American, American Indian, Asian, and Mexican American. Six titles are listed in this latter section

which relate primarily to New Mexican and Mexican folkdance. The bibliographies and general sources listed should be consulted for more information on Mexican Americans.

432. Moore, Rosebud. *A Critical Bibliography of Spanish Ballads in Spanish American Oral Tradition.* Master's thesis, Stanford University, 1935. 110 p.

This early thesis includes a classified guide and bibliography of all available Spanish ballads found in the oral tradition of Hispanic America. Fifty-three traditional ballads in over 226 versions are documented as to bibliographic source and classified according to motives, elements, themes, and origin in Spanish and European tradition. The first of three chapters contains the numerical classification and the list of versions by geographical regions. The second chapter classifies the variations by motives or elements and cites the bibliographic source. The final chapter discusses the general themes of each ballad and the Spanish and European roots. Ballads from New Mexico and California, identified by Arthur L. Campa and Aurelio M. Espinosa between 1915 and 1933, are cited throughout the work.

433. Rael, Juan B. "New Mexico Folklore Bibliography." *New Mexico Folklore Record,* 3 (1948-1949): 38-39. Annotated.

Sources on New Mexican folklore are mentioned in this short bibliography. The subjects covered are customs, songs, stories of saints, religious feasts, traditional herbs, remedies, and the *Penitentes.* Twenty-eight books, articles, and newspaper reports are cited with brief content descriptions. Review references are given for a few of the works. The sources date principally from 1948 with a few from 1947 and 1949. It is probably one of the earliest bibliographic works on New Mexican folklore in the annual publication of the New Mexico Folklore Society.

434. Robb, John Donald. "The J. D. Robb Collection of Folk Music Recordings." *New Mexico Folklore Record,* 7 (1952-1953): 6-20.

This is a listing of 1,096 recordings of Hispanic, Indian, and Anglo-New Mexican folk music. The collection was developed between 1942 to 1952 and housed in the Library of the University of New Mexico. The materials are available on a restricted basis to scholars and musicians. Hispanic melodies predominate since Robb concentrated his search in this area. A variety of types of folk music are included, some which originated in Spain or Mexico and some from New Mexico. Among the recordings are *romances, cuandos, décimas, canciones, corridos,* religious plays, religious ceremonial dances, and social dance tunes.

Each entry includes the title of the melody, performer, place, and date. The items are arranged in chronological order. An album of selections from this collection entitled *Spanish Mexican Folk Music of New Mexico* was released by Folkways Records and Service Corporation of New York.

435. Robe, Stanley L. *Index of Mexican Folktales Including Narrative Texts from Mexico, Central America, and the Hispanic United States.* Berkeley: University of California Press, 1973. (Folklore Studies, no. 26) 276 p. Index.

This is the first index to the traditional folk narratives of Mexican origin which are derived from European culture. Tales from indigenous tradition have been excluded for practical reasons. Contributing to the collection are tales from the well-established Hispanic areas of southern Colorado and New Mexico and certain Mexican settlements of more recent origin and urban character in other parts of the Southwestern United States. The classification system devised by Antti Aarne and revised by Stith Thompson in *The Types of the Folktale* was used as a guide by Robe.

The work is arranged in four sections: Animal tales, Ordinary folktales, Jokes and anecdotes, and Formula tales. Each section has numerous subdivisions. Descriptions of the tale types are in English, thus facilitating use by folklore scholars outside the Hispanic area. An extensive bibliography (pp. xv–xxi) on the Hispanic folktale accompanies the work. Approximately 145 entries are cited including indexes, reference devices, and narrative collections.

436. Roberts, Don L. "'The Archive of Southwestern Music.'" *The Folklore and Folk Music Archivist*, 9 (Winter, 1966–67): 47–52.
Collections in the Archive of Southwestern Music, housed in the Fine Art Library of the University of New Mexico at Albuquerque, are described in this article. The collections contain recordings of indigenous music of Indian, Spanish, Mexican and Anglo origins. Thirteen special segments of the archive are briefly summarized. Among these are the John Donald Robb collection of 2,200 songs from New Mexico, the majority being Spanish and Mexican in nature; the Rubén Cobos collection of Spanish and Mexican music, particularly strong in materials on the *Penitentes;* the Richard Stark collection of *velorios* and other Spanish American music; and other collections relating to Indian and Anglo folk and ceremonial music.

At the time this article was published the archive had been established for two years and was moderately funded. Numerous items were awaiting more detailed cataloging and description. Several of the collections described seem of immense value to students and scholars of Mexican and Mexican American folk music.

437. Segovia, Eloisa M., and Cindy Clayman Wesley. *Folklóricos regionales de México: A Textbook of Mexican Folk Dances.* Colton, CA: C and E Prensa, 1975. 200 p.
This listing of 38 dances represents all the various regions of Mexico. Each dance includes title, area of origin, special notes or equipment needed, basic steps, sequence and formation, history, costume description, musical recordings available. The dances are arranged according to level—beginning, intermediate, and advanced. The work is enhanced by illustrations; maps showing the place of origin in Mexico; a list of sound recordings; and a bibliography of selected readings on folk dances of Mexico. This is a highly useful text for dance groups or classes.

438. Simmons, Merle E. *A Bibliography of the "Romance" and Related Forms in Spanish America.* Bloomington: Indiana University, 1963. (Indiana University Folklore Series, no. 18) 396 p. Annotated. Index.
Popular narrative poems and songs of Spanish America, known as *romances* and *corridos,* are the subject of this excellent working bibliography. The entries are arranged within chapters by country and cover the scholarship up to the early 1960s. Items relating

to the folk narratives of the Southwest are found in the chapter on Mexico (pp. 203–287). As the compiler has pointed out, "Mexican folklore is not delimited, of course, by political boundaries of present-day Mexico . . ." Over 550 works are cited, including books, articles, theses and dissertations, chapters within books, and unpublished works which contain texts of the narratives and songs, bibliographies, studies, and folklore collections.

Because the systematic study of this genre in the United States was undertaken quite early in he century by Charles F. Lummis, Aurelio M. Espinosa, and their followers, many of the sources are directly pertinent to the folklore of the Mexican American.

439. Tully, Marjorie F., and Juan B. Rael. *An Annotated Bibliography of Spanish Folklore in New Mexico and Southern Colorado.* Albuquerque: University of New Mexico Press, 1950. 124 p. Annotated. Index.

An extensive guide to folklore of the Southwest; it includes titles published prior to 1948. The selection concentrates on books, book reviews, and articles located in the libraries of Stanford and University of California, Berkeley. Excluded are manuscripts in the possession of individuals. Approximately 700 entries cover such subjects as customs, dances, witchcraft, religious celebrations, drama, architecture, music, anthropology, and history. All items examined by the compilers are annotated with an evaluation of the folklore content. Those not examined are treated with brief entries only. An earlier version of this work was prepared as Tully's master's thesis at Stanford University. It was reprinted by Arno Press in 1977.

# Chapter 12

# *History*

Prior to the late 1960s, when courses on Mexican American history were first offered, historians had produced few sources to support work in the field. In filling the void, teachers and researchers resorted to materials from other disciplines, such as Sociology, Economics, and Anthropology, and relied heavily on publications pertaining primarily to the history of Mexico and of the Southwest. Subsequently, however, an impressive body of historical writings were produced as the field gained wider acceptance and increasingly attracted serious scholars. These developments are thoroughly documented and substantiated by Juan Gómez-Quiñones and Luís Leobardo Arroyo in "On the State of Chicano History: Observations on Its Development, Interpretations, and Theory, 1970-1974," a bibliographical essay included in this chapter, and by Carlos E. Cortés in "Chicanos: Historiography of a Conquered/Immigrant People."[1]

Although there have been some notable monographic studies published in recent years, most of the work in Mexican American history has appeared in periodical articles and dissertations. *El Grito, Aztlán,* and the *Journal of Mexican American History* have served as the main outlets for this research. Several other journals of greater circulation and coverage, such as the *Western Historical Quarterly, Labor History,* and the *Journal of Ethnic Studies* have also published articles of historical relevance to the Mexican Americans but only on an irregular basis. Occasionally a few journals—the *International Migration Review, Social Science Quarterly,* and *Pacific Historical Review*—have dedicated entire issues to Mexican Americans and their history.

In addition to the periodical articles, the teaching and research of Mexican American History are supported by an array of unpublished sources which include an extensive number of theses, dissertations, conference papers, and graduate students' research papers. Added to these should be *The Mexican American* and *The Chicano Heritage,* two reprint collections by Arno Press. These include previously published writings, new works, and original anthologies on a variety of topics of historical significance.

The first bibliographies and bibliographical essays specifically devoted to Mexican American history were published by a handful of scholars based in California. The bibliographical essays review the historiography and attempt to define the nature of Mexican American history by tracing its origins, establishing basic outlines, and analyzing its development. Of the published bibliographies, only two were issued separately. The others supplement texts or anthologies.

Most of the bibliographies in this chapter cover a limited period of Mexican American history and relate to a specific topic. A few others contain general sources from the Spanish colonial past to the present but these are somewhat superficial and more useful as introductory research guides. One exception is Luís Leobardo Arroyo's recent bibliography that demonstrates a new trend. His work, limited to historical writings published between 1970 and 1975, reflects the new scholarship and covers four centuries of Mexican American history.

Aside from the works discussed above, this chapter also contains a selection of background bibliographies and guides which place Mexican American history in a broader context and provide the foundation upon which it is built. Mexican American history is a field carved out of the historical experiences of several institutions, peoples, and political entities. As such, it is linked to areas outside its immediate domain. There are political links to imperial Spain from the 1500s to 1821, to Mexico from 1821 to 1848, and to the United States from 1848 to the present. The history of the Catholic Church in the Southwest, the missions, land grants, and contemporary Mexico are all intertwined with the history of Mexican Americans.

Among the background bibliographies are those which contain extensive selections of the literature about the Southwest, published between the sixteenth and twentieth centuries. Other bibliographies concentrate exclusively on sources relating to the history of the individual states of Texas, New Mexico, Arizona, and California. California has received the most attention from well-known book collectors and bookmen who compiled comprehensive works in the early part of the twentieth century.

Several special bibliographies of the background type identify sources on the Spanish press, the missions, the Church, the *Penitentes,* and the Mexican revolution and several works list the land grants of California and Texas. Other highly significant works in this chapter are the guides to the Spanish and Mexican archives, the land grant papers of New Mexico, the archives of the states of Texas, Arizona, and California, and the documents concerning the Southwest in the archives of Seville and Mexico City.

The *Historical Records Survey* publications have not been included in this chapter, with the exception of one which pertains substantially to the Mexicans of California. These works, gathered during the Depression years as part of the Work Projects Administration (WPA) programs, contain important primary source materials. They cover a vast number of documents but a thorough search should yield a great deal of information on the Mexican Americans in the manuscript collections, holdings of county archives, and public vital statistics for each of the states of the Southwest.

Two new works are in progress which will greatly facilitate research on Mexican American history and culture. The first item is the *Dictionary of Mexican American History,* coedited by Matt Meier and Feliciano Rivera. It will be published by Greenwood Press in 1980. The second is *The U.S.—Mexico Borderlands Sourcebook* which is mentioned in the footnote below. The publisher for the latter has not been announced. Although these forthcoming works are not bibliographies, historiographical and bibliographical essays will be included in each.

Additional historical works are found under the heading of History in the chapters on General Bibliographies and Library Guides. Occasionally, history materials are also found in the bibliographies in the chapters on Labor and Social and Behavioral Sciences.

1. Carlos E. Cortés, "Chicanos: Historiography of a Conquered/Immigrant People," *The Immigration History Newsletter,* 9 (November, 1977): 1-5. A similar article, by the same author, entitled "The New Chicano Historiography," is included in the forthcoming work *The U.S.-Mexico Borderlands Sourcebook,* edited by Ellwyn R. Stoddard, Richard L. Nostrand, and Jonathan P. West.

440. Arroyo, Luís Leobardo. *A Bibliography of Recent Chicano History Writings, 1970-1975.* Los Angeles: University of California, 1975. 45 p.
This is a bibliography of scholarly materials concerning Chicano history published between 1970 and 1975. The citations include some books and dissertations but most are periodical articles published in the United States. The chronological arrangement facilitates the search for particular items. The eight sections are arranged as follows: general works, historiographical and interpretative works, 1598-1822, 1822-1848, 1848-1900, 1900-1941, 1941-1974, and bibliographies.
This is one of the most recent bibliographies that brings together works related exclusively to history. It is unique in that it points out the trends in Mexican American historiography and a revival of interest in Mexican American history.

441. Bolton, Herbert. "Materials for Southwestern History in the Central Archives of Mexico." *American Historical Review,* 13 (1908): 510-527. Annotated.
Sources of early Southwestern history, prior to 1821, contained in the Archivo General, the Museo National, and the Biblioteca Nacional in Mexico City are discussed in this bibliographical essay. It describes the various holdings and their importance to the study of the Southwest. The essay also suggests the location of rich sources of materials for the post-1821 period in the Secretarías de Relaciones Exteriores, Guerra, and Fomento, on such topics as the Anglo-American colonization, the political disturbances in California and New Mexico between 1830 and 1840, and the Mexican-American War. Despite the date of this work it is still a valuable research aid for those concerned with the history of the Spanish Mexicans in the Southwest prior to 1848.

442. California. Office of the Surveyor General. "Corrected Report of Spanish and Mexican Grants in California, Complete to August 1, 1890." *Report of the Surveyor-General of the State of California, from August 1, 1888 to August 1, 1890,* pp. 41-59. (Sacramento, 1890)
This report serves as an updated register of land grants in California which were made by Spanish or Mexican authorities. The chart records approximately 600 grants which were given to Spanish Mexicans, Anglo-Americans and church officials. The information provided includes the name of the grant, confirmee, area, condition of the title, location, and number corresponding to the General Land Office Map. The register is arranged alphabetically by the name of the grants and is complete up to 1890.
Various earlier lists of land grants and supplements for California are found in preceding issues of the *Reports of the Surveyor-General of the State of California.* A list of land grants arranged by county appears in the 1879-1880 report, pages 33-54.
The land grants, most of which were owned by Spanish-surnamed Californians, are useful in historical, geographical, and genealogical research. The lists of the grants are available in large research collections, the California State Library, and a few can be purchased in microform. They are relatively neglected and untapped primary sources but

crucial to an understanding of the socioeconomic structure of California during the nineteenth century.

443. Carrol, H. Bailey. "Texas County Histories." *Southwestern Historical Quarterly*, 45 (1941-1942): 74-98, 164-187, 260-275, 341-361.
This is the first bibliography of histories of Texas counties, appearing in four consecutive issues of the *Southwestern Historical Quarterly*. The work was designed to offer a starting point for teachers, students, and laymen seeking historical information on the state. Each of the lists is arranged alphabetically by county. Books, pamphlets, theses, and articles are included. Most of the histories are of the reminiscent type. Those from counties with a large Mexican population are quite significant for historical and genealogical research on Mexican Americans in Texas.

444. Castañeda, Carlos Eduardo. *A Report on the Spanish Archives in San Antonio, Texas*. San Antonio: Yanaguana Society, 1937. 167 p. Index.
The Spanish archives located in the Bexar County Clerk's Office are indexed in this work. The materials consist of documents of the City of San Antonio extending from the time of its founding in the 1730s to the end of the Mexican rule in the 1830s. These documents were retained for legal purposes by the County Clerk's Office when most of the Bexar County archives were turned over to the University of Texas in 1896. Among the more than 2,000 documents are manuscripts related to land grants, deeds of sale, wills and estates, protocols, official correspondence between the officers of San Antonio and the home government, laws, decrees, royal orders, etc. There are also records of several Texas missions. The documents are listed in chronological order with a brief description of the type of material and the contents.
   A concise but informative history of San Antonio introduces the work and places the documents in their historical context. For additional information on the state of the archives, researchers should consult the work prepared by Richard G. Santos, *A Preliminary Report on the Archival Project in the Office of the County Clerk of Bexar County*.

445. Chapman, Charles Edward. *Catalogue of Materials in the Archivo General de Indias for the History of the Pacific Coast and the American Southwest*. Berkeley: University of California Press, 1919. 755 p. Annotated. Index.
This catalogue of 207 *Legajos* from the Archives of Seville contains 6,257 documents relating to the history of the Pacific Coast and the American Southwest. The majority of the documents concentrate on California with only a few hundred documents representing New Mexico, Texas, and Arizona. Each entry has a classification number, date, place, author, description or annotation, and other technical information. The chronological arrangement extends from 1597 to 1821. This guide, along with Ralph E. Twitchell's *Spanish Archives of New Mexico*, the Collection of Spanish Documents at the University of Texas, and the Bancroft Collection at Berkeley constitutes one of the best sources of primary materials on the Spanish period in the Southwest.

446. Chavarría, Jesús. "A Précis and a Tentative Bibliography on Chicano History." *Aztlán*, 1 (Spring, 1970): 133-141.
A discussion/outline of Chicano history and a bibliography are combined in this article. The first part proposes guidelines for the teaching of Chicano history as a preliminary

contribution to the ongoing debate regarding this field of study. The second part includes approximately 72 works which the author considers useful in covering topics in his outline. The works cited include books and articles dealing with subjects ranging from the pre-Hispanic period to the present. The selections are arranged in four sections corresponding to the course outline: Part I, Introduction to Chicano History; Part II, Mesoamerican Origins to the Independence; Part III, The Emergence of the Chicano, 1821-1900; and Part IV, The 20th Century and the Dawning of Consciousness. The sample course syllabus and bibliography are useful for teachers and students in Chicano Studies programs.

447. Chávez, Fray Angélico. *Archives of the Archdiocese of Santa Fe, 1678-1900*. Washington, DC: Academy of American Franciscan History, 1957. 283 p. Index.

This extensive calendar of over 3,000 mission documents and diocesan materials housed in the Archdiocesan archives of Santa Fe, New Mexico, includes documents dating from 1678 to 1900. The sources are classified in several categories: loose documents, books of patents, books of accounts, books of baptisms, books of marriages, and books of burials. Each entry generally includes the date, place where issued, names of individuals, type of document, and size.

This calendar is important for historical and geneological research in New Mexico. An appendix lists names of clergymen obtained from Ministration Registers. The author and subject index provides adequate access to the documents.

448. Colley, Charles C. *Documents of Southwestern History: A Guide to the Manuscript Collections of the Arizona Historical Society*. Tucson: Arizona Historical Society, 1972. 233 p. Annotated. Indexes.

A guide to one of the largest collections of historical materials on the history of Arizona, Northern Mexico, and the Southwest is provided in this work. The historical records relate to Spanish and Mexican colonization and culture, government, religious and social organization, mining, ranching, transportation, communications, business, biography, military, and Indians. Not included in the guide are the other holdings of the Arizona Historical Society: the more than 40,000 books and pamphlets, journals, thousands of photographs, newspapers, maps, and oral history materials. The entries of documents listed include letters, diaries, record books, decrees, legal cases, essays, etc. Most of the documents date from the 1800s, with a few from the 1600s, up to the late 1960s. Many of the documents are in Spanish by prominent Hispanic Americans from Arizona and northern Mexico. Included also is a particularly large collection of biographical files relating to individuals who arrived in Arizona prior to the Civil War. A list of the individuals follows the entry; many of the names are of Spanish origin. The biographical collection was compiled by Carl Trumbull Hayden, a former U. S. Senator of Arizona. The sources cited in this guide are rich in materials relating to the early history of Mexican Americans in Arizona and neighboring states.

449. Connor, Seymour V. "A Preliminary Guide to the Archives of Texas." *Southwestern Historical Quarterly*, 59 (January, 1956): 255-334. Annotated.

This is a catalogue of Texas history materials accumulated by the state government since

1835. The document entries are arranged in alphabetical order under the department or issuing agency as designated on each file. In view of the role Texas has played in the history of the Southwest and Mexico, many of the items mentioned are relevant to Mexican American studies. Excluded from the archives of Texas are the records of the General Land Office, the Attorney General's Office and the Court System. As the title indicates, this is an incomplete and initial effort to prepare a catalog of the Texas archives.

450. Cortéz, Rubén, and Joseph Navarro. "Mexican American History: A Critical Selective Bibliography." *The Journal of Mexican-American History,* 1 (Fall, 1970): 68–86. Annotated.
An excellent basic reference to Mexican American history materials in Spanish and English covering the period 1848–1970; it is thorough, critical, and selective. The first edition was published by the Mexican American Historical Society in 1969. Both editions arrange materials under the following headings: Background; Mexican American History: 1848–1970; and Non-Historical Sources. New items not listed in the earlier edition are marked with an asterisk.

451. Corwin, Arthur F. "Mexican Immigration History, 1900–1970: Literature and Research." *Latin American Research Review,* 2 (Summer, 1973): 3–24.
This article offers a superb review of the existing bibliography on Mexican immigration up to 1973; it analyzes studies by U. S. historians and social scientists, contains works which describe the Mexican position, points out research opportunities in the study of Mexican immigration, and cites bibliographical aids. This bibliographical essay is most helpful to students in selecting a topic and in initiating their research on immigration history.

452. Cowan, Robert Ernest. *A Bibliography of the History of California and the Pacific West, 1510–1906.* Together with the text of John W. Dwinelle's address on the acquisition of California by the United States of America. Columbus, OH: Long's College Book Co., 1952. 279 p. Annotated. Indexes.
This is a reprint of the 1914 edition published in San Francisco by the Book Club of California. Over a period of 20 years the compiler studied and collected California bibliography. At that time no complete bibliography on California had been published. This work, although only selective, includes 1,000 of the 7,000 most important printed sources on California and the Pacific West from 1510 to 1909. Excluded are documents, reports of institutions or corporations, speeches, addresses and ephemera. The sources cover the discovery, exploration, colonization, and evangelization of California, the period after 1848, the Gold Rush, the formation of state and local governments, Mexican land claims, and the early literature.
The arrangement is alphabetical by author. A section of supplemental bibliographic notes for the works cited is appended. The later revised and enlarged edition of this work covers California exclusively up to 1930.

453. _____. *A Bibliography of the Spanish Press of California, 1833–1845.* San Francisco, 1919. 31 p. Annotated.
The purpose of this bibliography is to provide a list of excessively rare specimens of early printed documents in California. Most of the documents are official proclamations of decrees, government policies, change of administrations, and assumptions of office. They are arranged chronologically from 1833 to 1845. Location symbols are given. Two thirds of these materials can be found in the Bancroft collection at the University of California, Berkeley. The annotations summarize the content and describe the physical characteristics of each item.

For Mexican American history this list is a valuable source of information for the period just prior to the transfer of California to United States jurisdiction.

454. _____, and Robert Granniss Cowan. *A Bibliography of the History of California, 1510–1930.* Los Angeles: Torrez Press, 1964. 4 vols. in 1. Annotated. Index.
The first edition of this work was published in 1933. It was inspired by the desire to update an earlier bibliography by Robert E. Cowan published in 1914. This title is essentially a different work; it covers California exclusively, adds new material, and extends the coverage to 1930. The plan of the work covers the same topics as the 1914 bibliography mentioned above. Volumes I and II contain the bibliographic entries; Volume III is the title, subject, and chronological indexes; Volume IV, added by R. G. Cowan in 1964 at the time of reprinting, contributes supplemental materials which "fill the gaps that time and discoveries have made."

This work and the 1914 bibliography are undoubtedly two of the most valuable tools for students of California history.

455. Cowan, Robert Granniss. *Ranchos of California: A List of Spanish Concessions, 1775–1822, and Mexican Grants, 1822–1846.* Fresno, CA: Academy Library Guild, 1956. 151 p.
A register of the land grants given to settlers in California between 1775 and 1846; 672 grants and concessions are listed. Each entry includes the name or names of the grant, the county where it was located, the names of the grantees, the date it was established, and the size of the grant. In addition, names of claimants after 1848 are included with the size of the claim and the date it was confirmed or patented. Appended are a list of the grantees, a list of the claimants, a county index, a chronological list of grants, a list of Spanish and Mexican governors, and a glossary of Spanish terms. This work is helpful for historical and genealogical research for the periods prior to 1848.

456. Coy, Owen C. *Guide to the County Archives of California.* Sacramento: California State Printing Office, 1919. 622 p. Annotated. Index.
This work is a guide to the county archives and a handbook. Part 1 deals with the care and use of the archives and Part 2, the largest, is the guide. Under the latter section the 59 counties are presented in alphabetical order and the records contained in their archives are listed according to the respective office such as County Clerk, Recorder, Superintendent of Schools, and the four fiscal officers—Auditor, Treasurer, Assessor, and Tax Collector. The period covered by this survey is approximately 1848 to 1919. Many of the records on naturalization, marriage, business, and schools contain a wealth of information on the early Mexican American communities in the State of California.

457. Díaz, Albert James. *A Guide to the Microfilm of Papers Relating to New Mexico Land Grants.* Albuquerque: University of New Mexico Press, 1960. 102 p.

Microfilmed records of land grants in New Mexico are listed in this classified guide. The work is divided into eight sections and consists of documents possessed by or housed in the U.S. Bureau of Land Management, Santa Fe, New Mexico; in the General Land Office of the National Archives; and in the National Archives Regional Office, Denver, Colorado.

Designed primarily as a finding device, it lists documents in the following categories—documents described in Ralph E. Twitchell's *Spanish Archives of New Mexico;* various indexes and record books kept prior to the establishment of the office of Surveyor General; records of the Surveyor General of New Mexico; and records of the Court of Private Land Claims. It has, in addition, an introduction which summarizes and describes the arrangement of the papers in 23 sections; an index to claims adjudicated by the U. S. Surveyor General and the U. S. Court of Private Land Claims; a reel-by-reel listing of the documents; and a selected bibliography. The selected bibliography constitutes an excellent aid to the study of the land grant problem in New Mexico.

458. Drake, Eugene B. *Jimeno's and Hartnell's Indexes of Land Concessions, from 1830 to 1846; also Toma de razón, or Registry of Land Titles for 1844–1845; Approvals of Land Grants by the Territorial Deputation and Departmental Assembly of California from 1835 to 1846; and A List of Unclaimed Grants Compiled from the Spanish Archives in the U.S. Surveyor-General's Office.* San Francisco: Kenny and Alexander, 1861. (Microfiche ed. by Lost Cause Press, no. 70, 841–843) 68 p.

This work, which has been reproduced on microfiche by the Lost Cause Press, brings together four earlier sources on land grants in California prior to the Gold Rush. Many individuals of Spanish surname are mentioned in these works. The first part consist of indexes to land grants made in California between 1830 and 1846. Included are the names of the grants, dates, and grantees. These indexes were found among the Spanish and Mexican Archives in the U.S. Surveyor General's Office. The second part is a registry of land titles for the years 1844–1845 and known as the "Toma de razón." Approximately 120 titles are listed with the names of the grantee, date, and location. The third document is a list of 279 land grants, owners' names, dates, and the final determination of California's Territorial Deputation and Departmental Assembly with regard to approval or rejection of the titles. The fourth and final document is a list of 44 unclaimed grants and concessions including the name of the grantee, name of the land grant, date, and location of the title.

This is one of several useful sources on land grants in the Southwest that serve as primary materials in historical and genealogical research of the Mexican period.

459. Elliot, Claude. *Theses on Texas History: A Check List of Theses and Dissertations in Texas History Produced in the Departments of History of Eighteen Texas Graduate Schools and Thirty-three Graduate Schools Outside of Texas, 1907–1952.* Austin: The Texas State Historical Association, 1955. 280 p. Annotated. Indexes.

This survey of M.A. theses and Ph.D. dissertations on Texas history, from 18 Texas Graduate Schools and 33 out-of-state schools, covers the period from 1907 to 1957.

Identified are 652 works dealing with topics in history and other disciplines ranging from the Spanish period to the twentieth century. Each entry includes author, title, degree obtained, year, length of work, institution, and abstract. It is an invaluable aid to scholars since much of the early research on the Mexican American has not been published. It is also an important source for students and thesis directors seeking to identify new research topics and to avoid duplication. Author and subject indexes are provided.

460. Gaer, Joseph. *Bibliography of California Literature: Pre-Gold Rush Period.* New York: Burt Franklin, 1970. (Reprint of 1935 ed., New York: Lenox Hill) (Burt Franklin: Bibliography and Reference, no. 389. American Classics in History and Social Science, no. 164) 69 p.
Included in this bibliography are works in Spanish, French, Dutch, German, and English, written and published up to 1849, that relate to the history of California. During this period in California history, prior to 1848 and the discovery of gold at Sutter's saw mill, the explorers and settlers in California left few, if any, printed records of fiction and poetry. Most of the written sources that have been preserved included letters, diaries and official records that are housed in libraries and archives. The most extensive and complete portion of the bibliography is that of the Spanish period (pp. 9–53). The compiler indicated that "For historical reasons, the major portion of the pre-Gold Rush literature is in Spanish." Approximately 600 titles are cited in this section. Although most of these have little significance to Mexican Americans today, the selections do provide historical background for the study of the early life of Spanish-speaking people in California. This bibliography is reprinted from the original edition in the University of Minnesota Libraries.

461. Gómez-Quiñones, Juan, and Luís Leobardo Arroyo. "On the State of Chicano History: Observations on Its Development, Interpretations, and Theory, 1970–1974." *Western Historical Quarterly*, 2 (April, 1976): 155–185.
This critical review of the state of the literature of Chicano history covers the period 1970 to 1974. The essay points out the published works and conference papers which gave rise to Chicano historiography. Mentioned are the scholarly journals which have published articles on Chicano history and the professional organizations and institutions which have given increasing attention to this new field of history. In addition, the important textbooks, documentary histories, bibliographies, anthologies, reprint collections, monographs, periodical articles and dissertations are cited. Occasionally works in progress are given reference. These sources are organized to demonstrate the trends in research and publishing in the field. The authors cite works and trends in social, labor, political, immigration, intellectual, cultural, biographical, local, and women's history. This is definitely a pivotal source for students and researchers working on topics in Chicano history.

462. Gonzáles y Gonzáles, Luís. *Fuentes de la historia contemporánea de México; libros y folletos.* México, D.F.: El Colegio de México, 1961. 3 vols. Annotated. Index.
Books and pamphlets published in Mexico and other countries on the 1910–1940 period of Mexican history are recorded in this major reference tool. The materials relevant to Mexican American studies can be found in Volume I under the categories: *México en*

*cifras, Historias generales, Migración,* and *Estructura social.* In Volume II the following are relevant: *Propiedad inmueble y reforma agraria, Agricultura y ganadería, Industria de transformación, Vida política interior,* and *Iglesia Católica.* Not much can be found in the third volume that is relevant to Mexican American studies. Although this work is in Spanish there are many citations to publications in English. Most entries include location symbols for libraries in Mexico.

463. Harding, George Laban. "A Census of California Spanish Imprints, 1833–1845." *California Historical Society Quarterly,* 2 (June, 1933): 124–136. Annotated.

This census of 74 California imprints enlarges upon Cowan's work, *A Bibliography of the Spanish Press of California, 1833–1845.* This checklist purports to include all known imprints other than sealed-paper headings and letterheads. A brief description is included for each item not in Cowan's earlier work. The items previously described by Cowan are so indicated. These imprints are, for the most part, official documents and are useful to consult for background information on the period just prior to the Anglo-American takeover in 1848.

464. Haro, Robert R. "A Bibliographic Essay." Supplement to *Pain and Promise; The Chicano Today,* edited and with an introduction by Edward Simmen, pp. 325–348. New York: New American Library, 1972. 348 p.

Literature relating to *La Raza* is treated in this lengthy bibliographical essay. The periods covered range from the pre-Columbian roots to the present day. The 130 works cited are organized under headings that record the historical, intellectual, cultural, and religious experiences of the Mexican Americans. Examples of primary and secondary works dating from 1897 to 1970 are analyzed. These include books, monographs, government publications, and films. The various sections are as follows: Mexico as a Nation; Modern Mexico; The Mexican American in the Southwest; Popular history of *La Raza; La Raza* comes of age; The Mexican American migrant; The land question and the *Alianza;* Community-urban studies; The Arts.

This is a valuable state-of-the-literature review which also points to areas of strength and vitality and areas in need of further research and investigation. This essay was first published in *Con Safos,* vol. 2, no. 7 (Winter, 1971).

465. Harwood, T. F. "Review of the Work of the Texas State Historical Commission." *Southwestern Historical Quarterly,* 31 (1927–1928): 1–32.

This bibliographical essay analyzes articles published by the Texas State Historical Commission and the *Southwestern Historical Quarterly* over a 30 year period. The works deal with the reminiscences of living witnesses of past events; early Texas history; the colonial period and revolution; the Republic of Texas and annexation; the period between annexation and the Civil War; Texas in the Confederacy; and Reconstruction. Included is a list of miscellaneous papers about Texas and some other papers relating principally to California. The topics covered are important to a study of the historical period in Texas prior to 1848.

466. Historical Records Survey, California. *Inventory of the State Archives of California, Department of Industrial Relations, Division of Immigration*

*and Housing*. San Francisco: The Northern California Historical Records Survey Project, 1941. 47 p. Annotated. Index.

Official documents of the Division of Immigration and Housing from the date of its creation to the late 1930s are inventoried in this work. Since Mexicans were an important immigrant group entering California, the files of this commission are of great significance to Mexican American studies. The files are arranged under seven headings. Of particular importance are those documents concerning Immigrant aid, Housing, Labor camps, Education and Field offices. The entries provide the official or unofficial title of the files with dates, size of documents, etc., while the annotations give detailed descriptions of subject content and form.

The inventory was initially prepared to serve the day-to-day needs of state officials and others requiring information from the public records. The manuscripts are important now as sources of historical data on the problems and experiences of the Mexican immigrants arriving in California.

467. Hoffman, Abraham. "Bibliography." In *Unwanted Mexican Americans in the Great Depression; Repatriation Pressures, 1929–1938*, pp. 189–200. Tucson: University of Arizona Press, 1974. 207 p.

This is a specialized selection of references that focus on Mexican Americans during the Depression years. It is the only bibliography available that concerns this particularly significant period in contemporary Mexican American history. The items are divided into Archival sources, Published works, Theses and dissertations. Approximately 300 citations are listed which were published between 1920 and 1940. The works reflect on such areas as immigration, labor, anti-Mexicanism, and urbanization of Mexican Americans. Particularly noteworthy are the special items relating to the repatriation during the 1930s with an emphasis on southern California.

468. Hoskin, Beryl Margaret, Doreen Van Assenderp Cohen, and Alice Ehlen Whistler. *The California Experience: An Annotated List of California Bibliographies based on the Collection of the Michel Orradre Library, University of Santa Clara*. Sacramento: California Library Association, 1977. 81 p. Annotated. Index.

Published and unpublished sources related exclusively to California history and life are found in this bibliography of bibliographies. The heavy emphasis on the Spanish period makes this work unique. All 164 items, from the rarest to the most current, are located in the library at the University of Santa Clara. Call numbers and location symbols are provided.

This listing of bibliographic resources complements the outstanding collection of Californiana in the Michel Orradre Library and are essential tools for the researcher in gaining access to the vast holdings.

469. Jenkins, Myra Ellen. *Guide to the Microfilm Edition of the Mexican Archives of New Mexico, 1821–1846*. Santa Fe: State of New Mexico Records Center, 1969. 26 p. Annotated.

This is a guide to the microfilm edition of the extant official administrative records of New Mexico from the Treaty of Córdova, 1821, to the occupation of Santa Fe by United States forces, 1846. The work consists of a description of the organization and content of the archives, location of the manuscripts, historical background of the Mexican administration of New Mexico, and roll notes. The 42 rolls are arranged numerically corresponding to the microfilm of the manuscripts. On the film the materials are in chronological order. Each entry has a descriptive annotation of the roll's contents. Most of the original documents are in the custody of the Archives Division of the State Records Center. Also included are the official documents in the Zimmerman Library, University of New Mexico, and the administrative records in the Bureau of Land Management in Santa Fe. A 144-page *Calendar of the Mexican Archives of New Mexico, 1821-1846* accompanies this guide and the microfilm.

These tools are essential to accessing the documents that contain the judicial proceedings, military records, land holdings, and fiscal information for the period prior to the signing of the Treaty of Guadalupe Hidalgo.

470. Jones, Oakah L. "The Spanish Borderlands: A Selected Reading List." *Journal of the West,* 8 (January, 1969): 137-142.
Some of the principal historical monographs and articles published on the Spanish borderlands up to 1968 are listed in this introductory compilation. It also includes a separate inventory of articles that have been published in the *Journal of the West* concerning the borderlands. This is a concise but useful resource for background material on the Mexican American which supplements Charles C. Cumberland's *The United States-Mexican Border: A Selective Guide to the Literature of the Region,* published in 1960.

471. Mecham, J. Lloyd. "The Northern Expansion of New Spain, 1522-1822: A Selected Descriptive Bibliographical List." *Hispanic American Historical Review,* 7 (1927): 233-276. Annotated.
This list covers 171 sources which constitute the nucleus of background materials essential for the study of the northern areas of New Spain during the period 1522-1822. All of the material, with a few exceptions, is located in the García Collection of the University of Texas. The list is arranged in three broad categories: General (1522-1822); Special: restricted areas and periods; and Frontier institutions. Within each category the material is subarranged by bibliographies, primary sources, and secondary sources. For the most part only the latest editions are noted.

472. Meier, Matt S. "Dissertations." *Journal of Mexican American History,* 1 (Spring, 1971): 170-190.
A selection of 299 theses and dissertations that have some bearing on Mexican American history are listed here. They span the years 1908 to 1970 and cover the colonial period to the present. The author was inspired to compile this list when presented with the lack of printed sources on the history of Mexican Americans. Thirty universities and colleges were surveyed. Most of the works are from United States institutions but a few are from Mexico. Of the ones prepared in the United States, the largest number are from universities in the West and the Southwest.

In spite of the compiler's efforts to identify historical research, a great many of the dissertations and theses are in the fields of sociology, economics, education, and anthropology. The period from 1848 to the present is the least well represented and there is a great deficiency in the area of social history, particularly since 1848. In spite of the shortcomings, this list is of value to students of Mexican American history.

473. _____, and Feliciano Rivera. "Bibliographic Essay." In *The Chicanos; A History of Mexican Americans,* pp. 281–292. New York: Hill and Wang, 1972. 302 p.

This bibliographical essay critically evaluates some of the major books on the Mexican American historical experience. The titles range from the scholarly to those of general interest. Selection was based on availability, coverage, and quality of the scholarship. Categories of materials included are general histories, source books, Amerindian background, the colonial Hispanic American experience, the Mexican period, the Anglo-American migration to the Southwest, migration from Mexico, and the contemporary period of Chicano history.

The bibliography supplements the text and also furnishes a general survey of the historical periods and the state of the literature.

474. _____, and Feliciano Rivera. *A Bibliography for Chicano History.* San Francisco: R & E Research Associates, 1972. 96 p.

Introductory materials for beginning students of Mexican American history are in this selective list. The citations are arranged in ten categories. Books and periodical articles are listed that deal with the Spanish colonial period; the Mexican period (1821–1848); the period from 1900 to the depression years; and the period from World War II to the present. There are also entries under various headings such as labor and immigration, civil rights, Mexican American culture and bibliographies. The most unusual part of this bibliography is the lengthy list of theses and dissertations. This substantial and highly pertinent bibliography should be included in core collections of Mexican American materials.

475. Navarro, Joseph. "The Condition of Mexican American History." In *Chicano; The Evolution of a People,* pp. 443–455. Edited by Renato Rosaldo. Minneapolis, MN: Winston Press, 1973. 461 p.

This bibliographical essay presents a definition of Mexican American history and a critical review of the related literature. The review is in two parts: Literature and its limitations, and History and other studies of man. The coverage of the section on the literature is limited to the period from 1848 to the present, in the United States. Approximately 28 titles are critically analyzed in terms of their accuracy, point of view, and usefulness to the study of Mexican American history. Many of the works examined are in the social sciences. This essay was reprinted from the *Journal of Mexican American History.*

476. New Mexico (Province) *Spanish Archives of New Mexico, 1621–1821.* Santa Fe: State of New Mexico Records Center, 1968. 182 p.

This work is the result of a microfilm project sponsored by the National Historical Publications Commission. It is an inventory of microfilmed documents in the Spanish archives of New Mexico from 1621 to 1821. The entries provide date, description, number of microfilm frames, and Twitchell number. (See Twitchell, R. E. *The Spanish Archives of New Mexico.* Cedar Rapids, IA: The Torch Press, 1914). The list is arranged in chronological order.

The guide by Myra E. Jenkins and the bibliography by Jack D. Rittenhouse supplement this work by covering the periods 1821–1846 and 1821–1880, respectively. The various sources which provide access to archival materials in New Mexico are among the most complete of all the states of the Southwest. Scholars of early Mexican American history will find a wealth of materials in these works for the study of the social and economic situation in New Mexico.

477. Ortego, Philip D., and Arnoldo De León. "Sources for the Study of Los Tejanos." *The Tejano Yearbook: 1519-1978; A Selective Chronicle of the Hispanic Presence in Texas,* pp. 103-107. San Antonio: Caravel Press, 1978. 107 p.

Works mentioned in this bibliographical essay were used to prepare a chronicle of the Hispanic presence in Texas from 1519 to 1978. Books, articles, and dissertations cited by the authors correspond to the five periods in the yearbook: The Deployment of Hispanic Culture in Texas (1519-1789), the Resilience of Hispanic Culture in Texas (1790-1836), Forging a Chicano Culture (1836-1900), The Mobilization of Chicano Culture (1901-1960), and the Dynamics of Chicano Culture (1961-1978). Although the references are few, the coverage uneven, and the presentation awkward and verbose, this source may be useful to historical research on significant events of Mexican and Mexican American experience in Texas, over an extended period.

478. Perrigo, Lynn. "Bibliography." In *Our Spanish Southwest,* pp. 403-472. Dallas, TX: Banks Upshaw, 1960. 498 p. Index.

Monographs on topics concerning the history of the Southwest are cited in this extensive bibliography. Those items listed under such headings as the Land of Cíbola, Conquest, Reconquest, Ranch, Mission, Presidio, Texas Independence, Anglo Infiltration, Revolution and Rebellion, and New Allegiance are of particular value to Mexican American studies. All headings in the bibliography correspond to chapters in the book and the items cited are supplementary to the text. A section of general background materials includes bibliographies, periodicals, guidebooks, and histories of Arizona, California, New Mexico, and Texas. The arrangement is difficult to use since the individual titles are listed consecutively and are not separated.

479. Ramos, Roberto. *Bibliografía de la historia de México.* 2nd ed. México, D.F.: Instituto Mexicano de Investigaciones Económicas, 1965. 688 p.

This is a comprehensive bibliography of scholarly works on the history of Mexico that includes sources in Spanish as well as other languages. In general, the references are indirectly related to Mexican American history and provide excellent background material. The titles are arranged in one alphabetical list by main entry. Without indexes, annotations, or a subject arrangement researchers must scan the entire bibliography. Location symbols are provided for each title.

This is a revised and enlarged edition of the first edition published in 1956.

480. _____. *Bibliografía de la Revolución Mexicana.* México, D.F.: Instituto de Estudios Históricos de la Revolución Mexicana, 1959-1960. 3 vols. Index.

Materials published up to January, 1960, on Mexican revolutionary movements from 1910 to 1922 are collected in this extensive bibliography. Included are books, pamphlets, and numerous Mexican government publications. The materials are mostly of Mexican origin but United States and European publications are also cited. Volume I lists materials published up to May, 1931; volume II contains items from 1931 to 1935; and volume III covers 1935 to 1960. This bibliography is the result of a thorough search of public and private libraries and collections in Mexico. In order to be more helpful to the researcher a location symbol is provided for each work. The sources cited provide excellent background material for research on Mexican migration to the United States.

This work was originally published between 1931 and 1940 but has been updated and revised with the materials included in Volume III. A subject index is provided.

481. Rittenhouse, Jack D. *The Santa Fe Trail: A Historical Bibliography.* Albuquerque: University of New Mexico Press, 1971. 271 p. Annotated. Index.

This bibliography covers published materials on the Santa Fe Trail, including items on microfilm or microfiche, for the years 1821–1880. A few works from the earlier Spanish period are also included. This bibliography indicates that the best collections of manuscript materials on the Santa Fe Trail are found in the Missouri Society Library; the State Historical Society of Missouri; the Kansas State Historical Society; the State Historical Society of Colorado; the New Mexico State Records Center; the Archives of Santa Fe; and Mexican archives. A special index is provided to the congressional documents cited. Many items, particularly those on the Mexican-American War and on United States-Mexican diplomatic relations, are relevant to Mexican American history.

482. Rivera, Feliciano. "A Selected Bibliography." In *A Mexican American Source Book,* pp. 39–53. Menlo Park, CA: Educational Consulting Associates, 1970. 187 p. Annotated.

For the study of the Mexican American, this manual or textbook covers the people, origin and background, cultural implications in the Southwest after 1850, migration, contemporary problems, and solutions. A supporting bibliography and texts of documents, such as the Treaty of Guadalupe Hidalgo, are included. The material is appropriate for high school to college-level instruction. The bibliography contains a core list of books, articles, reports, speeches, newspapers, and audiovisual materials. It supplements the interpretation of Mexican American history.

The earlier edition of this text, entitled *A Guideline for the Study of the Mexican American People in the United States,* published in 1969, contained facsimile copies of the Treaty of Guadalupe Hidalgo and the first Constitution of the State of California.

483. Rocq, Margaret Miller, *California History: A Bibliography and Union List of Library Holdings.* Revised and enlarged edition. Stanford, CA: Stanford University Press, 1970. 611 p. Index.

This is a fine reference source for locating California history materials. It contains over 17,000 items produced prior to 1961 and supplements the first edition published in 1950. Included are city and county histories and directories, great registers, histories of social movements, business and industry histories, biographies of prominent men and women, journals of pioneers, and records of fraternal societies, clubs, schools, chambers of commerce and more.

This edition contains the holdings of 290 additional libraries not covered in the first edition. Other helpful characteristics of this work are the list of bibliographies on California history and the list of special California collections. The location symbols of approximately 500 libraries both in and out of California assist the user in locating relevant materials.

484. Ross, Stanley R. *Fuentes de la historia contemporánea de México; periódicos y revistas.* México, D.F.: El Colegio de México, 1965. 2 vols. Annotated. Indexes.

Articles in newspapers and periodicals published during the *Porfiriato* and the Mexican Revolution are cited in this chronological listing. The coverage is limited to materials in Spanish published between 1908 and 1958 in Mexico and the border states of the United States. While many items are not directly relevant to the study of Mexican Americans, there are entries in each of the 15 major parts of the listing which relate to their background.

A list of 230 Spanish newspapers published in Arizona, California, Texas, and New Mexico during 1908-1958 makes this work even more useful to Mexican American studies. A geographical list by state identifies the location and holdings of Spanish newspapers in American libraries. Indexes to authors, names cited, places and institutions, and cross references are also of considerable help to the user.

485. Santos, Richard G. *A Preliminary Report on the Archival Project in the Office of the County Clerk of Bexar County.* San Antonio, TX: Office of the County Clerk, Bexar County, 196? 17 p.

A brief introductory description of the project undertaken to organize and preserve the historical documents of the Bexar County Archives is included in this report. The coverage extends from the time of the Spanish *conquistadores* through the period of Reconstruction which followed the Civil War.

The second section of the report is the "Brief Description of the Bexar County Archives." Part one lists the Spanish Mexican records, 1736-1836: land grants and sales, mission records, land transactions outside the county, wills and estates, rebel property, powers of attorney, contracts, agreements and receipts, protocols, military reports, custom house reports, and miscellaneous manuscripts and broadsides. Part two contains the early records in the Office of the County Clerk, approximately 1837-1925: records of Commissioners Court, cattle brands, survey records, marriage records, and others.

The final section is the microfilm key to the Bexar County Archives. The arrangement parallels that of the list of documents. The heading, reel number, contents, and total number of manuscripts are given for the Spanish Mexican Records. Similar information is provided for the early records from the nineteenth century.

Many of the manuscripts pertain to early Spanish or Mexican families in Texas. These materials are important for historical research and offer some assistance in genealogical work, as well. A copy of this report is available in the library of the University of Texas at Austin.

486. Shelton, Wilma Loy. "Checklist of New Mexico Publications." *New Mexico Historical Review,* 24 (1949): 130-155, 223-235, 300-331; 25 (1950): 57-72, 136-161, 222-241; 26 (1951): 64-67, 137-147, 225-241, 325-331; 27 (1952): 51-63; 29 (1954): 58-70, 124-153.

These checklists are chronological listings of all official New Mexican publications from 1850 through 1948. Included are constitutions, Attorney General's reports, Bureau of Immigration reports, proclamations, court records, associations and institutions of New Mexico, and other related materials.

This work complements Twitchell's *Spanish Archives of New Mexico,* which covers the period up to 1821, and Jenkins's *Guide to the Microfilm Edition of the Mexican Archives of New Mexico, 1821-1846*. Together they provide for a nearly continuous bibliographic record of the official state documents from 1685 to 1948.

487. Steck, Francis Borgia. *A Tentative Guide to Historical Materials on the Spanish Borderlands*. New York: Lenox Hill, 1971. 106 p. Annotated.
All aspects of the history of the Spanish borderlands from Florida to California are covered in this guide. The sections on Texas, New Mexico, Arizona, and California contain the most relevant materials for the study of Mexican Americans. A sizable portion of the entries are periodical articles ranging from the scholarly to the popular. The items listed were published prior to 1942 and concern the period 1689-1836, in Texas; 1581-1846, in New Mexico and Arizona; and 1769-1846, in California.
This guide was first published in 1943 by the Catholic Historical Society of Philadelphia. Although supplements were promised, none have appeared in the literature to date.

488. Swadesh, Frances Leon. *20,000 Years of History: A New Mexico Bibliography*. Santa Fe: The Sunstone Press, 1973. 138 p.
This bibliography was compiled in order to provide a listing that would reflect the multicultural richness in New Mexico. The materials are drawn from a period extending for approximately 20,000 years from the Paleo-Indian era and cover the Pueblos; Navajo-Apaches, Anglos, and Hispanics. The author cites what he considers to be the best published sources on cultural continuity and intercultural mingling. Relevant to Mexican American history are the items under the heading "Hispano" which is found in the subject categories of History, Anthropology, Archeology, Art-Folklore, etc. Many of the items classified under "Anglos" are related to Mexican Americans as well.
There is an author index, a list of all the appointed and elected governors of New Mexico from 1598 until 1974, and a list of museums and monuments in New Mexico. This work is appropriate for students and teachers in secondary schools and junior colleges.

489. Taylor, Virginia H. *Index to Spanish and Mexican Land Grants*. San Patricio, TX: General Land Office, 1976. 88 p.
This index is the first of its kind for the Spanish and Mexican land grants located in Texas between the Nueces and Rio Grande rivers. Prior to this work the grants were indexed, but each entry listed only the location by county, the size in *varas*, and the file number. In this special compilation each of the 300 grants is arranged in alphabetical order by the name of the original grantee or applicant. The entries, some more lengthy than others, provide fuller descriptions covering the location, name of the grant, size in acres, General Land Office file number, date of original grant by Spain or Mexico, name(s) of claimant(s), and date and result of confirmation by the Texas Legislature. In other instances information such as witnesses reports, patent date, location of copy of the title, and other pertinent data are recorded.
The preface gives a brief historical account of the grants, the legislation concerning claims, and the contents of the work. The copy examined was obtained from the University of Arizona Library, Tucson.

490. Tucker, Mary. *Books of the Southwest: A General Bibliography.* New York: J. J. Agustin, 1937. 105 p.

Tucker's work purports to be one of the first complete lists of books of the Southwest. All the items are in English. Books cited deal with Indians, missions, explorations, description of the country, natural science, travel, literature, music, and children's literature of the Southwest. Many of the titles are very old or even rare. Most are useful for background information on Mexican Americans. Many of the topics and items in this bibliography are not found in other sources of this type. This work is included as an example of the early bibliographical efforts to identify and collect material on the history of the Southwest.

491. Twitchell, Ralph Emerson. *The Spanish Archives of New Mexico.* Cedar Rapids, IA: Torch Press, 1914. 2 vols. Annotated. Index.

This is one of the most important guides to archival materials of the Spanish period in New Mexico. The documents are arranged roughly in chronological order. Volume I lists 1,384 documents pertaining to the claim and ownership of Spanish land grants in New Mexico which are housed in that state. Appended are lists of grants of allotments of land to the Pueblo Indians, a list of other grants, and a list of cases handled and disposed of by the Court of Private Land Claims. Volume II lists all other materials pertaining to the Spanish period which are housed in the Library of Congress. Included in volume II are approximately 20,000 numbered documents arranged in chronological order.

Items in both volumes are described in great detail and cover the period from 1685 to 1821. In 1690 most of the earlier archives of Santa Fe were destroyed by Indians in the Pueblo Rebellion. With a few exceptions the archives date from the eighteenth century and provide background material for Mexican American history. An author and subject index is included.

492. University of Texas, Austin. *Catalog of the Texas Collection in the Barker Texas History Center.* Boston: G. K. Hall, 1978. 14 vols.

Access is provided by this publication to an outstanding collection of 110,000 volumes including books, periodicals, pamphlets, and microfilm on Texas and the greater Texas region. The subject emphases are on the social and behavioral sciences, languages and literature, fine arts, and science and technology. Imprints in the collection range from the sixteenth century to the present with a concentration on materials from the nineteenth and twentieth centuries. Particularly notable are the materials from the special collections of Frank Kell on the Southwest; Earl Vandale on Texas history; and James Perry Bryan on Anglo-American colonization. The catalog is arranged in two parts in dictionary format: an author/title catalog and a subject catalog.

493. Velásquez, Pablo, and Ramón Nadurille. *A Selected Bibliography of Economic, Social, and Agricultural Development in Mexico.* México, D. F.: Instituto Nacional de Investigaciones Agrícolas, 1964. 22 p. Index.

This bibliography was specially prepared at the request of the United States Embassy in Mexico for a Rural Development Mexican/American Round Table Conference, held in 1965. It covers a selected list of 242 books, pamphlets, and periodical articles published on the social, economic, and agricultural development in Mexico.

Most of the items are English-language sources (Spanish and other foreign-language references are not cited) and are, for the most part, relevant to an understanding of the socioeconomic background of Mexican American immigrants. An asterisk adjacent to an item indicates important up-to-date material. The key word index provides subject access.

494. Wagner, Henry Raup. *Bibliography of Printed Works in Spanish Relating to Those Portions of the United States Which Formerly Belonged to Mexico.* Santiago de Chile: La Impr. Diener, 1917. 43 p.

Early Spanish-language imprints relating to the Southwestern United States, with a concentration on New Mexico and California, are described in this bibliography. The citations were selected from the bibliographies of the notable Chilean bibliographer José Toribio Medina. The 137 books and pamphlets, dating from 1553 to 1821, are arranged in chronological order. Although the works are not annotated, the lengthy titles and detailed bibliographical information provide adequate descriptions of the nature of the contents. Many of the items are official reports relating to the discovery and conquest, religious activities and the establishment of the missions, travel descriptions, frontier life, and the like. Other items include rules and regulations issued for the governance of the Southwestern provinces.

This bibliography and the one by Joseph Gaer, entitled *Bibliography of California Literature: Pre-Gold Rush Period,* contain primary sources that provide important historical data on the early life of Spanish-speaking people in the Southwest.

495. Wallace, Andrew. *Sources and Readings in Arizona History; A Checklist of Literature Concerning Arizona's Past.* Tucson: Arizona Pioneers Historical Society, 1965. 181 p. Index.

This bibliography is a revision of a series of checklists published in *Arizoniana* in 1963. The work is arranged in 15 sections, each compiled and prefaced by experts in the various fields. The sections include The Land; Peoples of the Far Past; Men of Spain; The American Pathfinders, The Miners, The Troopers, The Stockmen, Haulers and Travelers, The Homesteaders, Outlaws and Lawmen, The Statemakers, Builders of our Economy, Builders of our Culture, The Modern Indians, and Folklore and Fiction. Selected major books and articles are arranged chronologically in each section and the rare or scarce titles are so marked.

A special introduction to the general sources of Arizona's history was prepared by Bert M. Fireman, Executive Vice-President of the Arizona Historical Foundation. As Fireman points out, ''The first three hundred years of Arizona occupation and exploration belonged to Spain and Mexico...'' The sources listed in this work provide information on the historical background of Mexican American people in this state.

496. Waters, Willard O. ''California Bibliographies.'' *California Historical Society Quarterly,* 3 (July, 1924): 245–258. Annotated.

One of the earliest bibliography of bibliographies dealing with the history of California; works cited cover all aspects of California life from very early times to the beginning of the twentieth century. There are two sections: formal bibliographies in one alphabetical list and works containing bibliographical materials in another. Manuscripts and guides, along with lists of printed maps of the state, are included. The compiler, in a selective manner, has attempted to include most of the principal sources of information dealing with California up to 1924. Many of the works provide information on background sources for the study of Mexican American history, particularly during the nineteenth century.

497. Weber, Francis J. *A Select Bibliography of California Missions, 1765–1972*. Los Angeles: Dawson's Book Shop, 1972. 86 p. Annotated.
This bibliography lists 500 of the most important books and pamphlets on the missions of California. The coverage includes titles in Spanish and English published between 1765 and 1972. These are arranged by author in one alphabetical list. Among the works cited are essential historical and fictional accounts of the life and culture of the period prior to the secularization of the missions; biographies and diaries of important religious figures; illustrations of mission architecture; speeches and lectures commemorating special historical occasions; and guidebooks. Many of these sources are crucial to a study of Mexican American history in California before 1834.

This work, produced in a limited edition of 300 copies, was compiled to assist researchers in their quest for printed sources on the mission period. According to Weber, a disproportionately large quantity of materials were not included since they are merely sentimental descriptions with little historical value. The most worthwhile scholarly items were selected for this bibliography.

498. _____. *A Select Guide to California Catholic History*. Los Angeles: Westernlore Press, 1966. 277 p. Annotated. Index.
The post-mission period (since 1840) in California is the focus of this bibliography. The titles are arranged in eight sections: guides, printed works, periodical articles, church publications, unpublished materials, newspapers, diocesan and parochial directories, and archival depositories. Much of the material is not directly related to the Mexican American but there are many titles which could be useful in studying the Catholic heritage in California and the relationship between the Catholic Church and Mexican Americans of California. A 27-page preface critically reviews the bibliography of the history of the Catholic Church and its clergy in the state of California.

499. Weigle, Marta. *A Penitente Bibliography*. Albuquerque: University of New Mexico Press, 1976. 162 p. Annotated.
This is the most complete bibliographic work on the Brotherhood of *Penitentes*. It was originally prepared as an annotated bibliography which accompanies the author's dissertation. As such it is a companion volume to *Brothers of Light, Brothers of Blood: The Penitentes of the Southwest* (University of New Mexico Press, 1976). The bibliography contains 1,233 entries. The materials are arranged in five categories: Documents; General and comparative references; Books and other published materials; Anonymous newspaper items; Dissertations, theses, student papers, and unpublished manuscripts. This work serves as an invaluable aid to historical and religious research on the Hispanic Southwest.

500. Winter, Oscar Osburn. *A Classified Bibliography of the Periodical Literature of the Trans-Mississippi West (1811–1957)*. Bloomington: Indiana University Press, 1961. 626 p. Index.
Articles in 70 different periodicals devoted almost exclusively to the history of the Trans-Mississippi West, or a segment thereof, are recorded in this extensive bibliography. There are a number of subject headings and subheadings which are directly related to Mexican American history (e.g., Agriculture, Arizona, California, Hispanic Americans, Mexico, California Gold Rush, New Mexico, Texas, and others). A supplement covering the years 1957–1967, which surveys six additional journals, was published in 1970 with the collaboration of Richard A. Van Orman.

501.  Wright, Doris Marion. *A Guide to the Mariano Guadalupe Vallejo Documents para la historia de California, 1780-1875*. Berkeley: University of California Press, 1953. 264 p.

This guide to the materials in the Mariano Guadalupe Vallejo Collection is an alphabetical listing of the documents which comprise 36 volumes. The Vallejo collection consists of more than 10,000 manuscripts including letters and documents of the most prominent men in California during the first half of the nineteenth century. The manuscripts are divided into three groups. The first group (volumes 1-14) contains official papers, letters and documents sent to Vallejo, drafts of his letters to other individuals, and personal and business correspondence. The second group (volumes 15-27) is composed of military papers, pertaining in particular to the Presidio of San Francisco. A few papers concern the presidios of Monterey, Santa Barbara, and San Diego. The third group (volumes 28-36) is made up of a miscellaneous collection of family archives of some of Vallejo's relatives and friends.

Together the documents of the Vallejo collection cover a wide range of subjects and are particularly rich in the areas of military and mission history, economic history, immigration, colonization, and social history during the Mexican period in California. Each item includes the name of the author of the document, name(s) of related persons, date and place, and information indicating type of manuscript, e.g., a letter, a bill of lading, or a proclamation. The entire collection is housed in the Bancroft Library at the University of California, Berkeley. Photographic reproductions of documents may be obtained from the library.

# Chapter 13

# *Labor*

One of the most important and controversial subjects of Mexican American studies is Mexican labor in the United States. It has generated a voluminous amount of publications and has been the object of considerable debate within economic, political, and academic circles. From the late nineteenth century to the present, waves of Mexican immigrants have been a source of essential labor for American industries, particularly during periods of critical manpower shortages. Those who came prior to World War II worked mainly on the railroads, in mining, agriculture, meatpacking, and in the steel and automobile industries. Later arrivals gravitated either to agricultural fields or to service-oriented jobs in urban areas. In more recent years Mexican workers have found alternative employment in construction, crafts, Mexican food production, and the garment industry.

The presence of Mexican laborers in the United States, the continuing replenishment of this supply of workers, the roles of the United States and Mexico in promoting this labor force, and the nature of the industries hiring Mexicans have been topics of intensive interest to a wide range of academic researchers, labor unions, religious organizations, and government agencies. Over the years, studies, books, and articles have been published which detail the conditions, problems, and functions of the Mexican laborer. These publications, both scholarly and popular, have reflected the frequent and vitriolic arguments that have ensued over the need for Mexican workers, their effects on the labor markets and their rights, privileges, and legal status.

In spite of significant involvement in other sectors of the economy, the literature has emphasized the Mexicans' role in agriculture. This industry has employed Mexicans in greater numbers than other industries and has relied on them as the primary source of labor. Their participation in urban industries, railroads, or mining has been generally ignored; relatively few published references exist. The absence of such sources in the face of overwhelming coverage of agricultural matters has led to the popular misconception that Mexican labor has been exclusively engaged in agriculture. In reality, the percentage of Mexicans working in the fields has progressively diminished since World War II and the Mexican population increasingly resides in urban communities.

Research on Mexican labor in the United States is supported by numerous bibliographies which fall roughly into four categories: those which deal exclusively with Mexican laborers; those on agricultural labor in general; others on unionization in agriculture; and still others on the agricultural industry. The bibliographies cited in this chapter were

**167**

published from the 1930s to the 1970s, primarily by academic institutions and agencies of the federal government. For the most part, they were well prepared with complete and accurate bibliographical information. Except in a few cases, all were published separately and are easily obtainable.

The bibliographies dealing solely with Mexicans incorporate works which pertain to all aspects of their role as laborers. Among these, the earliest dates from 1948, but most are the products of the 1960s and 1970s. Some cover only a limited time period such as the Depression years. The majority mainly list sources on Mexicans in agriculture, with special emphasis on the *Bracero* program and the socioeconomic conditions of migrant workers. Only the work by Juan Gómez-Quiñones and Victor Nelson Cisneros, entitled *Selective Bibliography on Chicano Labor Materials,* qualifies as comprehensive in its coverage of Mexican labor in all types of industries and occupations.

The second category of bibliographies essential to research on Mexican labor consists of works on agricultural labor. Agricultural labor is a field that Mexicans have come to dominate to such an extent, particularly in the Midwest and Southwestern regions, that is almost impossible to write on the subject without reference to them. This category contains the largest number of bibliographies, many of which concentrate on the migratory workers. From the 1930s to the 1970s, the Department of Agriculture was the single most important source of bibliographies in this area. The first of these publications, *Agricultural Labor in the United States, 1915–1935,* by Esther M. Colvin and Josiah C. Folsom, was compiled in 1935 and subsequently updated at various intervals. Since the 1960s, other governmental agencies and academic centers have produced additional works of this type.

Bibliographies on unionization in agriculture constitute the third category of materials for the study of Mexican labor. They were issued in the latter part of the 1960s and the early 1970s. Much of the writing on unionization and the bibliographies themselves were inspired by the activities of the United Farm Workers union, led by César Chávez. The most comprehensive of these is an excellent guide to the extensive collection at Wayne State University on Chávez and his union. Other predominant themes in the literature are collective bargaining, labor laws, and organizing activities. Sources on unionization are still scarce, as reflected by the small number of works cited, but together the existing bibliographies provide a solid basis for further investigations.

A representative selection of bibliographies on the agricultural industry comprise the final category of resources necessary to an in-depth examination of Mexican labor. These works are included to assist researchers in identifying materials which place Mexican labor within the context of agricultural development in the United States. A great many of the sources listed in these bibliographies provide background information and comparative data on other ethnic groups which performed functions, in the rural areas, similar to those of the Mexicans.

Two additional works have been included which are not bibliographies but which facilitate access to primary sources on unionization. The first is a chronological index to *El Malcriado,* the official organ of the United Farm Workers union, and the second is an index to the manuscripts in the San Joaquin Valley Farm Workers Collection. Both collections are housed in the Library of California State University, Fresno.

Other sources on various aspects of Mexican labor can be found in the chapters on General Bibliographies, Library Guides, History, and Social Sciences. For a broader approach to the subject of Mexican labor, the following works should be consulted: the

*Bibliography of Agriculture,* a monthly index to the journal literature in agriculture, and the *Biological and Agricultural Index* (supersedes *Agricultural Index*).

502. Benedict, Murray R. *Agricultural Labor in the Pacific Coast States; A Bibliography and Suggestions for Research.* Berkeley, CA: Pacific Coast Regional Committee of the Social Science Research Council, 1938. 64 p. Annotated.

This selection of studies, prepared to facilitate the work of the Social Science Research Council, deals with problems of agricultural labor along the Pacific Coast. The items cited are classified under nine headings: Characteristics of the labor groups; Numbers of laborers needed; Wage rates and earnings; Living conditions; Labor relations in the field; Sociological problems; Relief problem related to employment and conditions; Selected area sources on California, Oregon, Washington, Arizona, Pacific Coast, Southwest, Pacific Northwest, and Utah; and Significant periodical articles and unpublished reports. Many government publications, both state and federal, and unpublished reports by state agencies are included. This bibliography covers all groups engaged in agricultural labor in the Pacific Coast states. Since Mexican Americans played a prominent role, much of the literature is of great relevancy to them.

This work is supplementary to a bibliography prepared by Orpha Cummings for the Giannini Foundation, under the title, *Research and Important Official Reports Relating to Agricultural Labor on the Pacific Coast,* published in 1936.

503. Cameron, Colin, and Joanne Edelson. *Farm Labor Organizing: An Annotated Bibliography.* Madison: Institute for Research on Poverty, University of Wisconsin, 1969. 62 p. Annotated.

This specialized bibliography concerns farm labor in the United States and crucial events in farm labor organizing. The arrangement is in four parts: the first and largest section contains materials on farm labor; the second part, on immigration; the third part, on labor unions and organizations; and the fourth part, on related topics and media (tapes and films). The listed items include government statistical sources; miscellaneous newsletters, radio stations and farm labor presses; bibliographies; addresses of sources; a glossary; and a list of films. In addition there are books, articles, reports, and government publications on special topics: characteristics and sociology of farm workers; employment of farm labor force; mechanization as it affects farm workers; housing, health, education and programs for farm workers; immigration; legislation and public policy; early attempts to organize; and contemporary grape strikes and boycotts. There is a separate section on the Mexican American.

504. Colvin, Esther M. and Josiah C. Folsom. *Agricultural Labor in the United States, 1915-1935.* Washington, DC: Bureau of Agricultural Economics Library, U.S. Department of Agriculture, 1935. (Agricultural Economics Bibliography, no. 64) 493 p. Annotated. Index.

505. _____, and Josiah C. Folsom. *Agricultural Labor in the United States, 1936-1937: A Selected List of References.* Washington, DC: Bureau of Agricultural Economics, U.S. Department of Agriculture, 1938. (Agricultural Economics Bibliography, no. 72) 205 p. Annotated. Index.

506. McNeill, John, and Josiah C. Folsom. *Agricultural Labor in the United States, 1938–June 1941: A Selected List of References.* Washington, DC: Bureau of Agricultural Economics, U.S. Department of Agriculture, 1942. (Agricultural Economics Bibliography, no. 95) 268 p. Annotated. Index.

507. Moats, Ruby W., and John McNeill. *Agricultural Labor in the United States, July, 1941–February, 1943: A List of References.* Washington, DC: Library, U.S. Department of Agriculture, 1943. (Library List, no. 4) 59 p. Annotated. Index.

508. Folsom, Josiah C. *Agricultural Labor in the United States, 1943–1952: A Selected List of Annotated References.* Washington, DC: Library, U.S. Department of Agriculture, 1954. (Library List, no. 61) 170 p. Annotated. Index.

The original bibliography by Colvin and Folsom and the successive complementary compilations, published by the Department of Agriculture, are devoted to the literature on farm labor in the United States. Over 3,000 books, reports, periodical articles and miscellaneous mimeographed items are included. They cover such topics as Mexican labor, immigrant labor, migratory labor, unions, child labor laws, mechanization and labor displacement, and many others of particular importance to research on Mexican migrant laborers in the West and Southwest.

Each work is arranged by subjects relevant to the material collected. The first work (1915–1935), spanning a period of concentration of Mexican labor in the agricultural development of the Southwest, dedicates a separate section to Mexican laborers. The second is essential for the study of the treatment of Mexican laborers during the Depression years, their living conditions, and social welfare programs. A notable portion of the third bibliography contains the Congressional committee investigations of agricultural labor by the House Select Committee on the Interstate Migration of Destitute Citizens, and the Senate Civil Liberties Committee, known as the La Follette Committee.

The fourth, produced during World War II, includes sources on farm labor legislation in the 1940s, farm labor controversies, and in general updates the earlier works. The final work deals mainly with hired agricultural laborers, government programs. alien labor, and strikes with an emphasis on the worker's status in the farm labor force.

Extensive annotations and detailed subject indexes enhance the usefulness of these bibliographies.

509. Consulting Services Corporation. *Migrant Farm Workers in the State of Washington; A Selected, Annotated Bibliography.* Vol. I. Washington, DC: Office of Economic Opportunity, 1966. 50 p. Annotated.

Secondary sources on agricultural migrant workers in the State of Washington are in this listing. The cited items were either published in the State of Washington or contain some special reference to that state. The publications originate from state and federal agencies, local government, and private organizations. These materials are now located in the libraries of the University of Washington, Seattle, and Washington State University. The categories under which items are listed offer a comprehensive picture of migrant farm labor: Socioeconomic problems, Education, Employment, Health, Housing and sanitation, Legislation affecting agricultural workers, Mechanization, the *Bracero* program,

Travel patterns, Social characteristics, Wages and income, and State and federal reports on farm labor. This bibliography is part of a four-volume work on migrants. Volumes 2–4 are studies conducted by the Office of Economic Opportunity.

510. Craig, Richard B. "Bibliography." In *The Bracero Program: Interest Groups and Foreign Policy*, pp. 207–224. Austin: University of Texas Press, 1971. 233 p.

This specialized supporting bibliography concentrates on the controversial *Bracero* programs from 1942 to 1964. It is the most complete listing of sources dealing with this aspect of Mexican labor in the United States. It covers government publications, theses and dissertations, books, articles, newspapers and periodicals, and provides a good selection, particularly in the area of government documents; 256 items are included that relate to immigration, migrant housing and other problems, legal issues, political process, conflicting interest groups, public opinion, international agreements, and farm labor. The bibliography opens the door to further research on this topic.

511. Fairbanks, Helen. *Collective Bargaining in Agriculture*. Princeton, NJ: Princeton University, 1969. (Selected References, no. 148) 4 p. Annotated.

Major works on collective bargaining in agriculture comprise this list of selected references. They are listed under three headings: Hired farm workers—background; History of organizing efforts; and Current situation and proposals for change. Although not a very extensive bibliography, the 18 selections are basic to research on the labor problems of farm workers, including Mexican American laborers. Books, monographs, articles and government publications are included. Addresses and prices are given for each item.

512. Fodell, Beverly. *César Chávez and the United Farm Workers; A Selective Bibliography*. Detroit: Wayne State University Press, 1974. 103 p. Annotated.

This bibliography was compiled to provide those interested in César Chávez, the United Farm Workers, and the various aspects of the agricultural strikes and boycotts with a wide selection of readily available publications. Materials included are books, articles, pamphlets, government publications, proceedings, reports, position papers, theses, and dissertations. The listed items refer specifically to César Chávez, the grape strike and boycott, the lettuce strike, the UFW or, prior to May, 1972, the UFW Organizing Committee, the Agricultural Workers Organizing Committee, and the National Farm Workers Association.

There are sources on the importation of foreign farm workers; previous farm labor strikes, and attempts to unionize workers; sources on child labor in agriculture; living and working conditions of migrant workers; agribusiness, farm labor contractors, agricultural mechanization, wages, unemployment and workmen's compensation; land grant colleges; use of pesticides and other chemicals in agriculture; activities of the migrant ministry and other church-related organizations; and federal and state legislation for farm workers. This is a revised and enlarged edition of a 1970 bibliography.

513. Folsom, Josiah C. *Migratory Agricultural Labor in the United States; An Annotated Bibliography of Selected References.* Washington, DC: Library, U.S. Department of Agriculture, 1953. (Library List, no. 59) 64 p. Annotated. Index.

This list of publications, arranged in 18 categories, concerns migratory agricultural laborers who habitually follow crops and obtain farm work through their own efforts. Items of interest to Mexican Americans are found under Immigrant labor—particularly Mexican; Migration, Recruitment, Placement and training; Legislation affecting migrants; Government programs; and Government investigations. This bibliography complements previous ones issued by the U.S. Department of Agriculture (nos. 64, 72, 95, and Library List no. 4) by Folsom, Esther Colvin, John McNeill, and Ruby Moats.

514. Fujimoto, Isao, and Jo Clare Schieffer. *Guide to Sources on Agricultural Labor.* Davis: Department of Applied Behavioral Sciences, University of California, 1969. 39 p. Annotated. Index.

Materials on agricultural labor published after 1960, with a few basic works from the pre-1960 period are cited in this guide. The items are divided into two parts. The first discusses research methodology using sources on agricultural labor and recommends indexes and guides; agencies and organizations, which can provide information related to agricultural labor; ephemeral materials; and bibliographies. The second part lists books and government documents under the headings of Overview of agricultural labor, Overview of California agricultural labor, and Technology and mechanization in changing agriculture as related to farms, farmers and workers (*braceros,* unions, etc.).

Although this guide does not specifically focus on the Mexican American, the subject and treatment are of obvious importance to this group. It is one of the best guides to sources on Mexican American agricultural labor. It is a revised edition of the authors' *Guide to Sources on Agriculture,* published in 1968.

515. Gilbert, William H. *Mexican-Americans and Mexicans in the United States Since 1945: Selected References.* Washington, DC: Legislative Reference Service, Library of Congress, 1965. 5 p.

This is an extremely selective list of general materials on Mexican American and agricultural labor, published since 1945. Materials are arranged in two parts under Nonperiodicals and Periodical references. More than half of the 47 items focus on the Mexican Americans as agricultural laborers and the *Bracero* program. No introduction is provided and no guidelines are stated on the preparation of this list.

516. Gómez-Quiñones, Juan, and Victor Nelson Cisneros. *Selective Bibliography on Chicano Labor Materials.* Los Angeles: Aztlán Publications, 1974. 29 p.

This is one of the more recent and comprehensive compilations on Mexican American labor. The bibliography is arranged by topics and within each section subarranged by type of publication: books, articles, dissertations and theses. The topics covered include general United States labor, the labor movement in Mexico, Chicano workers in industry and agriculture, and women workers. Additional information on Chicano labor can be found in the bibliographies, indexes, and statistical sources that are listed. The entries cover the period from the 1920s to the 1970s. Annotations and indexes would have increased the usefulness of this tool.

517. Guy, Kent. *Migrant Labor Law and Relations: Selected References, 1960–1969.* Washington, DC: Congressional Research Service, Library of Congress, 1969. 8 p.
Aspects of labor and the migrant worker are the concern of most titles in this bibliography. The 86 items are arranged in four sections—General materials, State studies (California, Colorado, Florida, Maryland, New Jersey, New York, Ohio, Oregon, Pennsylvania, and Wisconsin), Legal and legislative issues, and the Grape Strike at Delano, California, by the UFW Organizing Committee. The materials cited include journal articles, reports, and books. A short introductory paragraph describes the scope of the list and recommends additional Congressional Research Service publications which contain references to other aspects of migratory agricultural labor.

518. Hall, Carl W. *Bibliography on Mechanization and Labor in Agriculture.* East Lansing: Rural Manpower Center, Michigan State University, 1968. (Special Paper, no. 6) 18 p. Index.
This bibliography of periodical articles deals exclusively with the relationship between the mechanization of agriculture and farm labor. An extensive search for relevant articles identified approximately 150 items. Excluded, but still of consequence to the topic, are the numerous useful references to statistical data, census reports, manufacturers' data, and economic and labor information. This bibliography should only be used as a starting point for research on farm mechanization and labor.

519. Heslet, Mary R. *The Mexican Farm Labor Program: References, 1951–1965.* Washington, DC: Legislative Reference Service, Library of Congress, 1965. 14 p.
Predominantly official materials related to the study of Mexican farm labor for the period 1951–1965 are cited here. It is arranged in four parts, i.e., Congressional hearings, reports, documents; United States treaties with Mexico; Government publications; and Books, pamphlets and periodicals. Included are 116 items. No purpose, guidelines, or scope are mentioned. However, this work is a useful source of references on the importation of Mexican labor from the time of the Korean war to the end of the *Bracero* program.

520. ———. *Migratory Agricultural Labor: References to Federal Publications, Studies, and Reports, 1959–1968.* Revised by Helen N. Grubbs. Washington, DC: Legislative Reference Service, Library of Congress, 1969. 12 p.
This is a listing of 122 official publications arranged under the categories of congressional hearings and reports; publications from the following departments: Agriculture; Health, Education, and Welfare; and Labor; studies by the U.S. President's Committee on Migratory Labor; and U.S. treaties concerning agricultural labor. This bibliography was originally published in 1965 and covered the years 1959–1965. For references on nonofficial publications, other related bibliographies produced by the Legislative Reference Service should be consulted.

521. Hopper, Jean. "The Migratory Farm Worker: A Selected Bibliography." *ALA Library Service to Labor Newsletter*, 20 (Fall, 1967): 5–9.
Appearing in a newsletter sponsored by the American Library Association, this bibliography lists books, pamphlets, government publications, periodical articles, films, and

information sources on the migratory farm worker. While it relates to migrant laborers in general, most of the items are particularly appropriate for research on the Mexican Americans. The sections which are most helpful and unique are the lists of other sources of information on migratory farm workers and the 16 mm films. Brief content summaries of each film are provided, although none of the other entries are annotated. The materials cited constitute a solid base on which to build collections on migrant labor or on which to begin a literature search.

522. Jones, Robert C. *Selected References on the Labor Importation Program Between Mexico and the United States.* Washington, DC: Pan American Union, 1948. 7 p.

This concise bibliography actually forms part of a more extensive work, *Mexicans in the United States,* published by Jones in 1942. The smaller work covers materials on labor importation from 1900 to 1948. Five sections: General aspects; Agricultural labor; Railroad labor; Agreements, decrees and laws; and Mexican sources, contain chiefly articles with some books and government publications. Among the subjects treated are the effects of World War II on the labor market, and the United States and Mexican policies toward labor importation. This is an important source for the study of labor problems in both countries from an historical perspective.

523. Massa Gil, Beatríz. *Bibliografía sobre migración de trabajadores mexicanos a los Estados Unidos.* México, D.F.: Departamento de Estudios Económicos, Banco de México, 1959. 122 p.

This is a bibliography dealing with the problem of the migration of Mexican laborers to the United States. The materials cited were published between 1950 and 1958 in the United States. They include U.S. government publications, periodical articles, and citations from the *New York Times Index.* While the title of the bibliography is in Spanish, the entries are all English-language sources. Much of the material is arranged by subject and chronologically by date of publication.

524. Miller, Michael. "Mexican-American and Mexican National Farm Workers: A Literature Review." (Paper presented at the Annual Meeting of the Rural Sociological Society. San Francisco, August, 1975) 25 p. ED 111 563.

In this bibliographical essay Miller reviews the treatment given the Mexican American laborers and Mexican national farm workers in selected scholarly journals. The author chose 29 representative articles from legal, historical, social work, and social science journals. These date from 1960 to 1974 and are summarized and evaluated. The articles fall under the following categories: Migrant farm workers, *Bracero* program, Alien workers—"wetbacks" and commuters, and Labor immigration. The selection of articles is helpful in gaining a better understanding of the Mexican labor situation through recent research. A list of the articles appears at the end of the work.

525. Mortimer, Louis R. *Unionism and Collective Bargaining for Agricultural Workers: A Selective Bibliography.* Updated by Joseph Fulton. Washington, DC: Congressional Research Service, Library of Congress, 1974. 13 p. Annotated.

Unionization of agricultural workers is the subject of this list provided by the Library of Congress research service. The emphasis is on labor-management relations in agriculture. The materials are arranged in the following categories: Books and pamphlets, Periodical articles, Congressional hearings and reports, and Bibliographies. The 131 entries have been drawn from the catalog of the Library of Congress, *PAIS Index, Index of Legal Periodicals, Business Periodicals Index,* and *Biological and Agricultural Index,* up through July, 1974. This is a revised and updated edition of a Congressional Research Service bibliography by the same title, compiled by Louis R. Mortimer in 1971

526. Nordin, Dennis S. ''Graduate Studies in American Agricultural History.'' *Agricultural History,* 41 (July, 1967): 275–312. Index.
The purpose of this bibliography is to make known to researchers the many unpublished works by graduate students on American agricultural history. M.A. theses and Ph.D. dissertations are included. Over 1,100 entries are arranged under 18 major subject divisions. Items most applicable to Mexican Americans are found under the headings Regional and state agricultural history: California, Mountain, Southwest, and Pacific Coast; Agricultural labor: wage labor; and Crops: other crops. The titles listed are only supplementary to published sources on the history of agriculture and agricultural labor.

527. Reisler, Mark. ''Bibliography.'' In *By the Sweat of Their Brow; Mexican Immigrant Labor in the United States, 1900–1940.* Westport, CT: Greenwood Press, 1976. 298 p.
This excellent supporting bibliography focuses on Mexican immigrant labor in the United States. It was selected for inclusion because it accompanies the text in one of the best, and thus far the most thorough, historical accounts of this subject. The materials are arranged by type in the following sections: Archives; Manuscript collections; Documents, government publications and proceedings; Books; Articles and periodicals; and Unpublished sources. The items pertain to the first half of the twentieth century and cover immigration, agricultural labor, urban labor in industries, and the effects of the Depression years. This is a scholarly and comprehensive list for those interested in Mexican labor immigration.

528. Renton, Margaret A. *The Migratory Farm Labor Problem: A Select Bibliography.* Irvine, CA: Government Publications Department, University Library, University of California, 1975. (Government Publications Bibliography, no. 10) 32 p.
Government publications on migratory farmworkers in the University of California, Irvine, Library are the focus of this excellent listing. A total of 378 citations are organized under seven major sections with the items listed in alphabetical order by the issuing agency. It covers official documents by the State of California, U.S. Congress, Department of Agriculture, Department of Labor, and various other federal agencies. The documents deal with the migratory farm labor problem in general, and with education, employment, health, and housing. Also included are a few items on laws and statutes pertaining to migratory farm labor and a list of bibliographies on the migrant issued by various public agencies.

529. Ruesink, David C., and T. Brice Batson. *Bibliography Relating to Agricultural Labor.* College Station: Texas A & M University, 1969. 93 p. Index.

This bibliography generally includes materials published on agricultural labor in the United States between 1964 and 1969. The approximately 1,000 items listed are arranged in the following categories: Bibliographies, Books, Dissertations, Proceedings, Bulletins and unpublished works, Government publications, and Periodicals. The works are assigned subject designations depending on their content: e.g., General, Foreign, Government, Management, Migrant, Mobility, Outlook, Productivity, Seasonal, Supply, Unemployment, Union, Wages, Substitution, etc. This bibliography is in mimeographed form and was originally prepared for the Texas Legislature Committee on Wages and Employment for Agricultural and Small Business. For obvious reasons many of the items are particularly important to Mexican American labor research.

530. Schieffer, Jo Clare, and Isao Fujimoto. *The Social Implications of Agricultural Mechanization: A Bibliography.* Davis: Department of Applied Behavioral Sciences, University of California, 1969. 43 p. Annotated.

This mimeographed bibliography is the result of a thorough and systematic search for materials from the 1930s to 1968 on the social implications of mechanization and technology in agriculture. Although most of the materials are primarily from the 1960s, the entries relating to rural society date from the earlier period. The 399 entries are arranged in 11 subject areas including Social change and technology in agriculture; Agricultural technology: Technical materials; Technology and civilization: Forecast and analyses; Technology: Manpower implications; Technology and poverty; Social change and rural social change: general materials; and others. Many of the items are relevant to Mexican farm laborers due to their central role in the American economy and agricultural production. A useful feature of this work is the listing and description of the major indexes, journals, and organizations which were consulted in compiling the bibliography.

This is the first stage of a joint research project initiated in 1968 by the University of California at Davis, Cornell University, Louisiana State University, and Iowa State University.

531. Schlebecker, John T. *Bibliography of Books and Pamphlets on the History of Agriculture in the United States, 1607–1967.* Santa Barbara, CA: ABC-Clio, 1969. 183 p. Indexes.

One of the most extensive bibliographies on American agricultural history; it contains 2,042 books and pamphlets published from 1607 to 1967. Included are statistical works, biographies, and autobiographies of individuals involved in agriculture, and even some historical novels with themes relating to agriculture. Periodical articles and government documents have been excluded except in a few rare cases. This bibliography updates the work by Everett Edwards, entitled *A Bibliography of the History of Agriculture in the United States* (Washington, D.C.: U.S. Department of Agriculture, 1930). Approximately 70 percent of the titles in the new work were published since that date. For items directly related to the Mexican American the subject index should be consulted. Migratory labor, immigrants, and California farm labor seem to be the most pertinent subjects.

532. Sharma, Prakash C. *A Selected Research Bibliography on Mexican Immigration to the United States.* Monticello, IL: Council of Planning Librarians. 1974. (Exchange Bibliography, no. 672) 18 p.

This is one of the few Exchange Bibliographies that relates directly to the Mexican American. Most of the others deal with other minorities or ethnic groups in general. It contains nearly 250 selected references published mainly during the 1920-1967 period. The selected items are books, periodical articles, theses, dissertations, research reports, bulletins, mimeographed and other unpublished materials. Most of the sources are commonly cited works found in many other bibliographies on Mexican Americans. The lack of indexes and annotations makes this bibliography cumbersome to use.

533. Schideler, James H., and Lawrence B. Lee. *A Preliminary List of References for the History of Agriculture in California*. Davis: Agricultural History Center, University of California, 1967. 62 p. Index.
Sources for the history of agriculture in the State of California are listed in this comprehensive bibliography. The sources cover the Spanish and Mexican periods as well as the post-1848 years up to 1967. The focus is on individual industries, institutions, movements, politics, and leaders as well as such topics as land policy, land grants, colonies, labor, and Mexican agricultural labor. This bibliography comprises the third section of a project undertaken by the U.S. Department of Agriculture in cooperation with the Agricultural History Center at the University of California, Davis. The first section was entitled *A List of References for the History of Fruits and Vegetables in the U.S.*, compiled by Earl M. Rogers, and the second, *A Preliminary List of References for the History of Agricultural Science in the U.S.*, compiled by Carroll W. Pursell, Jr., and Earl M. Rogers.
    All three bibliographies are part of a plan to produce new works that would serve as revisions and updates of Everett E. Edward's, *A Bibliography of the History of Agriculture in the United States* (Washington, D.C.: U.S. Department of Agriculture, 1930). (Miscellaneous publication, no. 84).

534. Slobodek, Mitchell. *A Selective Bibliography of California Labor History*. Los Angeles: Institute of Industrial Relations, University of California, 1964. 265 p. Annotated. Index.
This extensive and selected bibliography on the history of labor in California was prepared to meet the needs of students and researchers with an interest in the labor movement and related fields. Included are pamphlets, articles, parts of books, selections from federal and state documents, and manuscript materials dating from the 1850s to 1963. With a few exceptions, the items listed are located in libraries of the San Francisco Bay area and Stanford University. While this bibliography was not compiled solely with Mexican Americans in mind, many of the entries are very significant to that group. One section on the Spanish and Mexican background contains items directly related to Mexican American history in California. Other relevant sources can be found in the index under the subheadings of Mexican agriculture, Mining, Food processing, Child labor, Supply of labor, Industrial workers of the world, and under specific industries.

535. Strange, Susan, and Rhea Priest. *Bibliography: The Mexican American in the Migrant Labor Setting*. East Lansing: Rural Manpower Center, Michigan State University, 1968. 26 p. Annotated. ED 032 188.
References dealing with Mexican American migrant laborers are cited in this work. The

275 entries date from 1928 to 1967 and include materials on cultural characteristics, education, employment, health, migrant farm labor, social change and adjustments, social welfare, and youth. The listed items are books, articles, reports, proceedings, and theses. No information is given as to the criteria for selection nor the purpose of the work.

536. Taylor, Paul S. "California Farm Labor: A Review." *Agricultural History,* 42 (January, 1968): 49–54.

This is one of the more important bibliographical essays on sources for the history of California agricultural labor. The author discusses the largely underutilized and unexploited sources such as the Federal Writers Project materials at the Bancroft Library, files of California newspapers, studies and reports of state bodies such as the Immigration and Housing Commission, reports of governors' commissions and committees and, most notably, the federal hearings of the La Follette Committee. In addition, organizations, dissertations, theses, monographic studies, and books are listed that provide information on various phases of agricultural labor. Although some of the materials relate to Chinese, Filipinos, and other immigrant groups, much of the information pertains to the Mexican American.

537. _____. *Material Relating to Agricultural and Maritime Strikes in California; Report and Key to Arrangements.* Berkeley: Bancroft Library, University of California, 1975. 6 p.

The Paul S. Taylor Collection, housed in the Bancroft Library of the University of California, Berkeley, is the subject of this guide. It is divided into six sections. The first section lists materials on or about the 1933 strike by cotton pickers in California. Included are original documents submitted to the Governor's Fact-Finding Committee, extensive newspaper and clipping files, field notes, reports on various cotton gins, notes on the hearings of the Committee, handbills distributed to the strikers, and various magazine articles. The second section lists 14 items on agricultural strikes and similar occurrences in cities of California during the 1930s. Most are clippings from newspapers, particularly the Tulare *Advance-Register.* The third section lists holdings related to the Salinas lettuce shedworkers' strike of 1936. It consist mainly of newspaper clippings and a file of the Salinas *Index-Journal.* The fourth section lists a document concerning the Sonoma County apple pickers' strike in 1935. The fifth section describes a small collection on the strike of sharecroppers in southeastern Missouri and eastern Arkansas in 1939. The sixth section contains references to copies of the *Associated Farmer;* clippings, pamphlets, and handbills relating to the labor initiative in the 1938 California election; clippings and pamphlets concerning maritime labor on the Pacific Coast; and materials relating to the I.W.W. in California for the years 1921–1923.

538. Turner, Howard B. *Imperial County, California: A Selected List of References.* Washington, DC: Bureau of Agricultural Economics Library, U.S. Department of Agriculture, 1941. (Economic Library List, no. 25) 77 p. Annotated. Index.

This is a selected list of references to the physical, agricultural, historical, and economic aspects of Imperial County, California, one of the important agricultural regions in the state. The bibliography is arranged in four broad areas: General, Agriculture, Irrigation and flood control, and Geography and geology. Of particular interest to Mexican American studies is the section on agriculture (pp. 9–23) which contains items relevant to the need for and use of Mexican labor in the production of certain crops. The call numbers given are for the U.S. Department of Agriculture Library.

539. U.S. Bureau of Labor Standards. *Selected References on Domestic Migratory Agricultural Workers, Their Families, Problems, and Programs, 1955–1960.* Washington, DC: U.S. Department of Labor, 1961. (Bureau of Labor Standards. *Bulletin,* no. 225) 38 p. Annotated.

The references in this bibliography cover governmental and nongovernmental sources dating from 1955 to mid-1960. Listed are documents on child labor, the community, migrants, education, employment, health, housing, income source, transportation, and welfare services. Many of the items included are reports of studies or surveys of migratory workers. Appended is a list of government agencies which provide information on current programs and developments.

This bibliography updates a 1956 publication by the Bureau of Labor Standards, entitled *Selected References on Migratory Workers and Their Families.*

540. Warnell, Katherine S. *Migratory Agricultural Labor: References to Books, Periodicals, and Films, 1959–1969.* Washington, DC: Legislative Reference Service, Library of Congress, 1969. 31 p.

This is one of the more recent listings from the Legislative Reference Service on migrant labor. Only nonfederal sources of information on migratory agricultural labor, published between 1959 and 1969, are included. The items cited are books, documents, periodical articles, and films covering such topics as *braceros,* California grape strike, education, income, health, housing, and welfare. The list of films on migratory labor gives the names of producers and distributors. This bibliography complements Mary Heslet's *Migratory Agricultural Labor: References to Federal Publications, Studies and Reports, 1959–1968* (Washington, D.C.: Legislative Reference Service, Library of Congress, 1969).

541. Yinger, Winthrop B. *César Chávez in "El Malcriado": 1965–1970 Compilation.* Fresno, CA: Library, Fresno State College, 1970. 8 p.

References to César Chávez in *El Malcriado* during the course of five years are listed chronologically in this index. The entries indicate date, page numbers, type of reference, title of essay, article, letter, or photograph. With the exception of nos. 1–10, all of the issues of *El Malcriado* published between 1965 and 1970 are housed in the Special Collections Department of the library at Fresno State College (now California State University, Fresno) and form part of the San Joaquin Valley Farm Workers Collection. This is a valuable reference tool for the study of Chávez and the United Farm Workers Union.

542. _____. *San Joaquin Valley Farm Workers Collection.* Fresno, CA: Library, Fresno State College, 1970. 11 p.

This is an itemized listing of materials in the San Joaquin Valley Farm Workers Collection which is housed in the Special Collection Department of the library at Fresno State College (now California State University, Fresno). The materials cover the period 1959–1970 and include ephemeral items (e.g., newspaper articles, bulletins, etc., a few new monographic publications, and bibliographies). The collection is arranged by the following subjects:

Agribusiness, The Arts, Agricultural Workers Freedom to Work Association, California Migrant Ministry, César Estrada Chávez, UFWOC Contracts with growers, Church documents, *Farm Labor* (a journal), Marches, Pilgrimages, National Advisory Committee on Farm Labor, National Sharecroppers Fund, National Farm Workers Association history, United Farm Workers Organizing Committee, and Miscellaneous sources and documents.

# Chapter 14

# *Linguistics*

Since the late 1800s there has been a continuous interest among linguists in the study of the Spanish language in the Western Hemisphere, particularly of the vernaculars of South America and Mexico. The impetus for much of the early works was provided by the Real Academia Española (the Spanish Royal Academy), and its various corresponding organizations in Latin America. However, the study of United States Spanish, as a subfield of American Spanish, received proportionately little attention from scholars until the middle of the 1960s.

Although the immense size and dialectal diversity of the Spanish-speaking population in the United States has provided a great deal of fertile ground for linguistic research, American linguists have practically neglected this area. Prior to the 1960s most of the work on Spanish in the Southwest was dominated by one man, Aurelio M. Espinosa. He concentrated his research on New Mexican Spanish and followed the approach of the Hispanic school. Since the mid-1960s, inspired by the Chicano Movement, a new generation of researchers turned their attention to sociological and educational aspects of Spanish in the United States. For in-depth reviews of the state of linguistic research on Mexican American Spanish, the reader is advised to consult Jerry R. Craddock's article in *Current Trends in Linguistics* and the introduction by Garland D. Bills in *Spanish and English of United States Hispanos: A Critical, Annotated, Linguistic Bibliography*. Both works are cited and annotated in this chapter.

Among the various Spanish-speakers in the United States, the Mexican Americans, as "the largest alloglottic minority," seem to have received the greatest attention.[1] Other groups such as the Puerto Ricans and Cubans in the United States have also gained some recognition, perhaps as a result of the socio-political ferment in the 1960s and a parallel resurgence of scholarly interest in the Mexican Americans, but not to the same extent.

As a result of the prior neglect, there are very few bibliographic sources available for research on Mexican American or Chicano Spanish. Likewise, because of this lack of sources, most of the general bibliographies and library guides on the Mexican American have not provided much assistance in identifying research on Mexican American Spanish.

Several important features are immediately apparent in the handful of bibliographies in this chapter. First, most of the works have not been separately published. Secondly, the majority of compilers are not native Spanish-speakers. Thirdly, and most important, they have all been produced by scholars in the field building somewhat systematically on the works of their predecessors. This has resulted in a rather tightly controlled bibliography.

A chronological survey of the existing bibliographies and bibliographical essays reveals that they span from 1911 to 1975 and fall roughly into three categories: those in the majority relate to the Spanish language in the Americas—works on United States Spanish occupy just a small subcategory within each bibliography; another group focuses on Spanish in the United States covering New Mexican Spanish, Spanish in the South and Southwest, and Chicano or Mexican American Spanish; and finally, the last group covers bibliographies on Mexican Spanish. These latter sources are useful in analyzing the influences on Spanish spoken by Mexican Americans since the Spanish of this group is considered by some to be a subdialect of Mexican Spanish.

The bibliographic foundation for sources on Mexican American Spanish was first established in 1941 by Madaline W. Nichols in her landmark work entitled *A Bibliographical Guide to Materials on American Spanish*. This work included United States Spanish as a subcategory. Prior to this publication research on Spanish in the Southwest was identifiable in only four bibliographic sources: two by C. Carroll Marden, one by Aurelio M. Espinosa, and another edited by Pedro Henríquez Ureña. The latter two are part of the *Biblioteca de dialectología hispanoamericano*.

Up to 1938 only bibliographic notes or preliminary bibliographies had been produced. By 1941, the year of Nichols's work, the tools of the linguist of Spanish in the Southwest included several general studies, local or regional dictionaries, vocabularies and word lists, Espinosa's works on New Mexico, and a few items on folklore and history.[2]

In 1954 Hensley C. Woodbridge prepared his model essay which served as a supplement to Nichols's bibliography. Many of the sources he listed were unpublished theses and dissertations. Following this, no bibliographies were produced on Mexican American Spanish for the next decade until Homero Serís devoted a special section to the United States in his work on Spanish linguistics. Six years later, in 1970, the works of Carlos A. Solé and Michael Fody III were published, extending the bibliographic coverage to 1969. In 1972 Solé issued a supplement to his 1970 work. The next year, 1973, Jerry R. Craddock's excellent article summarized the trends and state of the research up to 1970.

Another major landmark work was produced in 1975—*Spanish and English of United States Hispanos: A Critical, Annotated, Linguistic Bibliography,* by Richard V. Teschner, Garland D. Bills, and Jerry R. Craddock. It is undeniably the most thoroughgoing and comprehensive source, superseding all previous bibliographies. Few works if any escaped their attention. They specifically excluded educationally oriented materials on the Mexican American because a bibliography of Chicano-oriented applications in linguistics by Paul Willcott is in progress.

Throughout this century, the linguistic studies have tended to focus arbitrarily on specific geographical areas. Spanish of New Mexico and Texas received the most attention and that of Arizona and California the least. A few scattered unpublished theses can be found on Mexican American Spanish outside the Southwest, namely, on Mexican immigrant Spanish in Detroit, Chicago, and Seattle.

Topics covered by the recent literature of the "socio-linguistic revolution" include Pachuco, code-switching, English loan words, influence of United States Spanish on American English and on Amerindian languages in the United States, bilingualism and bilingual education, vernacular Chicano English, and social functions of language.[2] Syntax, phonology, grammar, folklore, and works of synthesis have received the least attention. No work on Mexican American Spanish has, as yet, achieved the scope of the research completed on the Puerto Ricans in *Bilingualism in the Barrio,* by Joshua A. Fishman and others.[3]

For additional sources on Mexican American Spanish, the chapters on Dictionaries, Education, and Folklore should be consulted.

1. Jerry R. Craddock, " Spanish in North America." In *Current Trends in Linguistics, Vol 10: Linguistics in North America,* ed. by William Bright, *et al.* (The Hague: Mouton, 1973), p. 475.

2. Craddock, "Spanish in North America," p. 468.

3. Joshua A. Fishman, Robert L. Cooper, Roxana Ma, *et al., Bilingualism in the Barrio,* Indiana University Publications. Language Science, Monographs, vol. 7 (Bloomington: Indiana University Research Center for the Language Sciences, 1971) 696 p.

543. Craddock, Jerry R. "Spanish in North America." *Current Trends in Linguistics,* 10 (1973): 467–501.

Accompanying this ground-breaking article is a bibliography of sources on Spanish as spoken in the United States. The major portion of the work refers to Mexican American Spanish, although coverage is complete for Puerto Rican, Cuban, *Isleño,* and Judeo-Spanish for the period 1953 to 1970.

The bibliography lists 195 entries arranged in alphabetical order. Works not examined by Craddock are marked with an asterisk. Books, articles, and dissertations which exemplify the new trends in socio-linguistics are most abundant. In particular, sources are cited on Pachuco, bilingualism, the social functions of language, place names, and studies of Spanish in various locales of Texas, New Mexico, southern Colorado, California, and Arizona.

This is one of the most important surveys of the linguistic research on Mexican American Spanish since Hensley C. Woodbridge's 1954 essay. It is essential to work in the field and helpful in identifying key works, unexplored areas, and comparative studies on other Spanish-speaking groups in the United States.

544. Davis, Jack Emory. "The Spanish of Mexico: An Annotated Bibliography for 1940–69." *Hispania,* 54 (Membership Issue October, 1971): 624–656. Annotated.

This bibliography lists 302 scholarly sources for the study of the Spanish language in Mexico. The work, spanning a 30-year period, incorporates all of the titles cited by Hensley C. Woodbridge in his "Annotated Bibliography" published by the *Kentucky Foreign Language Quarterly* in 1954. In addition, it continues and supplements the section on Mexico in Madaline W. Nichols's *Bibliographical Guide to Materials on American Spanish,* published in 1941 by Harvard University Press.

The listing of books and articles is comprehensive in scope for the period. Covered are general studies and works on lexicography, semantics, phonology, morphology, syntax, orthography, regional language, interlingual influence, argot-slang, language of individual authors, and place names. Of particular value are the interesting word and phrase studies and the list of dictionaries and vocabularies. Information concerning research in progress in the United States and Mexico is also provided.

545. Espinosa, Aurelio Macedonio. "Bibliografía" In *Estudios sobre el español de Nuevo Méjico*, pp. 24–42. Traducción y reelaboración con notas por Amado Alonso y Angel Rosenblat. Parte I. Fonética. Con nueve estudios complementarios sobre problemas de dialectología hispanoamericana, por A. Alonso. Buenos Aires: Instituto de Filología, Facultad de Filosofía y Letras, Universidad de Buenos Aires, 1930. (Biblioteca de dialectología hispanoamericana, no. 1) 472 p.

Accompanying the Spanish translation of the author's *Studies in New Mexican Spanish,* first published in 1909, is a scholarly bibliography on American Spanish. The original bibliography by Espinosa has been revised and updated by the editors of the *Biblioteca de dialectología hispanoamericana.* The additional works have been marked with an asterisk.

It is arranged in two parts. The first is a general list of the essential sources in Spanish, German, French and English which relate to the study of the Spanish language in the Americas. The second part is a bibliography on New Mexico. More than 300 entries include journal titles, dictionaries and vocabularies, linguistic atlas, regional grammars, language studies, folklore, histories, works of fiction, and a complete list of Espinosa's works up to 1930.

The majority of the general references are not concerned with Spanish in the United States but, nevertheless, serve as important tools for the serious scholar. The few selections relating to New Mexico, with the exception of the works by Espinosa, are mainly concerned with the folklore and history of the area. This bibliography demonstrates an early interest and awareness by Latin American linguists of the Spanish dialect in New Mexico. Espinosa's contributions were viewed as landmark works.

546. Fody III, Michael. "The Spanish of the American Southwest and Louisiana: A Bibliographic Survey for 1954–1969." *Orbis,* 19 (1970): 529–540. Annotated.

The purpose of this work is to supplement Hensley C. Woodbridge's "Spanish of the American South and Southwest: A Bibliographical Survey for 1940–1953," that appeared in *Orbis* in 1954. Fody's bibliography cites publications, dissertations, and master's theses which were produced between 1954 and 1969.

The works listed include studies of Spanish in the Southwest and Louisiana and studies on the influence of Spanish on English and Indian languages spoken in the areas covered. The items listed are arranged alphabetically under the following headings: Bibliography, General, California, Arizona, New Mexico, Texas, and Louisiana. The approximately 35 titles listed are extensively and critically annotated.

547. Henríquez Ureña, Pedro, ed. *El español en Méjico, los Estados Unidos y la America Central.* Trabajos de E. C. Hills, F. Semeleder, C. Carroll Marden, M. G. Revilla, A. R. Nykl, K. Lentzner, C. Gagini y R. J. Cuervo. Buenos Aires: Instituto de Filología, Facultad de Filosofía y Letras, Universidad de Buenos Aires, 1938. (Biblioteca de dialectología hispanoamericano, vol. 4) 526 p. Indexes.

This is a collection of scholarly studies of the Spanish language in Mexico, the United States, and Central America with supplementary bibliographies. The two sections which contain references of interest to Mexican American studies are the "Bibliografías particulares,'' nos. I and II. The first is entitled ''Sudoeste hispánico de los Estados Unidos'' (pp. xli–xlv) and the second is ''Méjico'' (pp. xlvi–lvii). The items are arranged in chronological order by imprint date and include works published between 1869 and 1936. Many early studies are included that do not appear in other bibliographies. Master's theses as well as books and articles are among the works cited. Other than linguistic studies there are works on folklore, songs, drama, slang, geographical place names, and vocabularies of Texas, New Mexico, Arizona, and Colorado. Scattered throughout the rest of the work are references to the Southwest. The indexes provide some access to these other sources.

In addition to the bibliographies, an important study in the main body of the work pertains to the Spanish of the Southwest. It is entitled ''El español de Nuevo Méjico,'' by Elijah C. Hills. This is an essential and noteworthy work for all serious students of Spanish philology.

548. Hernández-Chávez, Eduardo, Andrew D. Cohen, and Anthony F. Beltramo. ''Bibliography.'' In *El Lenguaje de los Chicanos: Regional and Social Characteristics Used by Mexican Americans*, pp. 238–256. Arlington, VA: Center for Applied Linguistics, 1975. 256 p.

Works of a linguistic nature dealing primarily with the speech of Chicanos and the influence of Spanish language on American English are cited in this specialized bibliography. Three hundred sixty-seven articles, books, and theses are arranged in one alphabetical listing. Subjects covered include: argot; syntax; bilingualism; place names; flora; surnames; archaisms; loan words; Western vocabulary; socio- and psycholinguistics; and others related to the Spanish spoken mainly in Arizona, New Mexico, Texas, California, and the Southwest in general.

The purpose of the work is to stimulate interest in the study of language used by the Spanish-speaking in the United States. Suggestions are made for areas in need of further study.

549. Hinojos, Francisco G. ''Selected Bibliography on the Pachuco.'' *Atisbos,* (Summer, 1975): 62–65.

This is an alphabetical listing of sources on the language of the Pachuco. Forty-seven items, including books, articles, ERIC documents, conference papers, and theses are listed. The titles, written or published between 1933 and 1972, cover such subjects as *Caló*, local and regional vocabularies, criminal argot along the border, the zoot-suit riots, anglicisms in American Spanish, and Mexican American youth gangs. The selection is quite comprehensive and presents varying opinions expressed over the years concerning the origins of this particular dialect. The bibliography is preceded by a discussion entitled ''Notes on the Pachuco: Stereotypes, History and Dialect.'' The author attempts to clarify certain misunderstandings and misconceptions concerning the Pachuco and his speech.

550. Keniston, Hayward. ''Notes on Research in the Spanish Spoken in the United States.'' *American Council of Learned Societies. Bulletin,* 34 (1942): 64–67.

The state of the literature on the study of Spanish in the United States is described in this brief bibliographical essay. The works analyzed are treated in chronological order from the earliest in 1894 to the late 1930s. Mentioned are approximately 18 articles, full-length studies, dictionaries, works on place names, and bibliographies which constitute the ground work for much of the linguistic research after 1940. Keniston points out the areas in need of further investigation, e.g., the relation between the Spanish in Mexico and that of the Southwestern United States. Richard Teschner has noted in his bibliography that the early works of Juan B. Rael are noticeably missing from this study.

551. Marden, C. Carroll. "A Bibliography of American Spanish, 1911-1921." In *Homenaje ofrecido a Menéndez Pidal,* vol. I, pp. 589-605. Madrid: Librería y Casa Editorial Hernando, 1925. 3 vols. Annotated.
This bibliography supplements the author's previous "Notes for a Bibliography of American Spanish," published in 1911. Although the works cited date mainly from 1911 to 1921, a few items published prior to this period are included. The same outline and arrangement of the earlier study are used in this bibliography. The section on Mexico contains 17 new titles and the section on the United States of America lists one study on Louisiana Spanish, seven entries for works by Aurelio M. Espinosa, and a New Mexico folksong published by Charles F. Lummis.

Again this work continues to reflect the paucity of linguistic research on Spanish in the United States. With the exception of the efforts by Espinosa, most scholars demonstrated more interest in the language and dialects of Mexico.

552. _____. "Notes for a Bibliography of American Spanish." In *Studies in Honor of A. Marshall Elliott,* vol. II, pp. 267-292. Baltimore, MD: John Hopkins University Press, 1911. 2 vols. Annotated.
This is one of the earliest attempts at a comprehensive bibliography of works related to the Spanish in the Americas. The items are arranged in six divisions: Spanish America (in general); South America (with subdivision by countries); Central America (with subdivision by countries); Mexico; West Indies (including Cuba, Puerto Rico and Curaçao); and the United States (New Mexico). The portions relating to Mexico and the United States contain materials of utility to research on the Spanish of the Mexican Americans. The 39 titles listed in these two sections were published between 1844 and 1911. The Mexican section contains citations to vocabularies, dictionaries, place name studies, prose, and verse written in popular dialect. The United States portion is limited to works related to the Spanish used in New Mexico, i.e., four works by Aurelio M. Espinosa, a text of *Los Pastores,* a study by E. C. Hill of New Mexican Spanish, and Charles F. Lummis's *The Land of Poco Tiempo.*

This bibliography, although offering some evidence of interest in the Spanish of the United States, actually indicates a neglect of the area by linguists of the period.

553. Nichols, Madaline W. *A Bibliographical Guide to Materials on American Spanish.* Cambridge, MA: Harvard University Press, 1941. 114 p. Annotated. Index.
This excellent work was one of the earliest reference guides to the literature on Spanish language in the Americas. Prior to the later bibliographies of Woodbridge and Teschner, this was considered to be the standard guide in the field. Since 1954 it has been updated by the two authors mentioned above.

The more than 1,200 citations are arranged geographically by country and subdivided by topics. The sections on Spanish language in the United States and in Mexico are helpful for research on the language of the Mexican Americans. The section on Mexico covers general studies, dictionaries and vocabularies, individual words, influence of other languages, toponymy, flora and fauna. The United States section includes general studies, dictionaries and vocabularies, and the influence of other languages. A useful list of official philological organizations and their publications and a bibliography of recommended bibliographies are also included.

554. Serís, Homero. *Bibliografía de la lingüística española.* Bogotá: Instituto Caro y Cuervo, 1964. (Publicaciones del Instituto Caro y Cuervo, no. 19) 981 p. Annotated. Index.
This comprehensive bibliography covers Spanish linguistics. Although the work is devoted to the entire Spanish-speaking world, the materials pertinent to the Mexican American are found in the section devoted to Spanish in the United States (pp. 752–758) and in Mexico (pp. 762–773). The titles cited in each section are grouped under headings such as bibliography, general studies, phonetics, syntax, lexicography, semantics, fauna and flora, place names, and personal names. The major works in English, German, and Spanish are mentioned: 60 titles are listed under the United States and 155 titles under Mexico. The items are selectively annotated in Spanish. This is an essential tool for research on the Spanish of the Mexican Americans and of the Southwest.

555. Solé, Carlos A. *Bibliografía sobre el español en América, 1920–1967.* Washington, DC: Georgetown University Press, 1970. 175 p. Annotated. Index.

556. _____. ''Bibliografía sobre el español en América: 1967–1971.'' *Anuario de Letras,* 10 (1972): 253–288.
Sources on the linguistic and dialectic development of Spanish in America are compiled in this bibliography. The majority of the items are arranged under country headings. The section on ''Estados Unidos de Norteamérica'' contains pertinent sources on the language spoken by Mexican Americans, subarranged geographically (*Estudios generales, Suroestes, Arizona, Colorado, Nuevo México, Texas, Florida, Louisiana,* and *otras regiones*). Included are 65 titles of books, articles, and dissertations which appeared between 1920 and 1967. Items are listed chronologically by state. As expected the listings for the states of New Mexico and Texas have the greatest number of entries. Critical regional and local studies, dictionaries, vocabularies, place name works, switching, phonetic developments, English influence, slang, and dialectal studies are among the topics covered by the references cited.
The bibliography is only partially annotated with concise descriptions of most of the major works. A reading knowledge of Spanish is essential in using this work since the introduction and brief annotations are in Spanish.
The 1972 supplement contains 327 additional titles mainly from 1967 to 1971, arranged in the same manner as the earlier work. The section relating to Spanish in the United States (pp. 272–273) cites nine new titles including works on the Pachucos, the Spanish of Texas, New York, and Los Angeles, to mention a few. The list of general studies which precedes the country listings may contain some useful citations for the study of Spanish in the United States.
A lengthy introduction written in Spanish describes the nature of the upsurge in interest in American Spanish and the state of the literature covered by the supplement.

557. Teschner, Richard V., Garland D. Bills, and Jerry R. Craddock. *Spanish and English of United States Hispanos: A Critical, Annotated, Linguistic Bibliography.* Arlington, VA: Center for Applied Linguistics, 1975. 352 p. Annotated. Index.

558. _____, Garland D. Bills, and Jerry R. Craddock. "Current Research on the Language(s) of U.S. Hispanos." *Hispania,* 60 (May, 1977): 347-358.
The purpose of this superb bibliography is to disseminate knowledge about the language and linguistic heritage of the Hispanic population in the United States and to focus attention on the strengths (and weaknesses) of the research in the field. The compilers have attempted to update and continue Hensley C. Woodbridge's "Spanish in the American South and Southwest: A Bibliographical Survey for the years 1940-1953," published in *Orbis* in 1954.
Included are 675 works arranged in the following categories: bibliographies, comprehensive/general studies and anthologies, sociolinguistics, textbooks, Spanish phonology, grammar, lexicon, onomastics and toponymy, English influence on Spanish, Spanish influence on English, English of a particular group, Spanish influence on Amerindian languages, and code-switching. More than half of the sources relate to the Mexican American. Also covered are Puerto Ricans, Cubans, *Isleños, Peninsulares,* and Sephardic Jews. Most titles have been critically annotated and, although linguistically orientated, represent a wide variety of disciplines: anthropology, sociology, education, folklore, literature, and psychology, to mention a few.
This is one of the finest and most comprehensive bibliographies available on the language of Mexican Americans. The enumerative supplement adds 253 items that appeared in print between January, 1974, and mid-January, 1977.

559. Woodbridge, Hensley C. "An Annotated Bibliography of Mexican Spanish for 1940-1953." *Kentucky Foreign Language Quarterly,* 1 (1954): 80-89. Annotated.
Covering the years 1940-1953, this bibliography continues the Mexican section of Madaline W. Nichols's *A Bibliographical Guide to Materials on American Spanish.* Included are books, articles and dissertations which relate to all the geographical areas of Mexico. The items cited are arranged in five sections: Bibliographies, General studies, Phonology, Descriptive studies, and Lexicography. The entries are partially annotated with short descriptions of the content. Excluded are works on style and Latin American Spanish as a whole.
This work and his other related bibliographies have served researchers well. The materials in this particular work contribute to an understanding of the influence of Mexican Spanish on the Spanish spoken by Mexican Americans, especially in the Southwest.

560. _____. "Spanish in the American South and Southwest: A Bibliographical Survey for 1940-1953." *Orbis,* 3 (1954): 236-244. Annotated.
This model bibliographic essay summarizes the state of the literature on the Spanish of the South and Southwest. The essay approaches the works geographically. Florida, Louisiana, Texas, Southwest, New Mexico, Arizona, and California are covered. The sections on Texas, New Mexico, Arizona, and California are the most relevant to the study of the language of the Mexican American. Research completed between 1940 and

1953 is discussed. Footnotes include additional materials not summarized in the text. Among the studies reviewed, lexicographic research predominates with only a few studies in the area of syntax and phonology. The titles cited indicate a growing interest in Spanish loan words and Spanish influences on American English. The author includes books, articles, theses, and dissertations in this survey.

It is useful as an introduction to the state of the research and literature of the period. This work updates that done by Madaline W. Nichols in *A Bibliographical Guide to Materials on American Spanish* in 1941.

# Chapter 15

# *Literature*

The distinct and separate identity of Mexican American literature, within a broader American context, is widely recognized today. Since 1970, attention has been given to the novel, poetry, drama, essay, and other genres of Mexican American literature. Early histories and bibliographies of American literature virtually ignored the written heritage of the Mexican American. Although folklorists and linguists gave some attention to the Spanish oral traditions in the Southwest during the first half of the twentieth century, emphasis in traditional literary circles was placed on the Spanish peninsular writers and their influence on American letters. Stanley T. Williams's *The Spanish Background in American Literature* exemplifies that tendency.[1] The proliferation of general and institutional bibliographies on the Mexican American during the 1960s and 1970s provided little assistance in identifying and defining Mexican American literature. The library guides, as discussed in an earlier chapter, frequently added to the confusion by listing many works by notable Mexican and South American literary figures.

Around 1970, a small number of scholars shifted their attention to this neglected area in American literature. Their recent bibliographies focus on the Chicano creative arts and literary "florecimiento."[2]

The special bibliographies selected for this chapter include works written by and about the Mexican American and thus provide a dual literary perspective—the Chicano and the "Chicanesque," or the Mexican American and Anglo-American views.[3] Among the selections are bibliographies of literature of the American West and Southwest; bibliographies of Chicano literature and criticism; and bibliographies of literary works by and about the Mexican American, with a pedagogical orientation.

In the first category, the bibliographies of literature of the West and Southwest share several characteristics, the primary one being that they contain works by the so-named "Chicanesque" writers.[4] Another characteristic is that all of the compilers are Anglo and the perspective they present is unquestionably Anglo-American. The works cited in these bibliographies recognize the presence of Mexican Americans, as characters in the historical drama of the region, but not necessarily as creators of the literature. Each of these bibliographies contains either chapters dedicated to the Spanish Mexican heritage or selections which speak of this heritage. However, the titles listed are usually in English and they depict the "Chicanesque" or Anglo-American image of the Mexican American and his customs. Most of the Southwestern bibliographies were produced in the 1950s and 1960s and cover more than a century of literary contributions. These compilations are still

191

important sources for the study of the Mexican American. They contain some of the major works of fiction, poetry, drama, and even folklore that represent one aspect of the literary reality of the region.

A counterpoint to the above are the more recent bibliographies and bibliographical essays written and published since 1970, which concentrate on contemporary Chicano literature from the 1960s to the present. This period, considered by Philip D. Ortego as the "Chicano Renaissance"[5] and recently referred to as the "florecimiento" by Juan Rodríguez, spawned numerous new literary works by Chicano writers.[6] The compilers of the recent bibliographies, both Anglo-American and Mexican American, have attempted to define Chicano literature in terms of authors, genre, and time periods. With the exception of three independently published works, all of these bibliographies have been issued as articles in such journals as *El Grito, Atisbos,* and the *Arizona Quarterly,* to mention only a few.

A third category of bibliographical works relating to Chicano literature are those with a pedagogical orientation. Among these are the listings of literature and other instructional materials for children and adolescents. They are the products of librarians', educators' and school officials' efforts to identify works of literary quality appropriate for bilingual-bicultural programs or units of classroom instruction. Compiled in the 1970s, these bibliographies were prepared in order to promote attitudes of respect and appreciation for Mexican American literature and culture. The titles are in English or Spanish, for the most part. However, many of the Spanish works are either translations of familiar children's literature in English or works written and published in Spain, Mexico, and Latin America. There is still a great need for new creative literature on the Mexican American experience for use in classroom instruction and curriculum planning. Other suggested readings and bibliographies for children are listed in the chapter on Education. Some of the library guides also devote a section to children's literature.

Increased awareness of Chicano literature has led to a corresponding increase not only in the compilation of bibliographies but also in conference programs and publications by such organizations as the Modern Language Association, the American Association of Teachers of Spanish and Portuguese, and the Pacific Coast Council on Latin American Studies. In the coming years, it is anticipated that many new research tools will be prepared in this area which will improve bibliographic access to Chicano literature and literary criticism. Several important works are in progress at this time. Ernestina N. Eger is compiling a comprehensive *Bibliography of Criticism of Contemporary Chicano Literature.* Her bibliographical notes have appeared regularly in *Carta Abierta.* This publication, edited by Juan Rodríguez, is one of the most important current sources of bibliographic information on the Chicano literary world. Julio A. Martínez has two works in progress. The first is a *Bio-bibliographical Directory of Chicano Scholars and Writers,* to be published during 1979 by Scarecrow Press; and the second is an *Encyclopedic Dictionary of Chicano Literature,* to be published by San Diego State University.

Most of the bibliographic activity in this area has been centered in academic institutions in the Western and Southwestern states—Texas, California, Arizona, New Mexico, and the State of Washington. These efforts are achieving nation-wide recognition for Mexican American writers as they assume a legitimate place in American literature.

1. Stanley T. Williams, *The Spanish Background in American Literature* (New Haven: Yale University Press, 1955), 2 vols.

2. Juan Rodríguez, "El florecimiento de la literatura chicana," In *La otra cara de México: Los Chicanos*, ed. by David Maciel (México, D.F.: Ediciones El Caballito, 1977), p. 348–69.

3. Cecil Robinson, *Mexico and the Hispanic Southwest in American Literature*, revised from *With the Ears of Strangers* (Tucson: University of Arizona Press, 1977), p. 349. Robinson referred to this perspective as "the view from within and the view from without."

4. Francisco A. Lomelí and Donaldo W. Urioste, *Chicano Perspectives in Literature: A Critical and Annotated Bibliography* (Albuquerque, NM: Pajarito Publications, 1976), p. 12.

5. Philip D. Ortego, "The Chicano Renaissance," *Social Casework*, 52 (May, 1971): 294–307.

6. Rodríguez, "El florecimiento," p. 348–69.

561. *Aspectos de la literatura Chicana/Aspects of Chicano Literature*. Berkeley: Chicano Studies Library, University of California, 1979. 12 p.
This brochure was prepared to accompany a traveling exhibit on Chicano literature, assembled by Richard Chabrán and Oscar Treviño. Both the exhibit and the brochure include 163 examples of the diverse forms of the Mexican American literary heritage as expressed in the drama, folklore, poetry, and prose. Selections are arranged in the following categories: Criticism, Drama, Newspaper clippings, Oral traditions, Periodicals, Poetry, and Prose.
The collection may be obtained for display purposes or the brochure may serve as a guide to the creation of a new exhibit utilizing the resources in local libraries.

562. Baird, Newton D., and Robert Greenwood. *An Annotated Bibliography of California Fiction, 1664–1970*. Georgetown, CA: Talisman Literary Research, 1971. 521 p. Annotated. Indexes.
Works of American fiction that include California in the setting are cited in this bibliography. It is not a guide to California authors, although many are listed. A total of 2,711 titles are cited. Among these 68 relate to Spanish California, 26 include Mexican Americans as characters, 33 are identified as dealing with Mexican California, and 16 cover the theme of migrant labor. Among the 33 novels and short stories in which the Mexican American is portrayed, only three are by Chicano authors. The remainder are products of Anglo writers and date roughly from 1891 to 1966. Each citation includes a short annotation describing the plot, locale, and book review sources. This work updates to 1970 the 1938 bibliography by Edgar Hinkel, entitled *Bibliography of California Literature. Volume 1. Fiction*. This recent work by Baird and Greenwood is one of the useful sources for research on the Mexican American in the "Literatura Chicanesca." Much of the fiction is historical and thus is valuable for gaining special insight into early California life. The works listed provide "the view from without," discussed by Cecil Robinson in *Mexico and the Hispanic Southwest in American Literature*. Although this perspective is frequently biased and inaccurate, it is, nevertheless, an integral part of American literature on the Mexican American.
Many of the titles in this bibliography are available in the California State Library, the Los Angeles Public Library, and other research libraries in the state.

563. Cárdenas de Dwyer, Carlota. *Chicano Literature: An Introduction and an Annotated Bibliography*. Austin: Departments of English and Mexican American Studies, University of Texas, 1974. 23 p. Annotated. ED 088 080.

This bibliography attempts to resolve certain questions surrounding the origin, nature, composition, style, and language of Chicano literature. Following a discussion on the topic is a bibliography of 57 titles including novels, short stories, poetry collections, Chicano and multi-ethnic anthologies, drama, and literary criticism arranged under these categories. The annotations provide descriptions of the content, reading level, and language. This is a collection of basic selections of Chicano literature.

564. Castro, Donald F. "Chicano Literature: A Bibliographical Essay." *English in Texas,* 7 (Summer, 1976): 14–19. ED 134 986.

Appearing in an issue of *English in Texas,* this bibliographical essay is devoted entirely to Chicano literature. The article presents various proposed courses that are appropriate for college or advanced secondary school students. The bibliography or list of sources is divided into five parts, each corresponding to one of the five proposed courses, i.e., Introduction to Chicano literature, Chicano short story and drama, Chicano poetry, Chicano nonfiction, and Chicano novel. The 35 books, many of which are anthologies, are evaluated in the essay as to their usefulness as texts for each course. The generic approach is regarded by the author as the best suited to the study and teaching of Chicano literature. The books cited are currently available and present a survey of writings by contemporary Chicano authors. Additional articles, dissertations, and chapters in books on literary criticism and the state of the art are also mentioned in the essay.

This essay and list of sources is helpful for selecting appropriate readings for courses on Chicano literature or for units on the Chicano in American literature courses.

565. Dobie, James Frank. *Guide to Life and Literature of the Southwest.* Revised and enlarged Dallas, TX: Southern Methodist University Press, 1952. 222 p. Annotated. Index.

This is a guide to the regional literature of the Southwest. The author prefers to consider this a collection, rather than a bibliography, of some of the books that make "good reading." The selections cover all facets of the Southwestern mosaic: the people, customs, humor, occupations, flora and fauna. The chapter on Spanish Mexican strains lists 45 entries. These include a sampling of some of the well-known classics in folklore, history, travel accounts, and fiction, many by Anglo-American writers, during the early part of this century. Listed with the works of Willa Cather, Anita Brenner, and Charles F. Lummis are the writings of Madam Calderón de la Barca, Cabeza de Vaca, and Bernal Díaz. Although dated, Dobie's selections provide an introduction to the study of the influences of Spain and Mexico on life and literature of the region. The selections are appropriate for secondary school and college-level readers.

566. Eger, Ernestina N. "Bibliographical Notes: Bibliography of Current Literary Criticism." *Carta Abierta,* 10–11 (junio, 1978): 2–4; 12 (noviembre, 1978): 2–7; 13–14 (diciembre, 1978): 2–3.

These current bibliographical notes, which have appeared regularly in *Carta Abierta,* respond to the increasing demand and need for more information on contemporary Chicano literary criticism. Although the arrangement of each list varies, the types of materials selected for inclusion are guided by similar criteria. Only works of criticism on Chicano and Mexican American authors are cited; Mexican and "Chicanesque" writers are excluded. Only criticism of the genres of the novel, short story, poetry, theater, and autobiography from 1960 onward are included. Articles, books, dissertations, conference papers, unpublished manuscripts, and works in progress are listed. Among these sources are bibliographies, literary history, theory, analysis, book reviews, interviews, and biographical works which relate to the topic of literary criticism. These bibliographical notes are preparing the foundation for a future comprehensive bibliography of criticism of contemporary Chicano literature.

567. Goodman, Elizabeth B., and Jacqueline N. Shachter. "Books about Spanish Americans." *Instructor,* 81 (January, 1972): 51.
This is a one-page list of recommended children's books with stories about the history and folklore of Mexico and the Mexican Americans of the Southwest. Selections are in English and Spanish. The list is arranged by language. Twenty-six titles in English include works on Father Serra, *piñatas,* California *rancheros,* and children's fiction. Twenty-seven titles in Spanish or Spanish/English include such selections as Berlitz for children, fiction, the Cat in the Hat in Spanish, riddles, and fairy tales. The works were selected by the compiler to ''help [Mexican American children] build their self-images.'' The materials are appropriate for a school or public library collection.

568. Hancock, Joel. "The Emergence of Chicano Poetry: A Survey of Sources, Themes, and Techniques." *Arizona Quarterly,* 29 (Spring, 1973): 57–73.
A discussion of the bibliographical sources of Chicano poetry as well as the predominant themes and techniques are combined in this article. As Hancock indicates, the most energetic efforts of the "Rennaissance of the Barrios" seems to be centered on literature. The author discusses the main Chicano journals, newspapers, anthologies, and collections of poetry by individual authors. Mentioned are seven journals and newspapers which have, with some regularity, published special sections or issues devoted to Chicano literature, and specifically poetry. Four anthologies and four collections of poetry are discussed in some detail. The poetry in these sources are analyzed in terms of content, influence, themes and techniques. Specific works are cited in the footnotes.

569. Haslam, Gerald. "¡Por la Causa! Mexican-American Literature." *College English,* 31 (April, 1970): 695–709.
This bibliographical essay focuses on the state of Chicano literature and criticism. The author reviews a few of the most notable Chicano writings, discusses trends, and points out factors which influence the thematic direction of the literature. Cited in the text are novels, short stories, essays, poems, and plays. Mention is made also of six selected periodicals which have accepted original works by Chicanos and articles on Hispanic American and Latin American heritage: *Southwest Review, New Mexico Quarterly, South Dakota Review, The Texas Observer, North Coast,* and *Arizona Quarterly.* The author reflects on the strong influence of Mexico in the life and creative efforts of Mexican Americans. The bibliographical citations for the works discussed in the text are found in the footnotes.

570. Kurtz, Kenneth. *Literature of the American Southwest: A Selective Bibliography.* Los Angeles: Occidental College, 1956. 63 p. Annotated.
This is a representative survey of the literature depicting the people, life and land of the Southwest. The compiler, in recognition of the fact that Mexican Americans are in-

adequately treated in literary works, includes several carefully selected sections on literature relating to Mexico and the Mexican heritage in the Southwest. Kurtz has accurately labeled his work a "reading list of a thousand books which express the American Southwest." The works are organized in 17 sections which include Bibliographies, Studies of Southwestern literature, The Regional Background, The Historical Background, Anthologies (prose and poetry), Poetry: Individual authors, The California-Nevada Scene, Days of the Dons and Missions of the Southwest, The New Mexico-Arizona Scene, Heroes and Villains: Frontier Fighters, Outlaws and Sheriffs, Home on the Range, Mining, The Indian in the Southwest, Mexicana, The Mormons, The Language of the Southwest, Some Southwestern Magazines. The titles date from ca. 1825 to the mid-1950s and are limited to publications in English. Among the titles are characteristic types of literature of the region; fiction, poetry, autobiography, biography, travel accounts, descriptive works, personal essays, and historical and cultural works which contribute to an understanding of life in the Southwest.

571. Lewis, Marvin A. "Toward a Bibliography of Chicano Literary Criticism." National Association of Interdisciplinary Studies for Native American, Black, Chicano *Newsletter*, 1 (April, 1976): 9–12.
This bibliography was compiled in recognition of the growing attention received by Chicano literature in recent years. The selections are from 1970 to 1975 and include journal articles, conference proceedings, dissertations, and review literature on Chicano literary criticism. The 49 items are arranged in three categories with the conference proceedings listed under the articles and the dissertations and reviews listed separately. Works in Spanish and English by Chicano and Anglo scholars are listed. The materials cover criticism of the novel, poetry, *Teatro Chicano*, historical surveys of the literature, the Pocho in fiction, and the roots and background of Mexican American literature. This bibliography is among the few works which have begun to pave the way toward the identification and definition of the true Chicano literature and its criticism. All the items cited are readily available in most research libraries with sizable Mexican American collections. With the exception of the four dissertations, all the other works are published in such periodicals as *La Luz, La Revista Chicano Riqueña, Cuadernos Americanos, Aztlán, El Grito* and others.

572. Lomelí, Francisco A., and Donald W. Urioste. "An Annotated Bibliography on Chicano Literature." *Latin America: Power and Poverty*, proceedings of the Pacific Coast Council on Latin American Studies, 4 (1975): 193–206. Annotated.
Sources on the Mexican American from a strictly literary perspective are cited in this bibliography. It covers a representative selection of works in the following categories: poetry, novels, short fiction, drama, anthologies, literary criticism, oral tradition in print, and journal articles. Most of the authors are Chicanos and the focus is on the Chicano experience. Extensive critical annotations are provided for each of the 52 works cited. The bibliography traces the Chicano literary expression from 1946 to 1975. It fills a gap, since most bibliographies on the Mexican American are heavily oriented toward the social sciences, literature of Mexico, or works by Anglo-Americans.

573. _____, and Donald W. Urioste. *Chicano Perspectives in Literature; A Critical and Annotated Bibliography.* Albuquerque, NM: Pajarito Publications, 1976. 120 p. Annotated.

This is perhaps the most complete and up-to-date bibliography strictly on Mexican American literature. Approximately 127 titles are mentioned from the earliest known Chicano novel, dated 1892, up to works published in 1976. It covers poetry, fiction, short stories, theater, anthologies, literary criticism, oral tradition in print, journals and their issues that relate to literature, arranged in this order. The bibliography was designed to further define and explore Chicano literature concentrating on works by Mexican Americans and by excluding works by Mexican authors. A special section entitled ''Literatura Chicanesca'' includes works by a few non-Chicanos written about the Chicano. An author index and a glossary of literary terminology and Chicano expressions are included to assist the user.

574. Los Angeles City School District. *Portraits; The Literature of Minorities: An Annotated Bibliography of Literature By and About Four Ethnic Groups in the United States for Grades 7–12.* Los Angeles: Los Angeles City School District, 1970. 69 p. Annotated.

The purpose of this work is to identify printed materials of literary quality by and about ethnic groups in the United States for students in middle and secondary schools. The focus is on literature concerning Black Americans, Mexican Americans, North American Indians, and Asian Americans. The materials cited are grouped under the headings of Fiction (novels, short stories); Poetry; Drama; Folktales and legends; Prose nonfiction (biographies, autobiographies, essays, letters, and speeches); and Anthologies. Each selection is annotated with description of the content and recommended level and use. Most of the selections concern Black Americans but a 1972 supplement includes more items relating to the Mexican Americans.

575. Major, Mabel, and Thomas Matthews Pearce. *Southwest Heritage: A Literary History with Bibliography.* 3rd revised and enlarged ed. Albuquerque: University of New Mexico Press, 1972. 378 p. Index.

This is a bibliographic review of works in English which relate to the different cultural strains of the Southwest, excluding California. The works span the period before the coming of the first Anglo-American settlers up to 1970. Drama, poetry, narratives, folk art and folklore, chronicles, journals, historical writing, biographies, autobiographies, children's literature, fiction, and other genre are arranged by four chronological periods. The items mentioned are critically analyzed in relation to the general literature on the Southwest. A selected bibliography of materials for general readers, bibliographic guides, and dictionaries is appended. Earlier editions of this work were published in 1938 and 1948. This excellent guide to the literature of the Southwest could be very useful as a source of background material for the study of Mexican American culture and history.

576. Martínez, Ernest A. *Chicano Children's Literature: Annotated Bibliography.* Rohnert Park, CA: Chicano Studies Department, Sonoma State College, 1972. 41 p. Annotated. ED 075 158.

Children's literature in Spanish and English that seems appropriate for bilingual-bicultural instruction is cited here. The 249 books are listed alphabetically by author and date from 1938 to 1972. Each entry is a brief bibliographic statement. Some items lack the necessary imprint. The works are rated on a scale of 1 to 5 using criteria such as literary merit, reality of characters, attitudes, existence of nostalgia and quality of illustrations. Grade level is also assigned to each work. For the most part the items selected are appropriate for primary through secondary school children. Certain titles such as Octavio Paz's *Laberinto de la Soledad* is more appropriate for college-level reading.

577. Powell, Lawrence Clark. *Heart of the Southwest; A Selective Bibliography of Novels, Stories and Tales Laid in Arizona and New Mexico and Adjacent Lands.* Los Angeles: Dawson's Book Shop, 1955. 42 p. Annotated. Index.
Fictional works about Arizona and New Mexico are listed in this selective bibliography. Most of the 119 entries provide accounts by Anglo-Americans of life in the Southwest. Many are descriptive of the Spanish and Mexican heritage. One such example is R. A. Summers's *Dark Madonna*, which used as a setting Tucson's "Little Mexico" in recounting the story of a Mexican family during the Depression. The works are arranged in alphabetical order in one list. A title index is provided. This bibliography is useful in identifying works that describe the Anglo-American's image of the Mexican American in the early part of the twentieth century.

578. Robinson, Cecil. "Bibliography." In *Mexico and the Hispanic Southwest in American Literature,* pp. 375–382. Tucson: University of Arizona Press, 1977. 391 p. Index.
This is a very thorough and informative revised edition of his earlier work entitled *With the Ears of Strangers; The Mexican in American Literature,* published in 1963. In addition to expanding the bibliographic coverage, Robinson adds a new chapter on Chicano literature (pp. 308–331), thus placing it in the context of modern American literature. Robinson writes that "... thanks to the Chicano movement, Mexican-American culture has been rescued at the eleventh hour ... " The supporting bibliography is arranged in alphabetical order by author. The selections include works of poetry, fiction, drama, and history by Chicano writers; literary and historical works by Anglo writers that demonstrate the influence of Mexico and the Hispanic Southwest; memoirs and personal narratives of early pioneers; and biographical and bibliographical studies of American authors. Approximately 200 books and articles are listed which are crucial to a study of Mexican American literature and the Hispanic literary heritage of the Southwest.

579. Rojas, Guillermo. "Toward a Chicano/Raza Bibliography; Drama, Prose, Poetry." *El Grito,* 7 (December, 1973): 1–85.
Literary works exclusively by Chicano writers are included in this bibliography. Excluded are titles published by Mexican authors. The selections cover the period 1965 to 1972 and were found in newspapers, journals, books, and unpublished manuscripts. More than 1,500 titles are arranged in three categories: Drama, Prose, and Poetry. Published and unpublished works are listed separately in each category. Forty-eight pages are devoted to poetry which is the most extensive of the three sections. The appendix contains a serials listing of Chicano/Raza Newspapers and Periodicals, 1965–1972. The list can be consulted when searching for the literary works cited in the bibliography. Approximately 158 journals, bulletins, newsletters and newspapers are included with publishers' addresses, known locations, and holdings statements. This is one of the most comprehensive bibliographies of Chicano literature up to 1972.

580. Salinas, Judy. "Recommended Resources for Teaching Chicano Literature and Culture." *Popular Culture Association Newsletter,* 6 (March, 1977): 62–75. Annotated.
This bibliographical work directs educators to the sources of materials that are essential in the preparation of an instructional program in Chicano literature and culture. The essay divides the sources into seven categories: Publishing houses and distributors; University Presses, libraries, and Chicano centers; Bibliographies; Anthologies on the Chicano and Chicano literature; Literature and cultural books; Journals and newsletters; and Films and audiovisual materials. This work combines the features of a directory, bibliography, and bibliographical essay in providing information on the special distributors and publishers of works in Chicano literature, the institutions which conduct research in the field, their addresses, and the types and titles of anthologies, series, journals, and individuals works that can be obtained from these sources. The sections on bibliographies and anthologies each list three titles, the section on literature and cultural books covers 15 works, including one by a woman writer, with lengthy annotations. Prices and distributors are indicated when known. The dozen or more significant journals and newsletters listed for the study of Chicano literature include *Books Abroad, De Colores, Tejidos, Revista Chicano-riqueña, Caracol, Aztlán, Grito del Sol, Mester, Carta Abierta* and several others. The concluding section on media materials mentions several films and two sources for further information. This article is particularly useful to librarians, as well as instructors, who are concerned with the acquisition of pertinent resources in the field of Chicano literature.

581. Schon, Isabel. *A Bicultural Heritage: Themes for the Exploration of Mexican and Mexican-American Culture in Books for Children and Adolescents.* Metuchen, NJ: Scarecrow Press, 1978. 158 p. Indexes.
This excellent selection of children's literature for kindergarten through twelfth grade is designed to promote attitudes of respect and appreciation for Mexican and Mexican American culture. The emphasis is on bicultural rather than bilingual works. The contents include a sample attitude survey, five chapters covering books on customs, lifestyles, heroes, folklore and historical developments and three appendixes. The approximately 265 works cited are primarily fiction although examples of biographical, historical, and artistic materials are also listed. Many of the selections are critically reviewed and evaluated in the text. The titles in each chapter are arranged by the appropriate grade level. Topics covered by the bibliography include food, stereotypes, self-identity, family, manners, heroes, folklore, art, Mexican history, and contemporary works on Mexican Americans. The appendixes contain additional readings and reference works. This is one of the more carefully selected listings of children's literature on Mexican Americans. It is highly useful for teachers in curriculum planning and in bilingual-bicultural programs.

582. _____. *Books in Spanish for Children and Young Adults: An Annotated Guide/Libros infantiles y juveniles en español: Una guía anotada.* Metuchen, NJ: Scarecrow Press, 1978. 153 p. Annotated. Indexes.
Prepared for teachers, librarians, and others who select books in Spanish for children and young adults, this bibliography lists books written since 1973 by Spanish or Latin American authors. None of the approximately 350 works are translations. The arrangement is by country of publication and subdivided by fiction, legends, poetry, songs, theater, history, and biography, as appropriate. The section on literature from Mexico (pp. 47–52) contains

22 titles on art, fiction, history and legends. Each item has been reviewed, evaluated, and extensively annotated. Grade levels are indicated. The appendixes lists reliable bookdealers in the United States and abroad who can provide the materials cited in this work.

This bibliography is useful for public, school and educational services librarians, as well as for teachers and parents in bilingual–bicultural programs. As perhaps the first extensive source of children's literature in Spanish, it fills a definite gap in the bibliographic resources.

583. Scott, Frank, Cesar Caballero, and Ida González. *Chicano Literature: A Selective Bibliography*. El Paso: University of Texas at El Paso, 1977. 17 p. ED 147 051.

This reference tool provides information on the literary contributions of Chicano writers. It is primarily a guide to the holdings of the University of Texas at El Paso Library. Call numbers are provided. Titles are listed under the headings of General works; Fiction— novels, short stories, and folklore; Drama; Poetry; Biographies; Book reviews; History and criticism; Bibliographies. Two additional sections have titles on children's literature and the Chicano in American literature. This is one of the few, if not the only, library guides that concentrates on literature and criticism of the Mexican American. Many of the general bibliographies and library guides contain only small sections on literature while emphasizing education and social sciences.

584. Sonnichen, C. L. *The Southwest Record in Books*. Rev. ed. El Paso: University of Texas at El Paso, 1969. 103 p.

Designed to provide sources for a course on life and literature of the Southwest, this selective bibliography cites books available in the library at El Paso. The emphasis is on works with literary value. While dealing for the most part with the Anglo-American heritage, pioneers, and cowboys, there is a special section on "The Spanish Heritage." Excellent references to material on the folklore of the Spanish Southwest are listed in this section. Most of the titles are in English. This bibliography is appropriate for students in secondary school through college level. An earlier edition was published in 1961.

585. Tatum, Charles M. "Toward a Chicano Bibliography of Literary Criticism." *Atisbos*, 2 (Winter, 1976–1977): 35–59.

This is one of the first, and perhaps the best, of the preliminary bibliographic surveys of literary criticism focusing on the ever growing body of Chicano literature. It is arranged in the following eight sections with critical comments and selections of the major works since 1960: Bibliographies; Background, general characteristics, and critical interpretations; Anthologies; Poetry; The Novel and short story; Drama; The Mexican, the Chicano, and non-Chicano literature; Journals. Two hundred four titles are cited, with the largest number in the section on the novel and short story. Tatum also lists a number of the more important Chicano publishers which produce works of literature and 19 non-Chicano journals and periodicals which occasionally include works of Chicano literature and criticism. It is evident from this work that most bibliographies on the Chicano have neglected literary criticism and that a comprehensive book-length bibliography on the subject would be highly desirable. It is anticipated that the work in progress by Ernestina N. Eger, entitled *A Bibliography of Criticism of Contemporary Chicano Literature*, will help in filling the gap in the future.

586. Trapp, Elizabeth A. Benedict. ''Chicano Literature: The Degree of Bibliographic Control.'' *Oklahoma Librarian,* 25 (July, 1975): 5–8, 33.

This article, which discusses the state of bibliographic control of Chicano literature, describes some of the difficulties in defining, identifying and locating literary works by Chicano authors. Cited are a number of sources which may be consulted in research on Chicano literature and the problems in their use. The author points to two special anthologies, an early work on oral tradition and folklore, library guides, special publishers, articles, and dissertations. It is unfortunate that the appendix lists only those bibliographies which are the least satisfactory in approaching the topic of Chicano literary expression and criticism—the library guides or bibliographies. Missing from the sources mentioned are the numerous newspapers and journals which have long been important outlets for Chicano writers. The article by Guillermo Rojas in *El Grito,* December, 1973, has been overlooked, as well as a number of other key publications on Chicano literature that were published prior to 1975. Although 1848 has been designated in this article as the acceptable beginning date for Chicano literature, no specific mention is made of bibliographic sources for the nineteenth century. This article is useful, nevertheless, in pointing out a few of the pitfalls one encounters in searching for creative works by Chicano literary figures.

587. Treviño, Albert D. ''Mexican American Poetry for the Secondary School Literature Program.'' *English in Texas,* 7 (Summer' 1976): 22–24. Annotated.

Included in this selection of contemporary Mexican American poetry are single works and anthologies which are appropriate for use in instruction at the high school level. The citations are arranged in the two categories mentioned. Each item is annotated with a concise description of the content. The poems selected correspond to the reading interest and maturity level of secondary school students. They are mainly in English with a minimal degree of standard Spanish vocabulary or regional dialectal forms and do not contain offensive words which often pose problems of censorship. Although more than half of the titles deal with aspects of the Mexican American experience or reflect on situations of particular interest to them, the bibliography is not designed to be a representative sampling of all Mexican American poetry. Nevertheless, it is a highly useful tool for teachers and school librarians.

# Chapter 16

# *Social and Behavioral Sciences*

In this chapter, bibliographies are presented that relate to the Mexican American in various areas of the social and behavioral sciences, with the exception of History and Labor. The voluminous amount of material, particularly on agricultural and migrant labor and on background history of the Mexican American, has necessitated that separate chapters be devoted to the latter two fields. The social science bibliographies, compiled during the past 30 years by scholars, private organizations, academic institutions, and agencies of the federal government, demonstrate an expansion of interest in the study of the Mexican American. They cover a broad range of subjects which are not unique to the Mexican American but are indicative of some of the problems, issues and experiences surrounding the study of this ethnic group.

Three categories of bibliographies can be identified among the works reviewed in this chapter. The first includes bibliographies which focus specifically on the Mexican American. Most of these are interdisciplinary and concern general social science materials, but a few have been identified that provide sources on school desegregation, politics, attitudes and images, counseling, social work, illegal aliens, and border problems. A growing interest in health topics has influenced the publication of a sizable number of bibliographies related to health care delivery and mental health in Mexican American communities.

The second type of bibliography includes socioeconomic literature on several minorities and ethnic groups. Mexican Americans are generally referenced in conjunction with Blacks, Asian-Americans, Native Americans, and occasionally Spanish-speaking immigrants such as Cubans and Puerto Ricans. These bibliographies cover a richer selection of topics than the previous category: minority businesses, marketing, employment problems, minorities in the legal profession, counseling, the aged, settlement patterns, housing, poverty, police relations, immigration, economic conditions, and civil rights.

In the third category the bibliographies do not emphasize any particular racial or ethnic group but instead concentrate on topics that are relevant to the contemporary socioeconomic dimensions of the culture of poverty: health and illness, discrimination in housing and employment, conditions of poverty, consumers, social legislation, and the family. These bibliographies are only a representative selection of the works available in this area. They have significance for research on the Mexican American since as a group many are living on incomes well below the low-income (poverty) level.

An overwhelming majority of the bibliographies in this chapter pertain to the fields of sociology and economics. The sources cited date from the late nineteenth century to the 1970s; some are journalistic accounts, others are scholarly studies, but for the most part they reflect prevailing attitudes held by Anglo-American social scientists toward Mexican Americans and other minorities. Up until the decade of the sixties most studies of minorities in the United States were based on the assumption that the social, economic, and educational problems were inherent to particular groups. Thus the "Mexican problem" was an expression frequently voiced by scholars and laymen who proposed solutions, some of which were sympathetic and others not. The unsympathetic writers were generally prejudiced by xenophobic sentiments.

During the 1960s and 1970s social scientists shifted their attention to undesirable socioeconomic conditions and their causes within society. Terms such as "underprivileged" and "disadvantaged" were used to characterize various minorities and ethnic groups. For a number of years most of this literature did not distinguish between the various minorities or tended to focus on the Black community. Undoubtedly, the Chicano Movement assisted in drawing more attention toward the long-neglected problems of Mexican Americans. In 1969 an extensive bibliography published by the U.S. Inter-Agency Committee on Mexican American Affairs, entitled, *The Mexican American, A New Focus on Opportunity: A Guide to Materials Relating to Persons of Mexican Heritage in the United States,* exemplified the new approach.

Apart from the disciplines of sociology and economics, the most prolific and productive area in the social and behavioral sciences relating to the Mexican Americans is psychology, particularly the applied fields. Since 1974 several bibliographies have been published on mental health and counseling.

The bibliographies in this chapter provide most of the initial sources for research on the Mexican Americans in the social and behavioral sciences. For more current publications the general social science indexes may be consulted (e.g., *Social Science Index, Public Affairs Information Service Bulletin, Psychology Abstracts,* and *Social Science Citation Index*).

588. Abraham, Pauline, *Bibliography: Indians of North America, Mexican Americans, Negroes—Civil Rights: An Annotated List.* South Bend: Indiana University at South Bend, 1974. 47 p. Annotated. ED 092 301.
Designed to assist teachers in selecting and acquiring materials related to civil rights issues, the selections are arranged in three parts by minority group. Included are books of fiction and nonfiction for junior and senior levels of high school. The annotations are both descriptive and critical. Sixty-seven titles for the study of civil rights and Mexican Americans are found on pages 18–31. The items selected are good basic works in the fields of literature, political science, and sociology, all directly related to Mexican Americans.

589. American Council on Race Relations. *Mexican Americans: A Selected Bibliography.* Chicago: The Council, 1949. (Bibliography Series, no. 7) 7 p.
This is one of the earliest bibliographies related exclusively to the Mexican American. It is arranged by type of material; books, pamphlets, reprints (M. A. theses, government publications, etc.), and periodical articles taken from scholarly as well as popular jour-

nals. The more than 100 selections, published from 1930 to 1949, are for the most part related to the history and socioeconomic status of Mexican Americans.

It is included here for its historical value since most of the entries have found their way into the numerous general bibliographies and library guides.

590. The American Jewish Committee. *Ethnic and Racial Groups in the United States: A Selected Bibliography.* New York: The Committee, 1968. 9 p. Annotated.

Selected references on various racial and ethnic groups including the Mexican Americans are listed in this concise bibliography. The 108 titles are primarily from the 1950s and 1960s and selectively cover Chinese, English, Germans, Greeks, Indians, Irish, Italians, Japanese, Jews, Poles, Puerto Ricans, Scandinavians, Scotch-Irish, Spanish-speaking peoples, Yugoslavs, and Negroes. An introductory section contains general background material on social change, intergroup relations, prejudice, and minority problems in general. The work is sponsored by the Blaustein Library, Institute of Human Relations.

591. *Articles Cited in Myers' Chronological Bibliography.* Berkeley: Chicano Studies Library, University of California, 1974. (Selected Collections of the Chicano Studies Library, no. 4) 13 p. Index.

This is an index by journal title and author to 123 articles, the majority of which are cited in the work by Dorothy S. Myers entitled *Chronological Bibliography of Articles in English Language Periodicals . . . which Indicate Attitudinal and Judgemental Viewpoints of Anglos . . . and Mexican Americans. . . .* All of the articles from 12 of the 111 journals in Myers's bibliography were assembled for the collection in the Chicano Studies Library at the University of California, Berkeley, and are available to patrons. The titles are arranged by journal and subarranged in chronological order. The materials span the period from 1835 to 1971.

This project was undertaken by Richard J. Cardella in 1973 for a class project at Berkeley under the direction of Herminio Rios, instructor.

592. Banks, Vera J., Elsie S. Manny, and Nelson L. LeRay. *Research Data on Minority Groups: An Annotated Bibliography of Economic Research Reports, 1955–1965.* Washington, DC: Economic Research Service, U.S. Department of Agriculture, 1966. (Miscellaneous Publications, 1046) 26 p. Annotated. Index.

Reports published by the Economic Research Service during the period 1955–1965 are listed in this bibliography. Ninety items are arranged geographically by state. Material relevant to the Mexican American can be located under the listings for California, New Mexico, and Texas. Topics of the works relate to socioeconomic development of all rural ethnic and minority groups: income, standard of living, migration, labor, health, and education. A number of items specifically concern Spanish Americans.

This bibliography is useful in comparing the situation of Mexican American rural poor with other minority groups. The lengthy annotations provide detailed content analysis.

593. Boner, Marian O. *The Merchant and the Poor: A Selected Bibliography.* Monticello, IL: Council of Planning Librarians, 1970. (Exchange Bibliography, no. 129) 5 p.

This is a specialized bibliography on the poor as consumers in the United States economy. The topics covered by the entries include credit, consumer education, and consumer legal rights. It is interesting to note that not one item refers specifically to Mexican Americans. However, most of the materials are crucial to a study of consumer problems in the barrio. Listed are sixty books, conference papers, periodical articles, publications by consumer interest organizations, and congressional hearings and legislation from the 1960s. This general work is included since there are no bibliographies which relate to the special problems and concerns of disadvantaged Mexican American consumers.

594. _____. *Poverty and Housing: A Selected Bibliography.* Monticello, IL: Council of Planning Librarians, 1970. (Exchange Bibliography, no. 128) 5 p.

Materials on the problems of housing availability for the poor are included in this selective list. The sources are relevant to most low-income ethnic and minority groups including Mexican Americans. The 56 entries were published in the 1960s and present an overview of the literature during the period of the War on Poverty. Twenty-eight of the items are government publications from the U.S. Commission on Civil Rights, the Congress, and the Departments of Justice, Housing, and Urban Development. Subjects covered by the materials include problems of slums, race, housing, politics, and legal rights in providing housing to the poor.

This is a good introductory source for students and others seeking information concerning legislation on housing and related problems associated with Mexican Americans in urban areas.

595. _____. *Social Legislation: A Selected Bibliography.* Monticello, IL: Council of Planning Librarians, 1970. (Exchange Bibliography, no. 130) 8 p.

This bibliography, on social legislation for lower-income groups, cites 98 items published mainly in the 1950s and 1960s. Topics covered by the sources include social programs to benefit the poor and legal provisions to improve their well-being. Nearly half of the books, reports, and conference proceedings are government publications issued by the Congress and various agencies. This work is useful in identifying sources of social legislation pertaining to disadvantaged Mexican Americans, although they are not mentioned specifically.

596. Booher, David E. *Poverty in an Urban Society: A Bibliography.* Monticello, IL: Council of Planning Librarians, 1971. (Exchange Bibliography, no. 246) 32 p.

Materials dealing with the programs proposed under the Johnson Administration in the War on Poverty are contained in this selected bibliography. Books, scholarly and popular articles, and government publications span the period from the 1940s through the 1960s. Although most of the items are not directed specifically toward the Mexican Americans, many are relevant to those living in poverty. Approximately 420 entries are organized under seven major headings: Theory and methodology; Grass root political behavior; Poverty and the poor; the War on Poverty: the Community Action Program; Selected newspaper and magazine articles; Bibliographies on poverty and the poor.

597. Boyce, Byrl N., and Sidney Turoff. *Minority Groups and Housing: A Bibliography, 1950-1970.* Storrs: Center for Real Estate and Urban Economic Studies, University of Connecticut, 1972. (General Series, no. 3) 202 p. Indexes.

This work includes sources dealing with minority housing problems in an urban environment: segregation, discrimination, availability, brokerage, cost and value, and government intervention through legislation and legal action. Most of the items cover the problems of disadvantaged minorities in general and are not exclusively related to Mexican Americans. However, the nature of the subject makes most references relevant. The bibliography is arranged in six subject categories. Books, pamphlets and reports, periodicals, legal periodicals, and government publications are listed separately within the subject categories. A section entitled ''Materials for Further Research'' cites reference works and agencies that are the most helpful in locating more up-to-date bibliographical information on housing.

This bibliography supersedes Stephen D. Messner's *Minority Groups and Housing: A Selected Bibliography, 1950-1967* (Storrs: Center for Real Estate and Urban Economic Studies, University of Connecticut, 1968.) (General Series, no. 1).

598. Brimmer, Andrew F., and Harriet Harper. ''Economists' Perception of Minority Problems: A View of Emerging Literature.'' *Journal of Economic Literature,* 3 (September, 1970): 783-806.

As a result of a survey of leading economic journals published in the United States between 1963 and 1969, this list of journal articles was produced. The articles relate to the economic problems of minorities and offer an overview of the efforts made by professional economists to study and report their findings and research. The minority groups covered include Negroes, Mexican Americans, Puerto Ricans, American Indians, and Orientals. As might be expected, most of the articles deal with the Negro, but a number of titles on Mexican Americans can be found under the subheading of Labor and Manpower.

599. Buenker, John D., and Nicholas C. Burckel. *Immigration and Ethnicity: A Guide to Information Sources.* Detroit: Gale Research, 1977. (American Government and History Information Guide Services, vol. 1) 305 p. Annotated. Indexes.

This interdisciplinary guide to the literature on immigration in the United States spans the colonial period to the present. Although the broadest possible coverage has been attempted, Afro-Americans and Native Americans are excluded. The Mexican American experience is treated in a special section (pp. 147-167). Books, articles, and dissertations from the 1920s to 1975 are listed with descriptive annotations. Other useful citations can be found in the chapter on ''General Accounts and Miscellaneous'' that deals with such topics as immigration to specific localities and the economics of immigration. Additional resources on the Mexican American are located in the final two chapters. One covers works on acculturation, assimilation, ethnicity, and restriction. The other combines a directory of centers, repositories, and societies that distribute and publish immigration materials with a list of United States census reports, other government publications, manuscripts, guides, and a concise list of representative ethnic journals.

Approximately 92 of the nearly 1,500 items relate specifically to the socioeconomic situation of the Mexican American. This work serves as a good initial source for research on the Mexican American and for comparative analysis of the numerous immigrant groups that comprise the American scene.

600. Bullejos, José. *Diez años de literatura económica: Bibliografía básica sobre la economía de México, 1943–1953*. México, D. F.: Instituto de Investigaciones Económicas, Escuela Nacional de Economía, Universidad Nacional Autónoma de México, 1954. 162 p. Annotated. Index.

Fundamental works relating to the economic problems of Mexico are cited in this bibliography. Included are the most important Mexican and foreign books, articles, and government publications, in Spanish and English, published between 1943 and 1953. Among the topics covered are mining, industry, foreign trade, foreign investments, oil, communications, and transportation. The literature on agriculture is too vast and, therefore, is not included.

The materials are all located in the main economic libraries of Mexico: the libraries of the Escuela Nacional de Economía, Secretaría de Hacienda; the library of the Nacional Financiera; and the library of the Banco de México. Some of the works are also in UNESCO's Centro de Documentación and in the Biblioteca de CEPAL. Research using these sources can lead to an understanding of the economic problems of Mexico that forced many of its citizens to immigrate to the United States.

601. Burg, Nan C. *Rural Housing and Rural Poverty*. Monticello, IL: Council of Planning Librarians, 1971. (Exchange Bibliography, no. 247) 23 p.

This listing of books, pamphlets, and periodical articles emphasizes rural housing and poverty. The topics cover poverty in a rural setting, solutions to housing shortages, and studies by the U.S. Departments of Agriculture, Commerce, and Labor. Most of the publications are centered in the 1960s. A few of the references provide historical background and several extend to the early 1970s. The 350 items are not directly related to Mexican Americans but, as a group experiencing problems of housing and poverty in rural areas, many items are relevant.

602. California. Ethnic Services Task Force. *Spanish Language Health Materials: A Selective Bibliography,* coordinated by Kamala Korzdorfer and Irene Yeh. Santa Barbara: California Ethnic Services Task Force, 1978. 41 p. Annotated.

Spanish language materials published between 1955 and 1977 on health-related topics are included in this bibliography. Although "designed for use by medium-sized public libraries in either initiating or expanding a Spanish language materials collection," the titles listed are actually supplementary to a core collection. The work is divided in two parts. The first part contains annotated selections of pamphlets, books, and government documents arranged in 14 subject categories: Resource persons; Alcohol and drugs; Consumer health information; Diseases; Human physiology; Medical care; Medicinal plants and herbs; Mental health; Nutrition; Pediatrics/Child care; Physical fitness; Pregnancy and childbirth; Sex education; and Woman's health. The second part, arranged in the same subject categories, cites works which were not available for examination. The annotations describe and evaluate the contents of each work and assign recommended reading levels. A vendor list is appended.

603. Chilman, Catherine. "Economic and Social Deprivation; Its Effects on Children and Families in the U. S.: A Selected Bibliography." *Journal of Marriage and the Family*, 26 (November, 1964): 495–497.
Materials in this bibliography focus on the effects of socioeconomic status on children of minority groups. Topics covered in the references relate to educational achievement of minority children, personality adjustment, consumer practices of low-income families, children in migrant families, racial identification, culturally disadvantaged, unemployed youth, child-rearing practices, social services, among others. The 84 entries are arranged in one alphabetical list. Most of the titles were published between 1954 and 1964. While not exclusively related to Mexican Americans, most of the cited periodical articles, government documents, and monographic studies contain information pertinent to this group.

604. *Counseling the Mexican American Client: An Annotated Bibliography of Journal Literature, 1964-1974*, by Vincent Noble, *et al.* Long Beach: California State University, 1974. 83 p. Annotated. ED 130 199.
This bibliography of professional journal literature concerning the counseling of Mexican Americans was prepared by graduate students at California State University, Long Beach. The 80 articles listed were published between 1964 and 1974. Most of these are in the fields of psychology, ethnology, sociology, social work, education, and anthropology. According to the compilers, the articles were found to be more descriptive than empirical and much of the literature consists of unsubstantiated opinions or observations. The bibliography serves to indicate gaps in the field of research and areas in need of further study.

605. Fariey, Lois J. *A Selected Bibliography: Health and Culture of Spanish-Speaking Migrant Labor*. Fort Collins: Colorado State University, 1966. 12 p.
Sources dealing with health aspects of Spanish-speaking migrant labor are arranged in one alphabetical list. It was prepared as a practical guide for the health practitioner. Most of the materials are periodical references not generally listed in other bibliographies. Many of the 180 entries deal exclusively with the problems of Mexican migrants and others are of a cross-cultural and comparative nature. A few of the items provide background information on Mexican American and fall into the categories of history, folklore, and culture. This bibliography is useful for students in health and social work programs.

606. Gagala, Kenneth L. *The Economics of Minorities; A Guide to Information Sources*. Detroit: Gale Research Co., 1976. (Economics Information Guide Series, vol. 2) 212 p. Annotated. Index.
This is a general summary of the basic research on economic conditions of "non-white" people in the United States: American Indians, Blacks, Mexican Americans, and Puerto Ricans. Included are books, journal articles, and government publications covering research in all areas of the social sciences, in addition to economics. Many of the materials cited are social and political studies conducted during the period 1965–1974 which provide economic information. Chapter 12 (pp. 177–185) concerns Spanish Americans. Sources on economic conditions, poverty, health, and agricultural labor are among the topics covered.

607. Gilbert, William H. *Mexican Americans in the U. S.; Housing, Education, Migrant Labor, etc.* Washington, DC: Legislative Reference Service, Library of Congress, 1964. 2 p.

This list of 28 books and articles, from popular periodicals such as *Reader's Digest, Saturday Evening Post* and *Newsweek,* deals with contemporary social and economic problems of Mexican Americans. The works were published between 1952 and 1961 and cover, in addition to the topics mentioned in the title, the *braceros,* integration, social status, health, and Mexican farm labor. There is no introduction to the list and no criteria given for the selection.

608. Gonzáles, Alex. *Minorities and the U.S. Economy.* Santa Barbara: Library, University of California, 1974. 112 p. Annotated. Indexes.

Works on economic problems of minority groups are collected in this bibliography. The materials are available in the library at the University of California, Santa Barbara. The entries are drawn primarily from business and industry literature and interdisciplinary sources. It is arranged in seven parts and includes books, articles, and government publications.

Part I provides materials on the socioeconomic background of minorities with emphasis on their economic development and their role in United States economic history. Part II contains materials dealing with policy issues, economic analysis, and the implication of public and private programs for minorities. Part III includes materials on minority manpower development, employment, and productivity. Part IV covers sources on the demographic profile of the minority market, income characteristics, market behavior, and marketing problems associated with minorities. Part V lists materials on minority activities and performance in the professions, small businesses and management, capital and corporate development. Part VI deals with materials on minority housing and welfare. Part VII provides a short bibliography of bibliographies for further study of minority economic problems. The specific minority groups covered are Blacks, Indians, Chicanos, and Asians.

609. Harding, Susan. *Bibliography on Mexican American Affairs.* Washington, DC: Legislative Reference Service, Library of Congress, 1968. 3 p.

This is a list on Mexican Americans prepared by the Legislative Reference Service in response to a request for a bibliography on Mexican American economic and social progress. It contains 23 books and articles dealing with their contemporary social, political, and economic problems. Most of the items are articles from popular periodicals such as *Newsweek, Nation,* and *Atlantic.* The topics include migrant laborers, civil rights, the Brown Power Movement, poverty, and Mexican American youth. This list supplements the other bibliographies on this group prepared by the Reference Service prior to 1968.

610. Haskett, Richard C., and Staff. "An Introductory Bibliography for the History of American Immigration, 1607–1955." In *A Report on World Population Migrations as Related to the United States of America,* pp. 85–295. Washington, DC: George Washington University, 1956. 449 p.

Prepared as a preliminary indication of the range of writings on American immigration, this bibliography covers a period of over 350 years and serves as a guide to further investigations. Nearly 2,000 titles are listed under topics corresponding to broad chronological periods of immigration, from 1600 to 1921. Attached to this is a listing of works which represent the approach to immigration since the passage of restrictive laws, from 1921 to 1955.

Work on or related to the Mexican immigrant can be located in the table of contents under General Works, 1607–1921, and the specific subdivisions of Latin Americans and Economic Aspects. A special section on Mexicans—labor and life in America—is included in the final portion of the bibliography entitled "The Narrow Gate, 1921–1955." In that section, works can be found on migrant laborers, labor agreements with Mexico, illegal migration, wetbacks, health services, *braceros,* Mexican migrant women, Spanish-speaking children, politics, discrimination and crime.

611. Hasse, Adelaire. *Index of Economic Material in Documents of the States of the United States: California, 1849–1904.* Washington, DC: Carnegie Institution of Washington, 1908. (Publication, no. 85: California) 316 p. Index.

This is one of the earliest economic bibliographies covering materials published in the period following the Mexican-American War in California. It lists only the printed reports of administrative offices, legislative committees, special commissions of the State of California and governors' messages for the period 1849–1904. The documents are economic in nature and deal with agricultural development, banks, industry, trade, and railroads. The items are arranged under topical headings. All documents are listed in chronological order and cross-referenced.

The documents are important for the study of the economic history of California. They serve as background for the study of many of the economic misfortunes of the Mexican Americans during the latter part of the nineteenth century. A copy of this work is located in the reference collection of the Bancroft Library.

612. *Hispanic Mental Health Bibliography II,* by Amado M. Padilla, *et al.* Los Angeles: Spanish Speaking Mental Health Research Center, University of California, 1977. 111 p. Index.

This is a revised and enlarged edition of the work by Amado M. Padilla and Paul Aranda entitled *Latino Mental Health: Bibliography and Abstracts,* published in 1974. The scope and coverage are similar. Included are all identifiable works in the fields of health, psychology, sociology, education, and anthropology that concern the mental health of the Spanish-speaking population of the United States. A majority of the items pertain to Mexican Americans or Puerto Ricans. Approximately 1,800 citations to journal articles, dissertations, government publications, books, conference reports, and unpublished manuscripts date from the 1920s to 1977. The materials were collected from the files of the National Institute of Mental Health Clearinghouse, *Psychological Abstracts,* ERIC, *Dissertation Abstracts,* and 38 specially selected journals. The bibliography is computerized and continuously updated by the Spanish Speaking Mental Health Research Center. Computer literature searches are available from the Center at the University of California, Los Angeles.

This is a unique and sophisticated tool that will provide researchers and practitioners with easy access to current data on the Mexican American and health-related issues.

613. Institute for Rural America. *Poverty, Rural Poverty, and Minority Groups Living in Rural Poverty: An Annotated Bibliography.* Lexington, KY: Spindletop Research, 1969. 159 p. Annotated.

This work was compiled to assist research on the subject of poverty in the United States. Although it contains approximately 1,000 items, it is only a selective and representative list of the numerous available resources. The materials are arranged under the three broad categories mentioned in the title. The table of contents, with numerous subdivisions, can be substituted for an index. The third general category, Minority Groups Living in Rural Poverty, includes the two subheadings: Spanish Americans in Rural Poverty and Migrants in Rural Poverty. Both of these sections contain items that are directly related to the social and economic status of Mexican Americans. Topics covered relate to discrimination, labor patterns, demographic characteristics, legislation, land reform, rural poverty, and the aged in rural poverty.

614. Institute of Labor and Industrial Relations. Research Division. *Document and Reference Text; An Index to Minority Group Employment Information.* Detroit: University of Michigan–Wayne State University, 1967. 602 p. Indexes.

A computer-generated KWIC index to the literature about employment problems of minority workers covered under Title VII of the Civil Rights Act of 1964; it lists and indexes published and unpublished materials on Blacks, Spanish-speaking, American Indians, Orientals, and women. The entries cover the period 1956–1966 and were obtained through a search of the catalogs of specialized library collections and the contents of more than 200 periodicals. Items directly relating to Mexican Americans can be found by the use of such key words as Mexican, Mexican American, migrant, farm, the names of states, etc.

Two appendixes are included. The first lists agencies administering fair employment practices acts and the second lists organizations concerned with minority group employment. The work is a product of an agreement between the University of Michigan, Wayne State University, and the Equal Opportunity Commission. A one-volume supplement was issued in 1971.

615. Jakle, John A. *Ethnic and Racial Minorities in North America: A Selected Bibliography of the Geographical Literature.* Monticello, IL: Council of Planning Librarians, 1973. (Exchange Bibliography, nos, 459–460) 71 p.

This bibliography is an initial survey of what geographers, social scientists, and planners have discovered about the place experiences of ethnic and racial minorities in North America. It is arranged in categories of geographical locations and ethnic and minority groups. There are 12 periodical articles and unpublished dissertations under the heading of Mexican and a few useful items under the heading of U.S.—West. The topic of this bibliography is unique and may be the only one on this subject related to the Mexican American.

616. Kinton, Jack F. *American Ethnic Groups and the Revival of Cultural Pluralism: Evaluative Sourcebook for the 1970s.* 4th ed. Aurora, IL: Social Science and Sociological Resources, 1974. 173 p.

Included in this bibliographic sourcebook are mainly sociological works on ethnic groups and ethnic relations. The materials are arranged in six sections: Ethnic group theory; Ethnic and quasi-ethnic groups; Immigrants and emigrants; Black Americans; Evaluative filmography on intergroup, ethnic, racial, and immigrant relations in transition; and a Directory of research and cultural centers. Each section lists books, articles, and reference works separately. Materials pertinent to the study of the Mexican American are found in a section under the heading Ethnic and quasi-ethnic groups. One hundred eighty-six items are listed in this special section. Dissertations completed between 1969 and 1973 are listed separately from the rest of the material. Many of the other sections contain print and nonprint materials related to the Mexican American.

The 1973 edition of this work is entitled *American Ethnic Groups: A Sourcebook.*

617. Lavell, Carr B., Wilson E. Schmidt, and Staff. "An Annotated Bibliography on the Demographic, Economic, and Sociological Aspects of Immigration." In *A Report on World Population Migrations as Related to the United States of America,* pp. 296–449. Washington, DC: George Washington University, 1956. 449 p. Annotated.

This is an invaluable bibliography on the social, demographic, and economic factors of immigration covering 29 nationalities and racial groups. Included are approximately 800 books, pamphlets, and articles listed under eight divisions: General works; International migration; Immigration to the United States; The Immigrant in the United States; Immigration and the nation; Immigration control; Immigration policy. A special section (pp. 354–359) is devoted to works on Mexican immigration to the United States. Other works relevant to this topic can be found under General works, Immigration policy, and the subsections relating to bilingualism, cultural adjustment, and demographic consequences. This work is useful as an initial source of standard materials and bibliographies on the problems, motivations, impact, and culture of the Mexican immigrant.

618. McClure, John. *The Police and Minority Groups: A Bibliography.* Sacramento, CA: Sacramento State College Library, 1969. (Bibliographic Series, no. 3) 9 p.

Selected materials on police and minority group relations available in the library of Sacramento State College are listed in this bibliography. Part 1 includes books and pamphlets, and Part 2 lists newspaper and periodical articles. The library's location symbols and call numbers are provided. While not totally concerned with Mexican Americans, the entries are of obvious usefulness since they cover the following topics: police and community relations, delinquency, minority rights, police brutality, and police training in race relations. This listing is now somewhat dated since it only covers publications from 1946 to 1969.

619. Metress, James F. *Mexican American Health: A Guide to the Literature.* Monticello, IL: Council of Planning Librarians, 1976. (Exchange Bibliography, no. 1129) 27 p.

A selection of cross-cultural and interdisciplinary materials on the Mexican American for the education of health professionals and students in health-related programs is offered in this bibliography. The purpose of the bibliography is to increase the understanding of the Mexican American subculture in order to improve health care delivery in Hispanic communities. The work is arranged in four categories: General cultural background; Health services and problems; Nutrition; and Medical anthropology. The recent guides such as this one, when compared to earlier bibliographies on health and the Mexican American place greater emphasis on the education of the health service personnel rather than solely on the Mexican American patient. The 361 items listed include books, articles, dissertations, government publications, and works in progress. All aspects of the history, literature, and culture; types of health services and problems; dietary problems and nutrition education; and folk medicine are covered. Reference books, bibliographies, and dictionaries are cited along with studies on migrants, aged, children, and the Mexican American family and community in general.

The largest number of citations are in the section on health services and problems, mainly from the 1960s and 1970s. A few titles written in Spanish are included. This is an important bibliographic contribution for research on diverse and complex health-related issues among Mexican Americans.

620. Molina, Alexis. *Minority Aged: A Bibliography.* New York: Institute for Urban and Minority Education, Columbia University, 1977. (Urban Disadvantaged Series, no. 49) 44 p. Index.

This bibliography cites references to sources of information on gerontological literature with specific emphasis on ethnic groups in Western societies. The 368 items are arranged in 14 sections. The first three sections refer to general materials, the cultural contexts of aging, and aging among ethnic, low-income, urban, and racial groups. The final 11 sections single out materials which refer to the specific group covered. The two sections which contain references of interest are the Spanish-speaking and the Mexican American. Included in these sections are articles, research papers, legislative studies, and a few books and monographs.

The area of Mexican American aged remains understudied. This particular bibliography attempts to make available the most current findings and to facilitate future research on the special problems and needs of this group.

621. Muñoz, Carlos, Jr. "Politics and the Chicano: On the Status of the Literature." *Aztlán,* 5 (Spring and Fall, 1974): 1-7.

The state of the scholarly literature which relates to Chicano politics is discussed in this critical bibliographic essay. To date no single bibliography exists on this topic, primarily because of the paucity of research in the field. The essay actually serves as an introduction to the volume which is devoted in its entirety to contributions on political issues concerning the Chicano. Muñoz contrasts the themes or categories of the nonacademic literature with that of the scholarly. Examples of each category are cited in the footnotes. Approximately 12 works are cited and briefly discussed. Recommendations are made for areas in need of further study.

622. Myers, Dorothy S. *Chronological Bibliography of Articles in English Language Periodicals, Chiefly in the United States, from Listings in Poole's Index and in Readers Guide to Periodical Literature, from Early 19th Century to 1971, which Indicate Attitudinal and Judgemental Viewpoints of Anglos Toward Mexico, Mexicans in the United States, and Mexican Americans; with some Citations of Articles Demonstrating Attitudes of Mexicans and Mexican Americans Toward Anglos and Toward Them-*

*selves.* Berkeley: University of California, 1971. (Student paper for Chicano Studies 124) 152 p.

This rather unusual bibliography is the result of a survey of 111 periodicals in search of articles regarding attitudinal and judgmental viewpoints of Anglos and Mexican Americans. The title is self-explanatory. In all, 93 articles found in 58 different periodicals are included. The periodicals range from the scholarly to the popular. They cover the period from the early nineteenth century to 1971. A coding symbol indicates whether an article is about Mexican or Mexican American attitudes toward Anglos. The arrangement is by periodical with the articles listed in chronological order. The list was prepared as a guide to the collection in the Chicano Studies Library at the University of California, Berkeley.

623. National Conference on Social Welfare. *Selected Bibliography on Mexicans and Puerto Ricans in Health and Welfare.* Columbus, OH: NCSW, n.d. (Publication, no. B0059) 15 p. Annotated.

Social welfare materials are the focus of this bibliography. The items were selected from among the National Conference on Social Welfare publications issued between 1924 and 1962. Included are works on migratory labor, Mexican immigrants, delinquency, and health, just to name a few. A useful feature is the list of libraries which have substantial NCSW publications. The National Conference has other similar publications in the areas of social welfare (e.g., bibliographies on transients, migrants, and travelers, urban development, and unemployment).

624. Navarro, Eliseo. *The Chicano Community; A Selected Bibliography for Use in Social Work Education.* New York: Council on Social Work Education, 1971. 57 p. Annotated.

The purpose of this reference tool is to point out the resources available to social work students and faculty in their study of life conditions in the Mexican American community. One hundred seventy-four titles are listed. The materials (books, articles, monographs, proceedings, and reports) are essentially well-known titles but they are coded to emphasize their social work aspects. The following subjects are utilized in coding: historical and background data; acculturation and culture conflict; issues and problems; power; politics and the Chicano community; Chicano organizations; economics and the Chicano community; social welfare and social work; the Chicano family; literature; and reference material. A list entitled "The Chicano Press" concludes the bibliography. Eight journals and newspapers are mentioned, with the publishers' addresses.

An earlier edition was published by the Graduate School of Social Work, University of Texas, Austin, in 1969.

625. Padilla, Amado M., and Paul Aranda. *Latino Mental Health: Bibliography and Abstracts.* Washington, DC: U.S. Department of Health, Education, and Welfare, 1974. 288 p. Annotated. Index.

A unique and exhaustive bibliography of literature in the fields of psychology and mental health; it consists of 497 periodical articles from *Pyschological Abstracts* (through 1972) and the files of the National Clearinghouse for Mental Health Information. References were also extracted from many other anthropological, psychological, psychiatric, sociological, and social work journals. All the cited articles concern people who are usually identified as Spanish-speaking, Spanish-surnamed, or of Spanish origin (with a few exceptions confined specifically to Mexican Americans and Puerto Ricans). All entries are followed by an abstract describing the content of the article. A subject index is provided to facilitate the search for materials on certain topics. Appended to the bibliography is a list of dissertations related to Latino mental health but without annotations.

626. Paulus, Virginia. *Housing: A Bibliography, 1960-1972.* New York: AMS Press, 1974. 339 p. Indexes.
This reference source was designed for those studying various aspects of housing—faculty, students, planners, developers, and government officials. The materials include books, journal articles, government publications, technical reports, conference proceedings, dissertations, and unpublished papers drawn from the literature of fields such as urban planning, economics, sociology, law, regional science, and public administration. Items relevant to Mexican Americans are found under the subject headings of Migrant labor housing; Minorities; Race as a factor in housing cost; Effects of race on property values; Minorities and housing markets; Public housing; and Racial aspects. For the period covered, this is a fairly comprehensive work.

627. Potter, Helen Rose. *Social and Economic Dimensions of Health and Illness Behavior in New Mexico: An Annotated Bibliography.* Albuquerque: University of New Mexico Press, 1969. 220 p. Annotated. Indexes.
Social and economic information pertinent to health and illness behavior in New Mexico is the theme of this specialized bibliography. Publications from the period 1950-1967, relating to all ethnic groups in the state, are emphasized. Many of the items are about Mexican Americans, particularly those under the headings of Folk Medicine, Health Behavior, and Spanish Americans. Four indexes are included: People of New Mexico Index; Selected Categories Index; Geographical Areas of New Mexico Index; and Health Facilities, Services and Manpower Index. A glossary of terms is provided. This is one of the best specialized bibliographies on New Mexico.

628. Reed, Katherine. *Mental Health and Social Services for Mexican Americans: An Essay and Annotated Bibliography.* Monticello, IL: Council of Planning Librarians, 1976. (Exchange Bibliographies, no. 1023) 37 p. Annotated.
The bibliography, which supports the essay, contains sources of information on mental health services for the Mexican American community. Included are 60 articles, conference papers, books, chapters from books, and unpublished papers that were prepared between 1959 and 1974. These sources are arranged first by general studies which have some bearing on mental health and related services for the Mexican American. The remaining entries are arranged geographically. Works on Mexican Americans in California, Colorado, New York, Texas/Southwest, Washington, D.C., and Washington State are listed. All entries have lengthy annotations which describe the content and conclusions arrived at in each work.

Topics covered by the entries are psychological and cultural problems, social services, mental health services, folk medicine, values and attitudes, delinquency, acculturation and family. Sources in this bibliography provide a survey of the literature on the problems, findings, and solutions involving one aspect of health care delivery service for the Mexican American.

629. Renton, Margaret A. *Mexico-United States Relations*. Irvine: Government Publications Department, General Library, University of California, 1976. (Government Publications Bibliography, no. 13) 23 p. Annotated.

This is a valuable source of United States, California, and United Nations official publications on certain aspects of United States–Mexico relations. The documents listed are held by the Library at the University of California, Irvine. The issues selected for coverage fall under four headings: U. S.–Mexico relations; Illegal aliens/undocumented migratory workers; Control of narcotics and illicit drugs; and Economic relations. These issues and the various items listed under them reflect for the most part contemporary and future concerns of the relationship between the two countries.

Most of the documents date from 1969. The exceptions are those documents on the *Bracero* program which are included for historical reasons. Not included are the numerous House and Senate Appropriations Committee hearings since these are available through the *CIS Index and Abstracts*. Of particular importance to Mexican American studies is the section on Illegal aliens/undocumented workers (pp. 2–7).

630. Riemer, Ruth. *An Annotated Bibliography of Material on Ethnic Problems in Southern California* (Preliminary Draft). Los Angeles: Hayes Foundation and Department of Anthropology-Sociology, University of California, 1947? 70 p. Annotated. Index.

This preliminary bibliography includes 376 items of "fragmentary materials" on the ethnic minorities of southern California. The materials cited were identified in a survey of library holdings in southern California. Emphasis is on unpublished materials which are rarely found in general bibliographies. Not all entries pertain to the Mexican Americans but those that do are very valuable, particularly because they are not widely known. Other groups covered include Japanese, Filipinos, Negroes, and Dust Bowl migrants.

Apparently no further work was done on this preliminary draft and it was never published in final form.

631. Ross, Stanley R. "Bibliography." In *Views Across the Border: the United States and Mexico,* pp. 427–451. Albuquerque: University of New Mexico Press, 1978. 456 p.

Articles in this text dealing with the United States–Mexican border are complemented by the bibliography. The references are arranged under three broad categories: Bibliographical references, Historical references, and Other published books and articles. Approximately 700 items are cited that cover the culture, politics, economic situation, migration, health, social conditions, psychological aspects, and ecology of the area. Although the bibliography focuses on the border, many of the titles represent a wider view of the Mexican American experience.

Most of the items were published in the 1960s and 1970s and manifest the contemporary problems of concern to social scientists with an interest in the Mexican American.

632. Salinas, Esteban, Ruth Bagnall, and William Kuvlesky. *Mexican-Americans: A Survey of Research by the Texas Agricultural Experiment Station, 1964-1973*. College Station: Texas A and M University, 1973. 8 p. ED 082 913.

This is a special bibliography of sociological references on Mexican Americans in Texas.

Listed are over 40 items (journal articles, student papers, reports, theses) which resulted from six research projects sponsored by the Texas Agricultural Experiment Station during the 1963–1973 period. The items are on the relocation of Mexican Americans, their ambitions, class mobility, school dropout rates, occupational orientation, and related topics. The six research projects are listed along with the names of directors, durations, title, and TAES project number. The publication was designed to publicize their findings and to increase public awareness of the research conducted by the Experiment Station on Mexican Americans.

633. Salinas, Guadalupe. "Mexican-Americans and the Desegregation of Schools in the Southwest," *El Grito*, 4 (Summer, 1971): 36–69.
References to legal cases involving Mexican Americans are contained in this bibliographical essay. The cases are in the areas of discrimination in employment; Spanish and Mexican land grant claims; public accommodation; administration of justice; and nonjudicial recognition. Most of the cases relate to Mexican American education. A supplementary section cites and discusses additional cases on civil rights issues (e.g., social welfare, voting, and migrant workers) and on educational rights. Complete citations for each case are provided in the footnotes.

This seems to be the only available reference source for legal cases which relate to Mexican Americans. This article was originally published in the *Houston Law Review*, in 1971. The supplementary portion was written for *El Grito*.

634. Sharma, Prakash C. *A Selected Research Bibliography on Aspects of Socio-economic and Political Life of Mexican Americans.* Monticello, IL; Council of Planning Librarians, 1974. (Exchange Bibliography, no. 695) 19 p.
Studies on the social, economic, and political life of Mexican Americans are listed in this concise bibliography. The 250 references to books, monographs, reports, articles, and periodicals cited were published during the 1930–1973 period. The majority of them relate directly to the Mexican American. Many of the items may be found in other more general bibliographies. This compilation indicates the growing interest, during the early 1970s, in the unique problems and patterns of life of Mexican Americans. Earlier exchange bibliographies presented only materials of overall interest to studies of minorities and ethnic groups or concentrated on specific problems of those groups.

635. _____. *Studies in Poverty: A Selected Bibliography.* Monticello, IL: Council of Planning Librarians, 1975. (Exchange Bibliography, no. 737) 12 p.
This listing includes 200 selected sources related to the traditional approach to poverty. The materials cover the causes of poverty and the physical manifestations of poverty in both urban and rural areas. Reference to the social and psychological aspects, and the general mental health of individuals plagued by poverty, are not included. Books, scholarly and popular articles and newspaper reports, published between 1935 and 1970, are listed. The arrangement is by type of reference. The materials are useful for background information on the causes and manifestations of poverty among the Mexican immigrants and Mexican Americans.

636. Susuki, Peter T. *Minority Group Aged in America: A Comprehensive Bibliography of Recent Publications on Blacks, Mexican Americans, Native Americans, Chinese, and Japanese.* Monticello, IL: Council of Planning Librarians, 1975. (Exchange Bibliography, no. 816) 25 p.

This is a guide to the literature on aging among various ethnic groups with books, articles, and reports arranged under headings for each group. A general introductory section focuses on cross-cultural and comparative studies of aging. Materials related to the Mexican American can be identified in this latter part as well as in Section III entitled "Mexican Americans." In this section the literature covers such topics as housing, communication, health, folk psychiatry, mental illness, rural aged Mexican Americans, federal programs, and the Mexican American elderly in Texas, the Midwest, and other locales. Of the approximately 152 items, 30 relate directly to the Mexican American. The compiler includes suggested areas in need of research. Although this list of materials on gerontology is sparce, it claims to be comprehensive.

637. Thompson, Bryan. *Ethnic Groups in Urban Areas; Community Formation and Growth: A Selected Bibliography.* Monticello, IL: Council of Planning Librarians, 1971. (Exchange Bibliography, no. 202) 18 p.

The literature on ethnic settlement patterns in urban areas is the subject of this bibliography. Emphasis is on the factors determining initial settlement, subsequent intra-urban migration, community growth and relationships of ethnic groups within the structure, and growth of urban environments. Approximately 355 books and scholarly articles are arranged in one alphabetical list. Mexican Americans are not included among the references to specific minority groups. However, the nature of the topic makes many of the items particularly relevant to them in comparative analyses.

638. Tompkins, Dorothy Campbell. *Poverty in the United States During the Sixties: A Bibliography.* Berkeley: Institute of Government Studies, University of California, 1970. 542 p. Annotated. Index.

This is one of the most comprehensive bibliographies covering all aspects of poverty. Cited are books, chapters of books, pamphlets, and periodical articles published in the 1960s. The 8,338 entries are drawn from the fields of social welfare, education, health, public administration, sociology, law, agriculture, and economics and they include materials from the collections of special libraries of the University of California, Berkeley. Much of this bibliography directly or indirectly relates to the socioeconomic conditions and problems of Mexican Americans. Helpful features of this guide are a list of all periodicals cited and a thorough author-subject index.

This bibliography certainly fulfills its purpose, which is to explore extensively the dynamics of poverty through the publications of the 1960s.

639. Trujillo, Roberto G., and Rosemary M. Stevenson. *Third World Students and Counseling: A Selected Bibliography.* Santa Barbara: Colección Tloque Nahuaque, Chicano Studies Library Unit and Black Studies Library Unit, University of California, 1978. 31 p.

This selective bibliography on minority counseling literature covers the period from 1965 through 1977 for Chicanos and Spanish-speaking groups, American Indians, Blacks, and Asian Americans. As one of the first works of this type, it was designed to identify the many difficult to locate resources on educational and community counseling for students, practitioners, and librarians. The citations, culled from numerous indexes, catalogs and subject bibliographies, reflect only a sampling of the coverage since the bibliographic control for this area is weak. Approximately 200 pertinent articles, dissertations, and books in the Chicano and multi-ethnic sections are applicable to counseling and the Mexican American.

The ERIC document numbers and call numbers for the items located in the library of the University of California, Santa Barbara, are provided as a service to patrons.

640. U. S. Department of Housing and Urban Development. Library. *The Mexican Americans: A Bibliography.* Washington, DC: The Library, 1970. 11 p.

Materials on the urban problems of Mexican Americans located in the library of the Department of Housing and Urban Development are listed in this bibliography. The materials are mostly articles from popular periodicals but also listed are a few books, monographs, reports, speeches, and many of the HUD publications. The 115 citations are arranged in alphabetical order. The library's call number is provided with each entry. The materials are chiefly in the social sciences and education, published between 1960 and 1970.

641. U. S. Department of Labor. *Mexican Americans: Selected References, 1967-1973.* Washington, DC: The Department, 1974. 22 p.

This is a selected bibliography of works in the social and behavioral sciences and history which relate to the Mexican American. With a few exceptions the items listed were published from 1967 to 1973. The books, articles, theses, dissertations, and government publications are arranged in five categories: General works, Employment, Education, History, and Bibliographies. The materials on agricultural labor are listed separately under employment. Materials on such topics as political involvement, health care, the Mexican American family, migrant labor, discrimination, educational achievement, and personality traits are included. It is useful as a guide to basic research and reference sources from the period.

642. U.S. Health Services and Mental Health Administration. *Spanish-Language Health Communication Teaching Aids: A List of Printed Materials and their Sources,* compiled by Robert N. Isquith and Charles T. Webb. Washington, DC: U.S. Department of Health, Education, and Welfare, 1972. (DHEW Publication, no. (HSM) 72-19) 55 p. Annotated. Index.

Selected Spanish-language health-related publications issued by various public and private agencies and corporations are cited in this catalog. More than 600 titles are offered by 91 different organizations. The entries include address, list of pamphlets, translation of Spanish titles, price, and order information, if available. A few of the items have brief content descriptions. None of the materials have been evaluated by the compilers and their inclusion does not indicate endorsement by the federal government. The subject index provides coverage for such areas as alcoholism, birth defects, consumer education, dental health, drug abuse, environmental health, communicable diseases, occupational safety, and the like.

This booklet is particularly useful for individuals and organizations participating in outreach programs for Spanish-speaking groups from lower socioeconomic levels. A companion work is the *Guide to Audiovisual Aids for Spanish-Speaking Americans; Health-Related Films, Filmstrips and Slides: Description and Sources* (DHEW Publication, no. (HSM) 74–30) issued in 1973.

643. U. S. Inter-Agency Committee on Mexican American Affairs. *The Mexican American A New Focus on Opportunity: A Guide to Materials Relating to Persons of Mexican Heritage in the United States.* Washington, DC: Government Printing Office, 1969. 186 p.

This is a comprehensive listing of books, reports, congressional hearings, conference proceedings, periodical articles, dissertations and other unpublished materials, bibliographies, and audiovisual media on the Mexican American. Appended to the bibliography is a directory of Spanish-language radio and television stations in the United States and a state-by-state listing of periodical publications of some interest to the Mexican American community. Many of the periodicals are official organs of Mexican American organizations. Although intended as a general bibliography, most of the material covers contemporary socioeconomic problems.

A revised edition of this work was published in 1971 by the U.S. Cabinet Committee on Opportunities for the Spanish Speaking, entitled *The Spanish Speaking in the United States: A Guide to Materials.* (See chapter on General Bibliographies.)

644. U. S. Office of Minority Business Enterprise. *Minority Business Enterprise: A Bibliography.* Washington, DC: Government Printing Office, 1973. 231 p. Annotated. Index.

As a preliminary effort by the Office of Minority Business Enterprise, Department of Commerce, this bibliography identifies works which relate to minority businesses. There are six basic parts: Bibliographies; Books and monographs; Articles; Reports and speeches; Directories; and Periodicals. Some topics covered by the index that relate to Mexican American business are assistance programs for minority firms; banking; business and urban development; Chicanos; consumer credit; consumerism, Spanish-speaking; economic development—Mexican American; management and technical assistance; and other general topics. Of particular interest in this work are the numerous directories, national and state, on minority businesses. Arizona, California, Texas, and New Mexico are among those states which have directories listed. Many of the titles are extensively annotated.

645. Von Furstenberg, George M. *Discrimination in Employment: A Selected Bibliography.* Monticello, IL: Council of Planning Librarians, 1972. (Exchange Bibliography, no. 297). 24 p.

This is a selection of references to the problems of discrimination in employment on the basis of race and cultural heritage. About 350 books and journal articles that focus on minority groups in the labor market are arranged in one alphabetical list. Specific reference to Mexican Americans can be located among the titles cited. Other information on this group can be gleaned from the sources related to specific industries and institutions (e.g., banks, supermarkets, and mines). The entries date mainly from 1964 to 1972 and treat discrimination in broad terms.

646. _____. *Discrimination in Housing: A Selected Bibliography*. Monticello, IL: Council of Planning Librarians, 1972. (Exchange Bibliography, no. 298) 7 p.

Listed in this bibliography are 92 books and articles on the topic of discrimination in housing. The items describe the causes, consequences, physical evidence, and solutions to housing discrimination against minorities, mainly Blacks. However, Mexican Americans have been victims of this problem as well. The sources listed can provide background information for in-depth studies on the topic as it relates to this latter group. This bibliography has been included because there is none in this subject area which relates specifically to Mexican Americans.

647. Wheat, Carolyn. "Selected Bibliography: Minority Group Participation in the Legal Profession." *University of Toledo Law Review,* (Spring-Summer, 1970): 935–981. Annotated.

This is the only bibliography available which deals specifically with minority groups (Blacks, American Indians, and Mexican Americans) in the legal profession. Approximately 153 entries are cited and arranged in five major categories. These include: Objective and relative measures of the shortage of minority group attorneys; Barriers to minority participation in the legal profession; Remedies: Breaking down the barriers; Evaluating the remedies; and Financing compensatory programs. Subtopics covered by the materials are discrimination, attitudes of minority students toward the legal profession, admissions policies, tests, impact of social class, the legal curriculum, among others. The items selected include articles, books, and government publications from 1960 to 1970 which are generally available. Additional sources of information, not in the bibliography, are suggested.

648. Winnie, William W., Jr., John F. Stegner, and Joseph P. Kopachevsky. *Persons of Mexican Descent in the United States: A Selected Bibliography*. Fort Collins: Center for Latin American Studies, Colorado State University, 1970. 78 p.

A selection of scholarly materials, mainly anthropological and sociological, related to Mexican Americans are cited in this bibliography. Colorado resources are emphasized. Approximately 1,000 entries, arranged alphabetically and dating from 1891 to 1970, have been included. The materials are books, periodical articles, M. A. theses, and Ph. D. dissertations. In keeping with the compilers' desire to list readily available materials, only dissertations completed in the State of Colorado are cited and no other unpublished materials are included.

Additional subjects covered are economics, psychology, political science, and education. Western history has been excluded. A list of bibliographies complements the list of resources. This is an important guide for serious research on the Mexican American.

649. Winters, William, Thomas A. Klein, and G. Allen Brunner. *Minority Enterprise and Marketing: An Annotated Bibliography*. Monticello, IL: Council of Planning Librarians, 1971. (Exchange Bibliography, no. 185) 39 p. Annotated.

This bibliography cites books, articles, and government publications on the subject of minority enterprises and marketing. Most of the items are on Blacks but there are some quite relevant to Mexican American consumers and businessmen. The list is the product of a study of entrepreneurship among minority groups, by a Task Force on Public Policy in Marketing from the American Marketing Association. Materials are arranged under ten headings which cover such topics as Constructing, manufacturing and wholesaling; Program initiation; Business expansion; Financial assistance; Managerial assistance; and Bibliographies.

Many of the references were drawn from a work entitled *Bibliography on Marketing to Low Income Consumers,* published in 1969 by the U. S. Department of Commerce, Business and Defense Services Administration.

650. Yanniello, William, and Helen Johnston, *Health Leaflets for Spanish-speaking Migrant Families.* Washington, DC: U. S. Public Health Service, 1960. (PHS Publication, no. 795) 12 p.

Health-related pamphlets in this list are useful for workers in public and volunteer agencies who deal with Spanish-speaking migrants. The materials are available from government departments and agencies such as the Public Health Service. The leaflets are in Spanish and English with a few in Spanish only. They provide health education information concerning accident prevention, maternal and child health, nutrition, sanitation, tuberculosis, and venereal disease. Each entry indicates the subject of the pamphlet and the address of the distributing agency. This is a companion list to the Public Health Service publication, no. 869, *Selected Films for Migrant Workers.*

# Chapter 17

# *Women*

Until recently Mexican American women were generally a silent and neglected minority within a minority. They quietly endured hardships alongside the men, suffered and toiled in the fields and factories, or worked toward equality for *La Raza*. But the written history of Mexican Americans has been primarily the history of activities and contributions of the men. The accomplishments of women have not been adequately recognized nor documented. Their personal concerns and aspirations often have been secondary to their dedication to the success of the Chicano movement as a whole. This position, as described by Elizabeth Sutherland in "Colonized Women: The Chicana," may have been a conscious one, fostered by a cultural background imbedded in Hispanic traditions.[1]

The late 1960s witnessed an increasing awareness within the Chicano Movement of the need for additional research on the Chicana and of participation by the Chicana in this research. The feminist movement, as well, has inspired courses on women which motivated and stimulated an interest in the Chicana and in her problems, needs, desires, and contributions. In comparison to the body of literature on Black and Anglo-American women, very little has been written by or about the Chicana. While the Chicana has played a role in the Chicano literary renaissance, few major literary works or autobiographies have been published by Mexican American women. The works that have been published are documented in a handful of bibliographies. General Mexican American bibliographies and library guides, aside from two or three, have not attempted to single out materials that particularly relate to women. Small sections on women appeared in a few of the Chicano bibliographies, such as the one by Juan Gómez-Quiñones, but these cite only a small sampling of published sources on Chicana feminism.

Throughout the 1970s students and faculty have sought materials in libraries on the Chicana. The traditional research tools (catalogs, indexes, and bibliographies) have not provided an adequate subject approach to this literature. The special bibliographies in this chapter attempt to bridge the gap between the general bibliographies and other research tools.

Two types of bibliographies are now available for researching topics on the Mexican American woman: the special bibliographies on the Chicana; and the bibliographies on women in general. Every identifiable bibliography on the Chicana has been cited, whether published or unpublished, but only a few of the general bibliographies on women, which have some bearing on the Chicana, have been selected. The characteristics of these bibliographies reveal the state of the literature on Mexican American women. They were all published or issued between 1973 and 1978, by academic libraries or Chicano research centers, and women in these institutions played a major role in their compilation.

It is encouraging to note that a number of special bibliographies on the Chicana have been prepared. These tools serve to point out the work that has been done as well as the lack of scholarly sources in certain areas. The Chicana bibliographies suffer from many of the same weaknesses of the general Mexican American bibliographies. They have often been prepared hastily and carelessly by inexperienced bibliographers, in response to the needs of researchers. Most of the lists are not published and, therefore, are difficult to obtain. The scope and purpose is often not clearly defined. Marginal and irrelevant items, unpublished student papers, and ephemeral publications comprise a substantial portion of the literature. Much of this literature is still polemical; the articles and papers seek to define the multiple causes of suppression and offer varied solutions. Health issues, education, and the family also have been topics of a small number of studies. However, the researchers in other areas related to the Chicana, such as history, politics, religion, literature, culture and the arts, must still rely heavily on background materials on Mexico, the Mexican woman, and other Third World women. And yet, the following bibliographies provide a vital service which justifies their mention and minimizes the importance of some of the flaws. The two bibliographies which might be considered the best to date were compiled at the Chicana Research and Learning Center in Austin, Texas, and the Chicano Studies Center, University of California, Los Angeles. Both are extensively and critically annotated and available through Educational Resources Information Center (ERIC).

The second type of bibliography essential to research on the Chicana is the general bibliography relating to women in the United States or Hispanic America. Several of the most recent examples of this type of compilation are mentioned in this chapter. Whether it be the ties with women in Mexico and Hispanic America, with other women or minorities in the United States, or with women in the labor force, each of the selected bibliographies provides access to supplementary resources touching on one of these dimensions of the Chicana's experience. Nevertheless, these bibliographies are not sufficient to thoroughly research topics on the Mexican American woman. Many bibliographies, even on women in America, include materials and subjects which are only indirectly relevant to the Mexican American woman. For more in-depth investigations, the major studies, periodicals, anthologies, and conference proceedings on the Mexican American must be consulted. The subject bibliographies and reference tools listed in other chapters will assist in identifying these supplementary sources.

1. Elizabeth Sutherland, "Colonized Women: The Chicana," in *Sisterhood Is Powerful: An Anthology of Writings from the Women's Liberation Movement*, comp. by Robin Morgan (New York: Random House, 1970), pp. 376–379.

651. Bickner, Mei Liang. *Women at Work; An Annotated Bibliography*. Los Angeles: Manpower Research Center, Institute of Industrial Relations, University of California, 1974. 1 vol. (unpaged) Annotated. Indexes.

652. _____, and Marlene Shaughnessy. *Women at Work, Volume II: An Annotated Bibliography, 1973–1975*. Los Angeles: Information-Publications

Center, Institute of Industrial Relations, University of California, 1977. 1 vol. (unpaged) Annotated. Indexes.

These selective bibliographies cover currently available materials on working women. Special efforts were made to include materials on nonprofessional women, women of minority groups, and women in the labor movement from an economic and sociological perspective.

The first volume, inspired by a course that the compiler offered on the subject in 1972, includes 600 scholarly books, monographs, journal articles, government publications and reports published in the United States between 1960 and 1973. The selections are arranged in eight sections: General, Education and training, Working women, Historical development, Occupation, Special groups of women, Public policy, and Bibliographies.

The second volume, covering the period 1973–1975, supplements the first volume and incorporates numerous studies which reflect the growing interest by the academic community in women in the labor force. The selections are arranged in eight categories: General, Historical development, Education and training, Working women, Occupations, Special groups of women, Public policy, and Bibliographies.

Sources directly related to the Mexican American woman are found under various headings in the subject indexes. Three other indexes, the author, title, and category, facilitate access to the entries in the bibliographies. A wealth of material on all aspects of women's occupations, problems, attitudes, legal rights, and status are indexes in these works. Special lists of general references consulted in compiling the bibliographies can be used to locate more current sources on women.

653. Cabello-Argandoña, Roberto, Juan Gómez-Quiñones, and Patricia Herrera Durán. *The Chicana: A Comprehensive Bibliographic Study*. Los Angeles: Chicano Studies Center, University of California, 1976. 308 p. Annotated. Indexes. ED 122 988.

654. Herrera Durán, Patricia, and Roberto Cabello-Argandoña. *The Chicana: A Preliminary Bibliographic Study*. Los Angeles: Chicano Studies Center, University of California, 1973. (Working Paper Series, no. 2) 52 p. Annotated. Index.

The comprehensive bibliographic study updates the preliminary work that was produced in 1973 and evaluates the most important materials on the Chicana. The 491 items are arranged under 18 subject headings: Films, Serials, General readings, Chicana and women's liberation, Civil rights, Culture and cultural process, Demography, Economics, Education, Family, Marriage and sex roles, Health and nutrition, History, Labor and discrimination in employment, Literature, Politics, Religion, and Social conditions. Included are books, periodical articles, journals, government publications, ERIC documents, films, dissertations and theses.

The preliminary bibliography represented the first stage in an ongoing project in the Chicano Research Library to identify materials on Mexican American women. It is one of the earliest works, if not the first, to be devoted strictly to the Chicana. All items identified at the time were included in an attempt to demonstrate the state of the literature on this subject. The 273 items are listed by type of material in this order: Books, Documents and papers, Articles, Theses and dissertations, Films, and Newspapers. The index provides access to such topics as academic achievement, Chicana movement, cultural characteristics, discrimination, family life, folk medicine, labor and women, legal rights, machismo, and many others.

Almost by necessity these bibliographies include a great deal of peripheral material which is, nevertheless, useful for background information and for comparative studies.

655. Common Women Collective. *Women in U.S. History: An Annotated Bibliography*, by Catherine Avril, *et al*. Cambridge, MA: The Collective, 1976. 114 p. Annotated.

The Common Women Collective, an outgrowth of the 1973–1974 Women's History Project in the Goddard-Cambridge Graduate Program, produced this bibliography as part of their work "towards a better framework for women's history." The bibliography contains approximately 450 titles of available books and periodical articles, which cover a broad range of topics. All entries are evaluated as to perspective, class conciousness, inclusion of traditionally omitted groups, writing style, documentation, and availability. Unpublished theses and manuscript collections are excluded. The work is arranged in 24 categories including General surveys, Historiography, Special groups such as Native American and Black women, and Chicanas, and specific time periods such as the Revolutionary War, the Depression, and the 1930s, to mention a few. The section on Chicanas lists only six works which relate to the Mexican American woman. Martha Cotera's *Diosa y hembra: The History and Heritage of Chicanas in the U.S.*, published in 1976, is not cited.

Several of the general and topical sections have relevant materials but for the most part the other selections do not pertain to the Mexican American, thus demonstrating the small amount of literature on the women of this ethnic group.

656. Concilio Mujeres. *Raza Women: A Bibliography*. San Francisco: The Concilio, 1974. 6 p.

This is a concise and hastily organized bibliography of works by, for, and about women of Hispanic background. The citations are arranged in three sections: Chicanas, España, and Mexico. The first section is subdivided into articles from books and magazines; pamphlets and journals; books; and articles from newsletters and newspapers. The second section includes articles from magazines; pamphlets and journals; and books. The third section on Mexico is subarranged by articles from magazines, newsletters and journals; books written by men; and books written by women. Included are 84 entries published between 1938 and 1973.

Most of the selections are popular and polemical, relating to the Women's Movement. Some, such as Fidel Castro's speeches, are not very relevant to the Chicanas. And inappropriately and curiously the work *Doña Perfecta* by the nineteenth-century Spanish novelist Galdos is included under Mexico. This bibliography lacks focus and gives no guidelines for criteria used in the selection. However, it is an early effort to draw attention to works on "Raza women." The weaknesses of this work demonstrate the need for more scholarly attention to this area.

657. Córdova, Marcella, and Rose Marie Roybal. *Bibliography on the Chicana*. Denver, CO: The Authors, 1973. 54 p. Annotated.

The purpose of this bibliography is to identify the literary accomplishments of Mexican American women. In actuality it is a compilation of materials by and about Spanish-speaking women. Presented are 308 titles, mainly articles, written by Chicanas about problems confronting Mexican Americans. The articles are from periodicals such as *La Luz, Regeneración, Con Safos, Los Conquistadores,* and *El Grito* which are generally not covered by the standard periodical indexes. A great majority of the items listed are directly related to the Mexican American experience, in general, and to that of the Chicana, in particular. The first part of this bibliography is annotated with short descriptions of the content of the materials.

Although numerous bibliographies on the Mexican American include books and articles relating to women, this is one of the few that has attempted to isolate the titles that relate specifically to works by and about the Chicana. A few forthcoming titles are mentioned. The arrangement is a bit awkward to use without an index.

658. Gutiérrez, Lewis A. *Bibliography on La Mujer Chicana.* Austin: Center for the Study of Human Resources, University of Texas, 1975. 20 p. ED 125 823.

This selection of references to the Mexican American woman was compiled from the collection of materials obtained by the Chicana Library Project. The purpose of the work is to stimulate further studies on the Mexican American woman by providing materials which reveal a better understanding of her experiences, activities, and motivations. One hundred eighty-six books, textbooks, articles and clippings, published between 1959 and 1974, are arranged under 26 subject headings: Art, Bibliographies, Business-employment, Chicano movement, Ecology, Economics, Education, Family, Farm workers, Feminism, Health, History, Immigration, Justice, Labor, Literature, Machismo, Midwest, Newspapers, Politics, Publications, Sexism, Socialism, Social studies, Sociology, and Third World women.

Although much of the material can be located in general bibliographies on the Mexican American, several of the categories list items that are specifically related to the Chicana and not found in other sources.

659. Haber, Barbara. *Women in America: A Guide to Books, 1963–1975.* Boston: G. K. Hall, 1978. 202 p. Annotated. Index.

Current books on American women, that could also serve as a core collection in Women's Studies, are cited in this excellent guide. The author is presently the Curator of Printed Books at Radcliffe College's Arthur and Elizabeth Schlesinger Library on the History of Women in America. She has selected for inclusion 450 of the most significant books on subjects and issues related to American women, published between 1963 and 1975. These works reflect the same principles and attention that were applied in the development of the collection at the Schlesinger Library.

In documenting the new feminism the following subjects are covered: abortion, Black women and Native American women, crime and imprisonment, education, feminism, health, history, law and politics, life styles, literature, the fine arts and popular culture, marriage and related issues, prostitution, psychology, rape, religion, sex roles, sexuality, and work. The bibliography does not attempt to cover certain areas which are, nevertheless, fundamental to research on American women. Omitted are fiction, poetry, drama, juvenile literature; highly technical professional studies; reference tools; and audiovisual media.

Although many of the general works on women have applicability to the study of some problems and issues related to Spanish-speaking women, no works are cited in this bibliography which specifically relate to this group. Haber writes that "There is not as yet a body of literature written by Spanish-speaking women in the United States." This statement could be contested. Numerous articles, bibliographies, chapters in books and dissertations have been written by and about the Chicana and Mexican American women but they have only found outlets for publication in journals, anthologies, and non-trade publications for the most part. These works include studies on the Chicana and the topics of health, religion, family, labor, crime, literature, politics, fine arts, and many others.

The limitations and scope that the compiler has imposed on this otherwise fine work have caused a segment of the second largest minority in the United States to remain unrepresented in the bibliography.

660. Knaster, Meri. *Women in Spanish America: An Annotated Bibliography from Pre-Conquest to Contemporary Times*. Boston: G. K. Hall, 1977. 696 p. Annotated. Indexes.

This lengthy work is the first and the most comprehensive bibliography published on women in Spanish America. Listed are 2,507 entries. It was motivated by a desire to facilitate access to a neglected area and to give impetus to scholarly research on Spanish American women. The arrangement follows the Library of Congress classification for subject bibliography. The broad subjects are subdivided by geographic region: Spanish America, Middle America, South America and Caribbean.

Materials on Mexican women are listed under all the subjects in the section on Middle America. Information can be found on the arts, literature, education, religion, family, health, psychology, history and the Women's Movement. Only two entries concern Mexican American women; however, the sections relating to Mexico provide excellent background material.

661. Mariscal, Linda. *Index to Material on La Chicana Oppearing(sic) in El Grito del Notre*. Berkeley: Chicano Studies Library, University of California, 1976. 4 p.

The title is rather self-explanatory. It is a mimeographed listing of articles which relate to the Chicana that were published in *El Grito del Norte* between October, 1968 and August, 1973. Fifty-five items were identified and arranged alphabetically by author. Most of the entries seem relevant to the Chicana and the Women's Movement with the exception of an untitled poem by Sor Juana Inés de la Cruz.

Although carelessly prepared, the listing is useful for those doing work on certain political and social aspects of Mexican American women.

662. *Mexican American Woman Curriculum Materials: A Selected Topics Bibliography of ERIC Documents*. Las Cruces: New Mexico State University, 1977. 80 p. Annotated. ED 152 474.

This guide to resources, research findings and developments related to the education of Mexican American women cites 106 items published between 1960 and 1976. These were drawn from *Research in Education* and *Current Index to Journals in Education*. Topics covered by the listing include learning motivation, integrated curriculum, cultural background, curriculum development, English as a second language, job training and cultural education. Many titles, although not specifically related to women, deal with the Mexican American in general.

663. *La Mujer Chicana: An Annotated Bibliography,* by Evey Chapa, *et al.* Austin, TX: Chicana Research and Learning Center, 1976. 86 p. Annotated. ED 152 439.
Publications by and about Chicanas are covered in this bibliography. This work is viewed by the Center as "a positive step in the documentation of the Chicana experience." Included are 320 books, articles, special journal issues, and unpublished manuscripts that are organized by topic. The most relevant categories are Chicana publications, Chicana feminism, Education, Health, History, Labor, Family, Politics and Social issues. Sections on Machismo and Third World women also contain some related items.
The appendix is a list of addresses of publishers and distributors for the material cited. Cross references, lengthy annotations, and a detailed table of contents enhance the usefulness of this work.

664. Oakes, Elizabeth, and Kathleen E. Sheldon. *Guide to Social Science Resources on Women's Studies.* Santa Barbara, CA: ABC-Clio, 1978. 162 p. Annotated. Indexes.
Research on women in the various areas of the social sciences is facilitated by this bibliography. It was compiled in order to provide "succinct evaluation of the social science literature on women" for professors in introductory courses. The selections are limited to books and collections of articles in journals and books. Coverage includes Anthropology, Economics, History, Psychology, Sociology, Contemporary feminist thought, Bibliographies, Journals, and Other Resources. Each discipline is preceded by a description of the state of the literature and subdivided into numerous categories according to existing material.
Works on the Chicanas which are scattered throughout the bibliography can be identified in the Subject Index. Approximately ten titles are directly related to this group. These basic works on Chicanas, appropriate for use by undergraduates, offer an overview of the immediate problems and issues concerning health care, family, labor, history, double oppression, welfare, and cross-cultural comparisons.
Audiovisual materials and unpublished sources, such as theses and manuscript collections, are not included. The annotations are descriptive and evaluative.

665. Portillo, Cristina, Graciela Rios, and Martha Rodríguez. *Bibliography of Writings on La Mujer.* Berkeley: Chicano Studies Library, University of California, 1976. (Publication, no. 2) 53 p. Index.
This bibliography is the result of efforts to identify materials pertaining to the Chicana in the Chicano Studies Library at Berkeley. The items listed are arranged in two parts. Part I includes 264 separately prepared works—reprinted articles, books, dissertations, and student papers. Part II lists 19 serials which regularly publish articles on Mexican American women, Mexican women, and women in general. Topics covered by the entries are primarily in the social sciences with a smattering of selections on art, literature, religion, and folklore. Call numbers are given for all the entries.
Numerous bibliographies are listed which provide information on a wider range of sources for in-depth research. This work is highly useful for the study of the Chicana.

666. Rios, Graciela. *Index to Social Conditions Section of the Chicano Studies Library as it Pertains to La Chicana.* Berkeley, University of California, 1975. (Student paper prepared for Chicano Studies 139) 11 p.

The items that relate to the Chicana in the social science literature of the Chicano Studies collection at Berkeley are analyzed bibliographically in this paper. Seventy-seven entries are arranged in four sections. The first two sections contain items on general social conditions of Chicanos. The last two sections include items on the Chicana by specific geographical location. The materials from the "stacks," i.e., books, theses and journal materials, are listed separately from the vertical file materials in each category.

The arrangement of this paper is somewhat unorthodox and confusing for the user. Topical subdivisions, a shelf list arrangement, annotations, or even a subject index would have greatly improved the utility of the listing. Nonetheless, many of the items provide the diligent researcher with material on the Mexican American woman, the Mexican American family, and other relevant themes.

667. Schlachter, Gail Ann, and Donna Belli. *Minorities and Women: A Guide to Reference Literature in the Social Sciences.* Los Angeles: Reference Service Press, 1977. 349 p. Annotated. Indexes.

This bibliography is especially strong on sources related to minority women, including Mexican American women. Divided into two sections; the first is devoted to Information sources—fact books, biographical and documentary sources, directories and statistical compilations—and the second covers Citation sources—indexes, abstracts, and bibliographies. The purpose of the work is to fill the bibliographic gap on minorities.

Over 800 annotated reference tools are included which provide access to people, places, events, organizations, statistics, media, articles and books. This guide would have been a more useful and unique work had the compilers concentrated solely on minority women. Many of the citations to the various minority groups, in general, are listed in other standard bibliographic tools. The sections on Spanish Americans and women have materials useful to research on the Chicana.

668. Southern Colorado State College. Library. *La Chicana: A Selected Bibliography of Material Concerned with the Mexican American Woman in Higher Education.* Pueblo: The Library, 1975. 6 p.

Supplementing the library's general bibliographies on Mexican Americans is this concise guide to materials and research on the Chicana in higher education. All of the items are available in the library at Southern Colorado State College. The 50 entries include books, general periodical indexes, periodical titles, government publications, ephemeral materials in the vertical file, and ERIC documents.

Relevant sociological, political, statistical, and economic studies are included in addition to materials in the field of education. Call numbers and suggested subject headings for books, articles, government documents, and the ERIC reports enhance the usefulness of this list for the library's patrons.

# *Author Index*

*The bibliographical entries and annotations have been indexed, but not the Foreword, the Introduction, nor the preliminary essay and footnotes of each chapter. The numbers in each of the three indexes refer to the item numbers and not pages.*

# Title Index

*The bibliographical entries and annotations have been indexed, but not the Foreword, the Introduction, nor the preliminary essay and footnotes of each chapter. The numbers in each of the three indexes refer to the item numbers and not pages.*

# Subject Index

The bibliographical entries and annotations have been indexed, but not the Foreword, the Introduction, nor the preliminary essay and footnotes of each chapter. The numbers in each of the three indexes refer to the item numbers and not pages.